From Pac-Man to Pop

Interactive Audio in Games and N

Edited by

KAREN COLLINS
University of Waterloo, Canada

ASHGATE

Published by
Ashgate Publishing Limited
Gower House
Croft Road
Aldershot
Hampshire GU11 3HR
England

Ashgate Publishing Company
Suite 420
101 Cherry Street
Burlington, VT 05401-4405
USA

Ashgate website: http://www.ashgate.com

British Library Cataloguing in Publication Data
Collins, Karen
    From Pac-Man to pop music : interactive audio in games and new media
    1. Computer game music – History and criticism 2. Sound effects music – History and
    criticism
    I. Title
    006.5

Library of Congress Cataloging-in-Publication Data
    From Pac-Man to pop music : interactive audio in games and new media / [edited by]
Karen Collins.
        p. cm. – (Ashgate popular and folk music series)
    Includes bibliographical references (p.   ) and index. ISBN 978-0-7546-6200-6 (alk. paper)
    1. Video game music–History and criticism. 2. Popular music–History and criticism.
I. Collins, Karen, 1973–

    ML3540.7.F76 2007
    781.5'4—dc22

                                                                    2007033749
ISBN 978-0-7546-6200-6 (Hbk)
ISBN 978-0-7546-6211-2 (Pbk)

Printed and bound in Great Britain by MPG Books Ltd. Bodmin, Cornwall.

Contents

PART 5   Audio and audience

List of figures

About the contributors

Rob Bridgett is currently Sound Director at Birmingham-based Swordfish Studios in the UK. Prior to that he spent four years as Sound Director at Radical Entertainment in Vancouver, where he was responsible for the audio on *Scarface: The World is Yours* (PS2, Xbox, PC); a project in which a full post-production sound design and mix was undertaken at Skywalker Ranch with Randy Thom. Work on other titles includes *Sudeki* (Xbox), *Serious Sam: Next Encounter* (Gamecube) and acclaimed Dreamcast racer *Vanishing Point*. www.sounddesign.org.uk. email: rob@sounddesign.org.uk

Anders Carlsson has been composing chip music for 15 years. He grew up active in the Swedish demoscene but is now more involved with records and live shows. He has a Bachelor's Degree in Media and Communication Studies and has used his studies in pedagogy to create workshops and lectures about chip music. www.goto80.com

Karen Collins is Canada Research Chair in Technology and Communication at the Canadian Centre for Arts and Technology at the University of Waterloo, where she is developing software tools for dynamic audio and teaching sound design and games development. www.GamesSound.com. email collinsk@uwaterloo.ca

Peter Drescher is a musician and composer with 20 years of performance experience. He has produced audio for games, the Web and mobile devices, and is currently Sound Designer at Danger, Inc., developers of the T-Mobile Sidekick. He lives in the San Francisco Bay Area.

Tim van Geelen is an aspiring sound designer and interactive music composer. Amongst other things, he has created interactive music and sound effect systems for the Architects of Air Luminaria sculptures and ArtEZ School of the Arts website. He is an active member of the Game Audio Network Guild and the Interactive Audio Special Interest Group. www.timvangeelen.com

Agnès Guerraz obtained her PhD in computer science from the University of Grenoble in 2002. Her research focuses on applying computational techniques to human interactions and developing novel interface technology. Her postdoctoral position at University College London examined haptic rendering algorithm based on texture data. Her recent focus at Xerox Research Center Europe has been on the development of statistical models to categorize documents. She has been a temporary Research Lecturer at INRIA France since 2006. In the Project WAM (Web Adaptation Multimedia), she focuses on rich graphic applications using interactive audio and multimedia template-based authoring tools keeping rich composition capabilities and smooth adaptability.

Norbert Herber is a musician and sound artist. His work can be described as Emergent music – an innovative generative style that uses artificial life systems to sustain continuous, real-time modification and adaptation. Using this approach he is focused on creating sound and music in digital environments for art, entertainment and communications. His works have been performed/exhibited in Europe, Asia, South America and in the United States. Current projects can be heard online at www.x-tet.com. Norbert is a Lecturer in the Department of Telecommunications at Indiana University, Bloomington and is currently conducting research as a PhD candidate with the Planetary Collegium at the University of Plymouth in England.

Kristine Jørgensen recently finished her PhD in Media Studies at Copenhagen University. Her dissertation entitled '*What are those Grunts and Growls over there?'* *Computer Game Audio and Player Action*, explores the functionality of computer game audio and how it influences player actions and behaviour in the game world.

Jesper Kaae holds an MA in Music Technology from Aalborg University in Denmark. He has composed a number of scores for video games and has written some computer programs based on interactive music.

Antti-Ville Kärjä works as a lecturer in musicology at the University of Turku. He earned his PhD in 2005 and is also an adjunct professor of the study of audiovisual media music in the Department of Music Anthropology at the University of Tampere. He is the secretary of the Nordic branch of the International Association for the Study of Popular Music and the vice-president of the Finnish Society for Ethnomusicology.

Erica Kudisch is a recent graduate of Vassar College. She is currently pursuing a PhD in Composition and Theory at the University of Pittsburgh, and is a founding member of Alia Musica Pittsburgh (www.alia-musica.org) and a principal with Undercroft Opera (www.undercroftopera.com).

Prof. Jacques Lemordant (PhD 1980) is member of the WAM Team which is working on multimedia documents at INRIA (http://wam.inrialpes.fr). He is also teaching XML technologies, multimedia programming and game design on mobiles at the Joseph Fourier University of Grenoble (France). Professor Lemordant was a scientific leader in European and national multimedia projects, has directed seven PhD students over the last six years, and has realized a prototype of a 3D (audio and video) conferencing system. He is now actively working in the field of 3D and interactive audio for mobile games.

Leonard J. Paul studied granular synthesis in depth from one of the primary pioneers of granular synthesis, Barry Truax. Since 1994, the author has often used granular synthesis in his own music, academically and in his work with video games.

He has been teaching video game audio at the Vancouver Film School for three years and has a 13 year history in composing music, sound design and coding for video games for leading gaming companies such as Electronic Arts and Radical Entertainment. He has spoken several times at the Game Developers Conference as well as contributing articles to Gamasutra.com on the topic of game audio. He was the composer for *The Corporation*, currently the highest-grossing Canadian documentary of all time, and has worked on many video games, including *Max Payne 2* (Rockstar, PC), *Tron* (Backbone/Buena Vista Entertainment) and *Death Jr. 2: Science Fair of Doom* (Backbone/Konami, NDS). www.VideoGameAudio. com. info@VideoGameAudio.com

Peter Shultz is a PhD student in music theory at the University of Chicago, where he teaches undergraduate theory courses. He received an AB summa cum laude in Music from Princeton University, with an undergraduate thesis on extended diatonic structures in the music of Béla Bartók. His dissertation research, currently in progress, centres on the meanings and functions of music in interactive contexts, and he enjoys choral singing and playing piano and trumpet.

Holly Tessler is completing a PhD dissertation at the Institute of Popular Music at the University of Liverpool. Her research is concerned with how the story of the Beatles is performed and is organized as an industrial process. Holly is a part-time lecturer in the School of Music at the University of Liverpool and has also taught in the Department of Media Studies at the University of Central England in Birmingham. She has recently been appointed as Research Assistant on an AHRC-funded project on mapping music within Merseyside. Research interests include music industries, music and technology and music and the legal system.

General Editor's Preface

The upheaval that occurred in musicology during the last two decades of the twentieth century has created a new urgency for the study of popular music alongside the development of new critical and theoretical models. A relativistic outlook has replaced the universal perspective of modernism (the international ambitions of the 12-note style); the grand narrative of the evolution and dissolution of tonality has been challenged, and emphasis has shifted to cultural context, reception and subject position. Together, these have conspired to eat away at the status of canonical composers and categories of high and low in music. A need has arisen, also, to recognize and address the emergence of crossovers, mixed and new genres, to engage in debates concerning the vexed problem of what constitutes authenticity in music and to offer a critique of musical practice as the product of free, individual expression.

Popular musicology is now a vital and exciting area of scholarship, and the *Ashgate Popular and Folk Music Series* aims to present the best research in the field. Authors will be concerned with locating musical practices, values and meanings in cultural context, and may draw upon methodologies and theories developed in cultural studies, semiotics, poststructuralism, psychology and sociology. The series will focus on popular musics of the twentieth and twenty-first centuries. It is designed to embrace the world's popular musics from Acid Jazz to Zydeco, whether high tech or low tech, commercial or non-commercial, contemporary or traditional.

Professor Derek B. Scott
Chair of Music
University of Salford

Preface

When I first set out to edit a volume of articles on games audio, my initial intent was, in a way, to see who I could find who was working in this area. It was with pleasant surprise, therefore, that I received submissions from around the Western world, and a wide variety of disciplines and backgrounds. The selected articles presented here were chosen to present an overview of a variety of aspects of games audio that I felt might provoke some thought and stimulate discussion in an interdisciplinary fashion, and introduce the reader to this subject area from a multiplicity of perspectives. I was especially pleased that some of the authors here came from outside of academe, and have taken the opportunity to discuss aspects of their practice, present some of the problems they face and suggest avenues that academics may help them to explore. I hope that the study of games audio can continue in such an interdisciplinary manner. Indeed, collaborative activity is much needed in the area, and industry groups have been very welcoming to academics, including the Interactive Audio Special Interest Group (IAsig) and the Game Audio Network Guild (GANG).

Much of the preparation that went into putting these chapters together came during my time as SSHRC Post-Doctoral Research Fellow under the supervision of Paul Théberge at Carleton University in Ottawa, and my gratitude goes to him, to the university and the Interdisciplinary Studies in Literature, Arts and Culture Department for their support, and to the Social Sciences and Humanities Research Council of Canada for funding my research. I would also like to thank my new department, the Canadian Centre of Arts and Technology at the University of Waterloo, for their support during the final stages of editing. My appreciation goes to the students, both in my own classes and in the times I have guest lectured at the Université de Montréal, who have been a driving force in getting a book out in this area. Heartfelt thanks goes to all of the authors involved for all of the work that they have put in.

Karen Collins

Introduction

Karen Collins

In 1983 my father brought home an IBM PC/XT. Although I recall being told that the machine was intended for work purposes (he was a mathematician), I distinctly remember having two games to play on the machine during the first few weeks the computer sat in our living room: *Frogger* (Sierra On-Line 1983) and *Floppy Frenzy* (Windmill Software 1982). *Floppy Frenzy* was a kind of educational game that was designed to teach us to keep our floppy disks away from dust and magnets, and aside from a few sound effects, I can't remember it having any music, but the *Frogger* tune (which varied on different 'platforms' – that is to say – on different computers or console machines) I can still bring to mind without any trouble at all. The simple tune that started the game, played through IBM's small speaker on one mono channel, must have been played back to me a thousand times over the following years as I, my family or my friends played the game.

Anyone who has played video games – or who has sat in a room while somebody else played a game – is familiar with the repetitive nature of games music. It is the bane of composers and players alike, who eventually resort to shutting the sound off to get a bit of peace. Games composers are well aware of the reputation of their craft as repetitive, incessant bleeping, and there have been many attempts to overcome the issue as well as this reputation. Not only are games music composers finally achieving more recognition for their work, but they are increasingly interested in tackling the problems of creating sound for a participatory, dynamic media; not only creating more variability in their soundtracks, but also ensuring that the music and sound effects are responding to the needs of the game and the game player. Many of the chapters in this book touch on or discuss in detail some recent thinking and approaches to these issues.

There are, of course, reasons why games music was (and to a lesser extent continues to be) so repetitive. Early distribution systems – floppy disks, cartridges and so on – had limited amounts of space available for memory and storage (see below). Most early games were coded by hand, and writing a few simple bars would be as cumbersome as several lines of code for a single instrument voice. The competitive nature of the industry (and short shelf lives for hit titles) meant that there simply was not enough time to write lengthy songs. Moreover, most early games music composers were not musicians, but were programmers, and although many were talented, their main focus was typically not on creating great music, but on game-play and on graphics. Not least of these problems was the fact that, unlike common uses of a film or television programme, a game would typically be played over and over, for hours and hours on end, as players 'died' and restarted a level. The timings were unpredictable, since some gamers might achieve a certain degree of skill that meant longer game-play, while others were stuck on the first few minutes of a game for hours or days. A brief history of the development of games audio and its technology will provide some context for understanding the chapters that follow.

A very brief history of games audio[1]

The earliest video games – those going back to what are allegedly the first, William Higginbotham's 'Tennis for Two' game of 1958, and *Spacewar!* of 1962 created at MIT – had no sound. Likewise, the earliest home consoles – such as the Magnavox Odyssey – were also silent. It was not long, however, before games were introduced into pinball arcades, and the very first mass-produced game, Nutting Associates' *Computer Space* (1971), included a series of different 'space battle' sounds, including 'rocket and thrusters engines, missiles firing, and explosions'.[2] Atari's *Pong* (1972), with its beeping paddle sound, was soon to follow.

It was Taito/Midway's *Space Invaders* of 1978 that was to introduce the idea of a continuous background soundtrack: four simple chromatic descending bass notes which repeated in a loop. Particularly notable, however, was the fact that, despite being the first to include a background track, the game's developers also recognized the need for the soundtrack to be dynamic – to interact with the player in some way. In this case, the music's tempo was affected by the player's progress in the game, with the four tones increasing in speed as the game progressed.

Most video games music at the time of the early arcade hits included one- or two-channel tunes either as quick title themes or two- to three-second in-game loops, although another important invention in games audio came quickly: the 'cut scene', an intermission cinematic, during which the player would sit back and watch, used as a reward for attaining a particular level. Tohru Iwatani's *Pac-Man*, the first game to incorporate a cut scene (Midway 1980), enjoyed its most musical times during these scenes, since typically the simultaneous playback of sound and player interaction was typically too taxing on the old processors, but cinematics were less demanding. *Pac-Man* also brought about a mass realization of the catchiness of sound in games – its infamous 'waca waca' in-game sound and opening two-channel title theme became the source of several gimmick songs in the 1980s, such as Weird Al Yankovic's 'Pac-Man', and Buckner and Garcia's 'Pac-Man Fever' which quickly led to an album of other games tunes, including 'Do The Donkey Kong', 'Ode to a Centipede', 'Froggy's Lament' and 'Defender'. Video games music may initially have been viewed as a gimmick, but it was soon to be taken more seriously.

Sound in games was slow to develop, however, as PCs in particular were considered business machines, and audio was not seen to have many business applications, and was therefore not a priority for computer developers. Nevertheless, there were many progressive ideas introduced to the audio programming of 8-bit machine games, and 8-bit games developed a unique aesthetic that is still enjoyed by gamers and music fans today. The majority of 8-bit machines (and early arcade

---

1   This history is an abbreviated version of that published in Karen Collins, 'From Bits to Hits: Video Games Music Changes its Tune', *Film International* 13 (2004): 4–19.

2   See the flyer for the game at The Arcade Flyer Archive, http://www.arcadeflyers.com/ (accessed 10 June 2007).

and pinball machines) used sound chips known as programmable sound generators (PSGs). Early PSGs used analogue synthesis, or subtractive synthesis, which starts with a waveform created by an oscillator, and uses a filter to attenuate or subtract specific frequencies. It then passes this through an amplifier to control the envelope and amplitude of the final resulting sound. PSGs offered little control over the timbre of a sound, usually limiting sounds to single waveforms (typically square waves) without much ability to manipulate that waveform.

It was Commodore who fully recognized the importance of gaming to the home computer market, taking computers out of their formerly specialty stores and putting them into department stores and toy centres. In 1982, after the success of its VIC-20 model, Commodore released its 64K model, which would go on to become the best-selling computer of all time, selling an estimated 22 million units. The C64 was originally conceived of as a games computer, and the graphics and sound remain evidence of this. The sound chip (called SID, Sound Interface Device) was a three-voice plus noise generator chip, created by Robert Yannes, who had helped engineer the VIC-20, and would later go on to create the Digital Oscillator Chip for the Apple IIGS. Unlike other PC chips at the time, each tone on the chip could be selected from a range of waveforms – sawtooth, triangle, pulse and noise. Each tone could also be subjected to a variety of effects and programmable filters including ring modulation. *Frogger*, released in 1981 in the arcades, and 1983 for the IBM PC and C64, reveals the great differences between the machines of the times. The PC could only handle a short two-channel title tune and level intro song, with the rest of the game remaining limited to sound effects. The Commodore 64 on the other hand had a continuous background medley, including 'Yankee Doodle' and 'Camp Town Races'.

Commodore had directly taken on the popular home consoles of the era, including the Mattel Intellivision, the ColecoVision and the Atari Video Computer System (VCS, later known as the 2600) which saw limited success when it was first released in 1976. In 1980, however, Atari licensed the arcade hit *Space Invaders*, which became a best seller and helped to spur on the sales of the VCS. Eventually, over 25 million VCS systems were sold, and over 120 million cartridges.[3] The sound chip in the VCS was known as the TIA (television interface adapter), and also handled graphics. The audio portion had two channels, with an awkward 'polynomial counter' to determine frequencies. A base tone was set, and then randomly divided by the system clock into 32 other note options, meaning many notes were quite out of tune, and making writing music on the Atari very difficult. Even title themes were rare, and if anything a few notes which sounded completely random might be thrown in as a title song. Many Atari VCS tunes sounded like atonal melodies strung together, with no real discernible rhythm.

Nintendo improved on the 8-bit console sound with the release of the Nintendo Entertainment System, or NES, sold in North America beginning in 1985. The NES used a built-in five-channel sound chip with one waveform for each channel – two pulse waves, a triangle wave, a noise and a sample channel. The NES came pre-packed with the game *Super Mario Bros.*, a game which would push its composer

---

3   See William Hunter, 'The Dot Eaters Videogame History' (2000): http://www. emuunlim.com/doteaters/play3sta1.htm (accessed 10 October 2004).

Koji Kondo into the spotlight in Japan. Kondo quickly mastered the limitations of the NES sound chip, managing to fill out its three tone channels with a clever use of percussion, catchy melodies and smooth looping capabilities that used slight variations to keep the song from getting monotonous as in earlier games. Most NES songs consisted of a melody, thickened out with a second channel, a bass line and percussion. Most Nintendo songs were melody-based, but some composers explored other possibilities, including Hirokazu 'Hip' Tanaka's soundtrack for the *Metroid* game, which intentionally avoided melody-based songs, instead opting for a science-fiction film music style, where sound effects and song blur together to create an eerie atmosphere.

Recognizing that gamers and musicians wanted decent quality sound from their PCs without having to go out and buy new computers, add-on third-party FM sound cards began to develop in the mid 1980s. Sound cards were designed with the gamer in mind: they generally had a joystick game port which could double as a MIDI port with an adapter. The first popular PC sound card was produced by the small Canadian company Ad Lib Multimedia in 1986. The use of FM synthesis techniques meant that game developers could now use a wider range of instruments and sounds. To boost sales, the Ad Lib card was packaged with software capable of playing back MIDI files ('Juke Box'), a MIDI sequencer program equipped with 145 pre-set voices ('Visual Composer') and an FM synthesis program to design sounds or instruments ('Instrument Maker').

MIDI, a protocol defined in 1983 to allow musical devices (synthesizers, keyboards, sequencers, mixing desks, computers) to be compatible in a standardized format, revolutionized the possibilities for games composing. Only commands, rather than actual sounds, are transmitted, meaning file size is very small. A MIDI command might, for instance, tell a synthesizer when to start and stop playing a note, at what volume and what pitch, and what voice, or sound, to use. The fact that MIDI was stored in code, rather than sampled sound, meant that it was a great benefit to games, since memory space was limited on the early systems. Although by the early 1990s most home computers had FM sound cards supporting MIDI, many of these sound cards were cheap, and the FM synthesis made the MIDI music sound disappointing. When CD-ROMs came out, MIDI in gaming was largely abandoned, and with it the notion of dynamic music, which would react to player and game engine input. Nevertheless, CD-ROM technology ensured that there was more room for music in games: previously most games had shipped on 3.5 inch floppy disks, and, perhaps more importantly to the game music composers, since CD-ROM audio was not reliant on a sound card's synthesis, composers could know how the music would sound on most systems, unlike with chip-based sound, which could vary greatly.

CD-ROM technology was incorporated into many of the 16-bit home consoles. The first real 16-bit console was the 1989 release by Sega, the Genesis (known in Europe as the MegaDrive). The Genesis produced many games ported from successful Sega arcade games like *Space Harrier*, *After Burner* and *Ghouls 'N Ghosts*. The system originally came packaged with the arcade hit *Altered Beast*, but soon took on Nintendo's *Mario* with their *Sonic the Hedgehog* character. The Genesis also had superior sound over the NES: it had a similar PSG chip to handle effects and the occasional music part, as well as a Yamaha FM synthesizer chip, which had six channels of digitized stereo sound.

With the Genesis leagues ahead of the NES in capabilities, Nintendo realized that they would also have to build a 16-bit system to compete. By 1991, they had developed their Super Nintendo Entertainment System (SNES). The SNES sound module, built by Sony, consisted of several components, the most important of which was the Sony SPC-700, which acted as a co-processor with its own memory. It was essentially a wavetable synthesizer that supported eight stereo channels at programmable frequency and volume, and effects such as reverb, filters, panning and envelope generators, and with a preset stock of MIDI instruments. Wavetable synthesis uses preset digital samples of instruments, usually combined with basic analogue waveforms, creating more 'realistic' instrument sounds.

After attempts to continue working with Nintendo on a CD-ROM-based system failed, Sony went off on their own and developed their own system, the Sony PlayStation, a console which was cheap and easy to program, and therefore saw the support of more games designers. The PlayStation was enormously successful, selling over 85 million units, most likely due to its affordability and the massive library of games available. The sound chip was capable of 24 channels of 16-bit sound at CD-quality sampling rate, and allowed for real-time effects like ADSR changes, looping, reverb and pitch modulation. The PlayStation's CD-ROM drive could also play audio CDs, and in fact there were some games in which it was possible to pause the game and replace the game's audio with the player's own audio CD, a function which is now built into all Microsoft Xbox 360 consoles.

Nintendo bypassed the 32-bit machines altogether, going straight to a 64-bit release in 1996, the Nintendo 64 (N64). The N64 surpassed the PlayStation in capabilities, if not in popularity. The main processor controlled the audio, producing 16-bit stereo sound at a slightly higher sample rate than CD quality. Some games supported surround sound, and this was enhanced with the third-party add-on release of RumbleFx 3D Sound Amplifier. With the release of the 128-bit machines in the late 1990s (including the Sony PlayStation 2, the Sega DreamCast, the Nintendo Game Cube, the Xbox and so on), games were able to produce DVD quality audio, with multichannel surround sound. With large DVD-ROM games, music for a single game could fill several audio CDs, such as *Final Fantasy IX*, which was released as a four-CD set.

The latest generation of games consoles and computers (referred to typically as 'next gen' consoles) have eliminated many of the technological difficulties of earlier games. Games audio is often now recorded with full orchestras and choirs, and it has become quite common for games soundtracks to now be released as commercial music CDs or to be sold on iTunes. Although the technology is now there, the tools are not, and the more dynamic aspects of games audio (player participation, non-linearity and so on) have only begun to be explored.

Games that use music as the primary narrative component, such as *Dance Dance Revolution*, have been immensely popular, and offer many areas for interesting exploration and future development. The bizarre game *Vib Ribbon*, for instance, released in Japan in 2000 for the PlayStation, allowed the user to put in his or her own music CDs, which would then influence the generation of maps in the game.

The game scanned the user's CD and made two obstacle courses for each song (one easy and one difficult), so the game was always as varied as the music the player chose. Many other types of games are now beginning to explore the potential of including more dynamic musical elements, which is explored by many of the authors in this volume. The implications of this participatory and non-linear aspect of games audio are vast in terms of how scholars may approach games audio in the future, and the authors here hint at some of the directions that can be taken.

The current state of games audio research

As Erica Kudisch shows in her annotated bibliography at the end of this book, despite thirty years of technological development in games, academic research into games audio has been slow to develop. There have been but a handful of academic articles published, often in conjunction with or in comparison to film music. The authors in this book come from disparate disciplines: psychology, business/industry studies, popular music(ology), computer science, communications and so on. This is, perhaps, how a new discipline should begin; with a variety of theoretical perspectives and practices that can create a diverse spectrum in which discussion and opinion can clash, develop and grow. As authors such as Ronald H. Sadoff and Rick Altman have shown in the case of film sound, at least in the early stages of research in a new area, it is necessary for academics to work with those in industry and to consult primary sources in order to understand the impact that processes and practice have on production.[4] With this in mind, the structure of the book that follows this Introduction is such that it interweaves articles by those in industry with research by academic scholars, many of whom are also practitioners themselves.

The book is divided into five sections. The first part, 'Industries and synergies', addresses the growing synergy, or mutually beneficial collaborative activities between video games and the popular music industry. The multibillion-dollar video games industry, while experiencing a slight fluctuation every five years or so when new consoles are typically released, has been increasing in worldwide dollar value at a time when other cultural industries, particularly the popular music industry, are decreasing. The ties between these two industries are now strengthening, as the popular music industry views games as a way to market music to its target groups, while the games industry can use popular music to appeal to specific markets, to reduce production costs and to open up new uses for music in games.

In the first chapter, 'The new MTV? Electronic Arts and "playing" music', Holly Tessler explores this relationship between the games industry and popular music, asking whether games will replace television as the primary form of media for exposure to new music. By focusing on the enthusiastic utopian vision of Electronic Arts executive Steve Schnur, Tessler explores games as a new distribution channel for popular music. In Chapter 2, 'Marketing music through computer games: the case of Poets of the Fall and *Max Payne 2*', Antti-Ville Kärjä narrows this focus with

---

4   See Rick Altman, *Silent Film Sound* (New York, 2007); Ronald H. Sadoff, 'The role of the music editor and the "temp track" as blueprint for the score, source music, and scource music of films', *Popular Music* 25/2 (2006): 165–83.

a case study of the growing synergistic relationships between the music and games industries. Kärjä asks whether the success of Finnish indie rock band Poets of the Fall in 2005, despite little in the way of a marketing campaign, may be related to the use of one of their songs in the first person shooter (FPS) game, *Max Payne 2: The Fall of Max Payne* (Remedy Entertainment 2003).

Another recent platform for music in games is in the area of mobile (cellular) telephones, which is the subject of the second section of the book, 'Ringtones and mobile phones'. Although many early mobile phones contained games, these games were generally without sound, and since that time, sound has developed in fits and starts amongst a confusion of standards and platforms. Although mobile phones are, in a sense, audio devices (primarily for voice, but also increasingly as multimedia devices), sound in mobile games remains fairly primitive in comparison to their console, PC or online counterparts. Part of the reason for this slow development has been the fact that mobile games are often consumed in public, and therefore audio has played a secondary role to image in games, with phone companies such as Nokia warning developers, 'The game should be playable without the sounds. Allow silent starting of games. If intro music is implemented, there must be a way to switch it off. Prompt for sound settings at the start of the game … Do not include loud or high-pitched sounds, have sounds on as the default, [or] use sounds that are similar to ring tones and alert tones'.[5]

One of the areas of music in which mobile phones have excelled has been ringtones, as phones have expanded from polyphonic chip-tunes to MP3 file formats. The ringtone industry is currently valued at about $4.5 billion worldwide, and makes up approximately 12 per cent of all music sales. Some have touted ringtones as perhaps being able to save the music industry, and trade magazines such as *Billboard* now regularly track ringtone sales. Ringtones can cost as much as three times the price of regular music downloads, and are useful as a marketing tool for selling albums and singles. As mobile phones are increasingly capable of playing MP3 files, however, consumers are less enthusiastic about paying high prices for tracks that they may have already purchased on iTunes or another Internet music service. In Chapter 3, 'Could ringtones *be* more annoying?', Peter Drescher, industry composer and sound designer at Danger, Inc., first presents a speech that he gave in 2004, and then looks back at how rapidly the industry has changed, and where it may soon lead.

Lacking the tools that are available to console or PC games developers due in part to so many competing standards, music in games has remained behind in fidelity and responsiveness, particularly in terms of how the audio reacts to and interacts with the mobile game player. Working at the French National Institute for Research in Computer Science and Control (INRIA), Jacques Lemordant and Agnès Guerraz have, within their research as part of Project WAM (Web, Adaptation and Multimedia), explored tools development for mobile devices, which they present in Chapter 4, 'Indeterminate adaptive digital audio for games on mobiles'. Here they

---

5   Nokia Corporation, 'From Beeps To Soundscapes: Designing Mobile Game Audio' (2005): http://sw.nokia.com/id/e2b3d80a–5ea7–453b–978e–1814310b4639/From_Beeps_To_ Soundscapes_Designing_Mobile_Game_Audio_v1_0_en.pdf (accessed 10 June 2007).

describe some of the common problems of mobile audio formats, and explore how game audio developers can build complex dynamic soundtracks for mobile games.

Though mobile phones are still struggling with conflicting standards and tools, current games consoles have to a large extent overcome many of the constraints that were experienced in previous games machines, and attention is increasingly turning towards the aesthetics and style of games audio, specifically how the music interacts with and adapts to the needs of the game-play and the game player. I have elsewhere defined this aspect of games music as dynamic, or audio that changes in relation to what happens in the game, encompassing both interactive and adaptive audio.[6] Interactive audio refers to sound events that occur in reaction to a player's input. In other words, the player can press a button to make the player jump, and the jumping elicits a sound. Adaptive audio, on the other hand, occurs in reaction to game-play, in terms of being set to occur in response to timings or other parameters set by the game's engine, rather than directly in response to the player. For instance, in *Super Mario Bros.* (Nintendo 1985), there is a timer that causes the music to increase in tempo when the time on a level begins to run out. The dynamic aspects of games music are an important distinguishing factor from more linear music such as that of film or television media. The third section of the book, 'Instruments and interactions', presents three chapters which address the issue of composing for dynamic media. Each of these chapters is written by authors who compose dynamic music, whether for games, Internet, or multimedia installations.

In Chapter 5, 'Theoretical approaches to composing dynamic music for video games', Danish game and Web composer Jesper Kaae provides a theoretical argument for plundering music's history, particularly the twentieth-century avant-garde, to search for approaches to variability and adaptability, which he distinguishes as two main requirements of dynamic music. Variability, or a kind of random sequencing, is used in games to increase the lifespan of a piece of music, which may need to be repeated hundreds of times for the player. By variably sequencing the music's component parts, the music becomes less repetitive. Adaptability, on the other hand, he defines as encompassing the interactive and adaptive elements of music described above.

In Chapter 6, 'Realizing groundbreaking adaptive music', Dutch sound designer Tim van Geelen provides a practical look at the problem of composing for games, giving us examples of the functions and uses of dynamic music in games and explaining some of the tools involved in creating dynamic audio in what he terms 'parallel composing', or composing songs in a linear fashion in layers that can be interchanged. Chapter 7, 'The composition-instrument: emergence, improvisation and interaction in games and new media' by interactive composer Norbert Herber, describes a composition-instrument conceptual model of a work that can play and be played simultaneously, bringing in examples from contemporary games such as Nintendo's *Electroplankton* (Nintendo 2005), in which a user can work with the game interface to create music.

---

6   Karen Collins, 'An introduction to the Participatory and Non-linear Aspects of Video Game Audio', in Stan Hawkins and John Richardson (eds), *Essays on Sound and Vision* (Helsinki, 2007).

The fourth section of the book involves new 'Techniques and technologies' that have arisen in the most recent generation of console releases (Xbox 360, PlayStation 3 and the Nintendo Wii). The integration of the audio into a game, particularly how games music interacts with other audio elements in a game (such as dialogue, sound effects and ambience), poses many interesting problems for games audio developers. Unlike in linear media where audio is mixed in a post-production model to a fixed image, game timings and interactions are unpredictable, and mixing must essentially be accomplished in real time. Mixing involves the interplay of all the audio components in a game to ensure that there is no overlap between frequencies, including deciding which elements should be emphasized, and which should be de-emphasized in the mix. In Chapter 8, 'Dynamic range: subtlety and silence in video game sound', Rob Bridgett, the sound director at Swordfish Studios, explores interactive mixing in real time, and discusses the problem of dynamic range in current games audio, suggesting some ways in which to overcome these issues.

Of course, another issue in games sound is the need for more variation in sound effects. Playing 40 hours with the same gunshot sound, or the same footsteps, can get very repetitive for the player, leading to listener fatigue, and the player's desire to turn off sound altogether. Leonard Paul, a games and film composer working at the Vancouver Film School, addresses the issue of repetition by introducing us to granular synthesis in Chapter 9, 'An introduction to granular synthesis in video games'. In granular synthesis, sounds can be constructed from smaller grains of sound which could be adapted in real time in a game, so that no sound effect would play back in the same way twice. He takes us through a tutorial using an open-source real-time graphical programming environment, PureData, and gives us examples of how such an application could be used in games sound effects, ambience, dialogue and music to ensure the player gets enough variation to keep sound in games interesting.

Finally, the last section of the book, 'Audio and audience', addresses the uses and users of games audio. The leading industry organization, the Entertainment Software Association, claims that over 75 per cent of heads of households in the United States now play computer or video games.[7] They also claim that games are now almost evenly divided in terms of gender (slightly more males), and that the average age of gamers is increasing as the first generation ages and buys machines that they share with their children. But audiences vary considerably depending on genre and platforms, as does the music, and how music is used in these games also varies. The final section of this book, then, asks whether or not audio has an impact on players, what this impact is and what may be some of the alternate uses for games audio.

For instance, despite some of the advances in games sound technologies, there have been some musicians who have coveted the older chip-tune aesthetic of the earlier 8-bit games era (roughly 1975–85), and who create music from older sound chip technology. These composers embrace the many constraints of the older chip technology, which was often limited to simple (typically square) waveforms, few channels and low memory. While chip-tunes, or 'micromusic', have been around for many years, growing out of the computer 'demoscene', there has been a recent

---

7 See the Industry Facts at the Entertainment Software Association's website, http://www.theesa.com/facts/index.php (accessed 5 June 2007).

surge in popularity for this music, particularly now, a time when there has been a general increased nostalgia for old video games (witnessed in recent art exhibits and books such as *I Am 8-Bit* and a documentary called simply '8-Bit'). In Chapter 10, 'Chip music: low tech data music sharing', chip-tunes composer Anders Carlsson of Sweden's Goto80 takes us through the history of the demoscene and chip music, and explores the implications of the recent success on the scene.

Chapter 11, Kristine Jørgensen's 'Left in the dark: playing computer games with the sound turned off', explores the impact that games sound can have on the player. Drawing on her PhD thesis work which tested male gamers responding to games with and without sound, she challenges some of the assumptions about games audio and its functions and uses in different genres, ultimately determining that game usability is affected significantly by audio, but that this is to some extent dependent on genre. In Chapter 12, 'Music theory in music games', Peter Shultz asks what kinds of skills and concepts rhythm-action games (music-based games) entail. He explores the systems of notation in music games, thus exploring games music as a potential avenue for education.

PART 1
Industries and synergies

Chapter 1

The new MTV? Electronic Arts and 'playing' music

Holly Tessler

In October of 2004 I attended the MusicWorks conference in Glasgow, Scotland. In several days' worth of seminars, discussions and question-and-answer surgeries, the most memorable talk came from Steve Schnur, ostensibly an outsider to the world of music, as he was in attendance as a delegate representing video game publisher Electronic Arts. I call Schnur's presentation memorable because it was dazzlingly multimedia-focused. He showed promotional clips of soon-to-be-released video games with new and exclusive music from big-name artists; in this instance, Snoop Dogg's version of 'Riders on the Storm', licensed for use in Electronic Arts' (EA's) *Need for Speed Underground*. Schnur's talk was high in what Scott Donaton calls 'emotional capital': intellectual property designed 'to elicit emotion and create connections'.[1] Indeed, that is precisely what had taken place in this half-hour demonstration/promotion/advertising sales pitch. To me, and to others, who, having grown up on *Frogger* and *Pac-Man*, at first only saw a seemingly peripheral relationship between video games and popular music, Schnur's talk was convincing. Beyond the audio-visual pyrotechnics, Schnur's MusicWorks presentation was compelling, if not outright provocative, for another reason as well. The clear message put across was not just in Glasgow, but also at trade shows such as MIDEM,[2] as well as in trade publications like *Music Week* and *Billboard* and broadsheets like the *Financial Times* and *The Guardian*. Schnur has called video games 'one of the most important breakthroughs in the history of the music industry ... What MTV used to be: ushering in trends and creating the new "cool".'[3] Schnur reasoned that 'music video first appeared in 1981, and, since then, a generation has been raised with an expectation of visuals attached to audio.'[4] He continued that video games, like MTV and rock' n' roll music:

> Fight many of the same battles ... [They] continue to develop with the same fierce spirit and 'screw you' swagger. They court the same controversies. They ... hold great festivals.

---

1   Scott Donaton, *Madison and Vine: Why the Entertainment and Advertising Industries Must Converge to Survive* (Ohio, 2004), p. 52.
2   MIDEM (*Marché international de l'édition musicale*) is the world's largest music industry trade show.
3   Steve Schnur, 'Video games and music have a strong relationship', *Music Week*, 1 November 2003, p. 16.
4   Schnur, 'Video games and music have a strong relationship', p. 16.

They can empower us, obsess us and, hopefully, continue to always surprise and challenge us. And no matter how old you are, your parents will still never understand.[5]

Schnur extended this analogy even further, drawing parallels between the technological advances of popular music and video games:

The Atari can be considered the gramophone of our culture. Our Sega and Nintendo game cartridges are another generation's 8-track tapes and LPs. Sony's original PlayStation may seem as quaint and almost prehistoric as an Elvis movie today ... The themes from 'Pac-Man', 'Donkey Kong', 'Super Mario' and 'Zelda' are as crucial to our consciousness as the riffs from 'Johnny B. Goode or 'Satisfaction' ... 'Def Jam Vendetta' remains as conceptually groundbreaking as the Who's 'Tommy'. We remain the same force for change. Today, games can be our Beatles, our Sex Pistols, our Nirvana ... So are videogames the new rock'n'roll? I say absolutely, yes, videogames are the new rock'n'roll. Videogames are the new hip-hop. They are the new house, heavy metal, R&B and punk. They are our culture. They are us ... Videogames will become the new radio ... [and] the new MTV.[6]

To support this rhetoric of the importance of video gaming, Schnur made reference to a number of interesting statistics. For instance, he argued that 60 per cent of all North Americans and 40 per cent of all Europeans play video games.[7] He asserted that there will soon be a worldwide household penetration rate near to 70 per cent for video game consoles and, interestingly, he cited a consumer survey which determined that Americans, on average, spend about 75 hours more per year playing video games than they do watching rented videos/DVDs, watching television or listening to the radio.[8]

It is undeniable that video games are big business, with worldwide sales estimates of around $28 billion (USD) each year,[9] but does that really make gaming the new MTV? The new rock 'n' roll? The new hip-hop? Beyond the catchy rallying cry, which is undeniably seductive, the argument Schnur is ultimately making is that video games are new cultural and industrial intermediaries, forging new customer-motivated and consumer-driven business partnerships. EA has become so embedded in various entertainment industry deals and initiatives, the parallel to MTV is especially clear in one particular aspect: it becomes difficult to determine if video games exist to promote popular music, or, if the EA model is fully extrapolated, if popular music exists to promote video games. The most evident comparison which can be made between video games and music video remains implicitly unarticulated by Schnur or any of his counterparts: the impact of the video game industry on the vertical integration of the music industry. Drawing similarities between music video and video games in this regard makes for some interesting discussion. For

---

5   Steve Schnur, 'Playing For Keeps: Videogames Have Changed The Way We Hear Music', *Billboard*, 6 November 2004, p. 10.

6   Schnur, 'Playing For Keeps: Videogames Have Changed The Way We Hear Music', p. 10.

7   Schnur, 'Playing For Keeps: Videogames Have Changed The Way We Hear Music', p. 10.

8   Schnur, 'Video games and music have a strong relationship', p. 16.

9   Aaron Weiss, 'From Bits to Hits', *NetWorker*, March 2004, p. 23.

instance, Banks has written 'Music video functions at the major record labels can be divided roughly into three areas: production, promotion and retail distribution.'[10] I would assert that video games can be understood as following a similar trajectory. Each of the following sections will detail key developments spearheaded by EA, which first underscore the centrality of video games in all facets of the contemporary popular music industry, but also aim to evaluate whether the EA strategy is unique, reproducible or even sustainable within the contemporary entertainment and cultural industries climate.

Video games and the production of popular music

Like music video before it, video games as a new medium for popular music have become so noteworthy because of their almost seamless integration into record companies' infrastructure. In terms of production, many major video game publishers, but in particular EA, have become gatekeepers, if not fully-fledged A&R[11] functionaries, for both major and independent record labels by presenting new and exclusive music to gamers worldwide. The UK industry trade paper *Music Week* estimates between 3,000 to 4,000 songs were submitted by artists and labels around the world to EA in hopes of inclusion on the soundtrack to *FIFA 2005*.[12] One-quarter of those songs which made the final cut onto the game soundtrack came from independent labels.[13] But unlike music video, which polarized the bifurcation between major and independent record labels,[14] video games as a new medium for facilitating the production of popular music embrace tracks from both sectors with equal zeal, as they seek to include artists and songs that 'drive the game while enhancing the gaming experience'.[15] Indeed, Schnur credits EA for helping to break (then) indie acts like Franz Ferdinand, Arctic Monkeys and The Streets,[16] reasoning that 'Videogames take chances with new music where radio does not.'[17]

There is perhaps no more evident case for the power of video games as a new medium and production channel for popular music than EA's series of virtual-world-building games, *The Sims*. Characters in the games speak to each other in a language known as 'Simlish', purportedly a fractured combination of Ukrainian

---

10 Jack Banks, 'Video in the Machine: The Incorporation of Music Video into the Recording Industry', *Popular Music* 16/30 (1997): 293–309, p. 294.

11 The Artist and Repertoire division of a record company, which is responsible for the scouting, acquisition and development of artists.

12 Music Week 2004/6.

13 Scott Banjeree, 'The Labels Have Seen EA Games Break New Bands: The Last Word: A Q&A with Steve Schnur', *Billboard*, 15 May 2004, p. 86.

14 Banks, 'Video in the Machine: The Incorporation of Music Video into the Recording Industry', p. 16.

15 Schnur, 'Video games and music have a strong relationship', p. 16.

16 Stuart Miles and Adam Sherwin, 'Sir Cliff is displaced by a halo', *The Times*, 27 November 2004, p. 45. Senay Boztas, 'Computer games the new MTV for bands', *The Sunday Herald,* 21 November 2004, p. 8. Michael Paoletta, 'EA Scores One For New Music With "Madden"', *Billboard*, 13 August 2005, p. 10.

17 Steve Schnur in Paoletta, 'EA Scores One For New Music With 'Madden', p. 10.

and Tagalog.[18] Through recording and licensing deals with EA, a variety of well-established musical acts have re-recorded Simlish-language versions of their hits for various Sims games. Howard Jones has remade a Simlish-language version of his 1985 hit 'Things Can Only Get Better' and Depeche Mode have released a Simlish version of their single 'Suffer Well' from the 2005 album *Playing the Angel*. Both tracks were included in the soundtrack for *The Sims 2*. Similarly, the Black Eyed Peas have recorded 9 of 15 tracks from their 2005 album *Monkey Business* in the virtual language for *The Urbz: Sims in the City*.

The Simlish experience is just part of a larger strategy by EA and other video game publishers to introduce new and previously unfamiliar music to a worldwide audience. Maissa Dauriac, music supervisor at Syncope Entertainment, supports EA's involvement with labels to produce new music: 'With a [videogame] soundtrack you need to offer the audience an original song that is not available anywhere else but on that soundtrack.'[19] As Stanley suggests,[20] video games publishers are, in effect, 'programming the radio station of the future', establishing a partnership that is beneficial to both the gaming and music industries. Record labels get tremendous amounts of promotional airplay for their artists and music, while video games publishers enhance the 'value-added' experience of their titles through the utilization of new music.

Video games and the promotion of popular music

In terms of promotion, it becomes a debatable question whether video games are reliant on popular music, or whether popular music is reliant on video games. Banks wrote of the role of video promotion departments in record labels as being ones that use:

> Video clips to get favourable public exposure for their artists. These divisions distribute a label's video clips to music programme services and also plan marketing campaigns for artists that often include promotional contests on MTV or other shows. These executives make arrangements for their label's artists to be guests on outlets like MTV or BET and develop short promotional spots featuring the artist to air on these services.[21]

The parallel between the promotional function of MTV and video games is clear in this regard. Schnur has said:

> Our first discussions were based on 'what if'. What if we could break bands? What if we could be a part of your [record labels'] weekly internal discussion where you used to talk about the MTV plan, the radio plan, the touring plan, the press plan? Would we ever get

---

    18 Mark Brown, 'Depeche Mode try a new style: en dough cheeky-a-vunch', *The Guardian*, 4 March 2006, p. 13.

    19 In Patrick Klepek, 'Frag to the music: Record labels, games publishers see licensed music as booming biz', *Computer Gaming World*, 250, April 2005, p. 33.

    20 T.L. Stanley, 'Music world hits new high note', *Advertising Age*, 75/21 (2004), p. 4.

    21 Banks, 'Video in the Machine: The Incorporation of Music Video into the Recording Industry', p. 294.

to the point where the labels would talk about the EA plan? I can tell you we're there. The labels vie for a spot in EA games.[22]

EA's push to see video games as another legitimate promotional outlet for popular music appears to be succeeding. For instance, one of EA's top-selling titles, the snowboarding adventure *SSX3*, sold around five million copies worldwide.[23] Average game-play statistics demonstrate that a typical video game will be shared by 2.5 people, who play for 50 hours each, and each song on the title's soundtrack will pop up around twice an hour.[24] Based on these numbers, EA estimates each song on the *SSX3* soundtrack will have been heard about 500 million times worldwide at the end of the game's lifecycle, which is far more airplay 'than a number one record around the world' will receive.[25]

EA makes further reference to a 2003 study which indicated that in consumers aged 13–32, '49% learned about – and bought – a CD by a new artist after hearing a song in a game'.[26] In support of this claim, EA's release of American football bestseller *Madden NFL* has proved itself adept at helping to promote new music. Schnur cites the 2003 version of the game for boosting sales of Good Charlotte's song 'The Anthem'. The song was included on the *Madden* soundtrack in August of 2002, a month prior to release of the band's album *The Young and the Hopeless*. Epic Records has been quoted as saying the advance publicity for the song and the band through the video game increased sales 'considerably'.[27] Blink-182's single 'Feeling This' on Geffen, released on *Madden 2004*, shares a similar history. The 2004 edition of the game was released three months ahead of the band's radio release of the single and 'By the time it got to radio … Geffen was in a very confident position that they had a song that was not only a hit, [they] had a song that was going to garner requests. To date it is the most successfully researched record that Blink has put out.'[28]

It would appear that the shared demographics between video gamers and consumers of popular music make for a comfortable relationship where benefit flows in both directions, from video games to popular music, but also from popular music to the game publisher. Kamau High notes a growing market demand for video game music.[29] Music has become a feature – and selling point – of video games, just as much as video games help promote popular music. This can be very likely attributed

22 Cited in Banjeree, 'The Labels Have Seen EA Games Break New Bands: The Last Word: A Q&A with Steve Schnur', p. 86.

23 Schnur, 'Video games and music have a strong relationship', p. 16.

24 Boztas, 'Computer games the new MTV for bands', p. 8.

25 Schnur, 'Video games and music have a strong relationship'; Boztas, 'Computer games the new MTV for bands', p. 8; Kate Fitzgerald, 'By the demo: music for the ages', *Advertising Age*, 74/30 (2003), pp. 3–4.

26 Schnur, 'Video games and music have a strong relationship', p. 16.

27 Fitzgerald, 'By the demo: music for the ages', p. 3.

28 Schnur in Banjeree, 'The Labels Have Seen EA Games Break New Bands: The Last Word: A Q&A with Steve Schnur', p. 86. Radio relies on record research to determine audience preferences about artists, songs, genres and so on.

29 Kamau High, 'In search of all the young men with big bulging wallets', *Financial Times*, 24 May 2005, p. 14.

to the fact that many of today's musicians are themselves video gamers, and the lure of being affiliated with a video game has all the appeal and none of the stigma of other music licensing opportunities. For instance, in 2005 Sierra Entertainment released *50 Cent: Bulletproof* where players 'fight, shoot and bludgeon their way through life' in a semi-biographical video game adaptation of the rapper's life.[30] Similarly, EA's *Def Jam Vendetta*, released in 2003, is a street fighting/wrestling/ story-telling game where players fight 'real life' artists from the Def Jam roster including DMX, Method Man and Ludacris. In the same type of cross-promotional synergy, game publisher Atari and Motown Records collaborated in 2004 on the debut of *Transformers*, a video game based on the popular toy of the same name. Players who progress successfully through the game unlock both the debut single, 'Wishbone', from new act Dropbox, as well as their cover of the *Transformers* theme song as a reward for winning the game. The music video for 'Wishbone', directed by Nigel Dick, also features footage from the game.

Not to be overshadowed, platform providers like Sony, Microsoft and Nintendo also exploit this cosy relationship between popular music and gaming to promote their own hardware releases. Nintendo's annual Fusion Tour combines live performances from developing and established acts like Hawthorne Heights, Evanescence, Fall Out Boy, Panic! At The Disco and My Chemical Romance with an opportunity for concertgoers to play brand-new Nintendo game releases. In a slight twist on the live-performance *oeuvre*, Microsoft, in promoting its Xbox console, sponsors 'Game With Fame' events where gamers have the chance to battle online against actors, professional athletes and musicians like Chris Cornell and Rihanna.

Kamau High notes the emergence of music from video games as emerging cultural events entirely of their own prestige.[31] Specifically, he cites the popularity of orchestral performances of music from the video game series *Final Fantasy* being sell-out attractions in Chicago and Japan. Similarly, the Video Games Live touring event has performed music from games such as *Halo*, *Tomb Raider* and *Myst*. All of these cross-promotional events and partnerships underscore the vibrancy and dynamism of, as well as the potential for, a wireless, online entertainment medium that encompasses popular music, video gaming, hardware, software and portable technologies like mobile phones and MP3 players. The following section of the chapter explores some of the retail implications of this 'hypermedium'.

Video games and the distribution of popular music

In further consideration of Schnur's assertion that video games are the new MTV, it is again helpful to return to Banks's discussion of the role of video music in played in extending the role of distribution of popular music. He writes:

> The record labels have collaborated with MTV to gain greater control over the distribution and exhibition of music videos ... The mutually beneficial arrangement allowed MTV to

---

30 Kamau High, 'Industries in tune to woo young fans', *Financial Times*, 6 September 2005, p. 14.

31 High, 'In search of all the young men with big bulging wallets', p. 14.

pick video clips featuring hit singles and major recording stars for its exclusive use that would probably increase its ratings, while record companies could get guaranteed exposure for their artists that might not otherwise get airplay ... The primary objectives of these accords was to control jointly the emerging distribution system for clips. These agreements created a degree of vertical integration through contractual agreement by forging links between the production of clips (commissioned by labels) and the distribution of clips through exposure media (MTV). These contracts were a way that record companies could get exposure for their artists while also insuring the stability and strength of MTV.[32]

Banks's primary assertion, that record labels and video music channels collaborated in mutually beneficial contractual arrangements, is plainly echoed in EA's own recent dealings with the music industry. EA's first direct venture into the music business, EA Trax, established in 2002, formally integrated licensed music into the gaming experience with the aim of enhancing the playing experience. First utilized in EA's range of sports-oriented titles, games came loaded with 'a selection of songs from established and emerging artists, picked specifically for each game'. EA Trax is more than a kind of 'sonic wallpaper', however. Its music is both non-diegetic and diegetic in use, accompanying 'menu screens, replays, and specific game modes, as well as pump[ing] from the sound systems in stadiums and arenas'.[33] While EA claims the primary aim of EA Trax is to create a more intense game-play, from the outset the idea also had clear and further industry implications.

Not content to simply provide a new cross-promotional conduit between music and video games, through its next music-oriented venture, Next Level Music, EA expanded even further the vertical integration of the music industry.[34] In 2004 EA and music publisher Cherry Lane announced a teaming up to create Next Level Music, a company 'that will sign established as well as emerging new artists, acquire publishing catalogs, produce original music and further develop EA's rich catalog of music'.[35] More than just an innovative music industry practice, Next Level Music is also significant as it draws an 'analogous relationship' to the partnerships between music publishing companies and motion picture studios in the early decades of the twentieth century. Simply, in the same way both music publishers and film studios saw the shared benefit of utilizing music in film, EA and Cherry Lane are both plainly aware of a similarly favourable partnership in this century.

Next Level Music makes manifest the opportunity to exploit popular music in video games in entirely new markets. For instance, video game soundtracks are now given sales awards in the same style as recorded-music albums and singles. EA's

32 Banks, 'Video in the Machine: The Incorporation of Music Video into the Recording Industry', p. 297.

33 Electronic Arts, 'EA TRAX Pumps Up Gameplay with Hot Artists and Fresh Music', *Electronic Arts* (2005), http://www.easports.com/articles/trax.jsp (accessed 12 May 2007).

34 Tim Wall describes vertical integration in the record industry as 'the joining of companies at different levels' in the production process starting with the signing of artists and musical composition, moving through the recording, copying, distribution and retail sectors. *Studying Popular Music Culture* (London, 2003) p. 89.

35 Cherry Lane Music Publishing, 'EA and Cherry Lane Music Enter Joint Venture' (2005), http://www.cherrylane.com/clpub/html/body_newsdtl.cfm?fSYSID=45&fNewsDeta il=True (accessed 12 May 2007).

NBA Live is the top-selling video game soundtrack of all time, earning a platinum record from *Billboard* magazine and the Recording Industry Association of America (RIAA), for selling over one million units.[36] Similarly, EA competitors Rockstar Games, in conjunction with Interscope Records, have released a top-selling series of music soundtracks in support of the *Grand Theft Auto* (*GTA*) series of car-chase video games. Kline et al. see cross-promotional deals like Next Level and *GTA* as being just the preliminary steps in video games and popular music emulating a 'Hollywood marketing model' consisting of 'soundtracks, product tie-ins, and media events'.[37] They argue these deliberately and carefully researched campaigns cultivate a subcultural 'symbolic field' which places emphasis not on just one product or another, but instead on an overall lifestyle, noting 'Rockstar sponsors nights at leading clubs in New York and London, promotes a line of skateboarder clothing, and commissions graffiti artists to design packaging for its games.'[38]

Indeed, Kline et al.'s supposition seemed to presage an even broader expansion plan by video game publishers, who have begun moving beyond terrestrial promotional campaigns into the virtual world as well. In 2005 EA entered into its third music industry deal. This time EA partnered with Nettwerk, a Canadian independent record label and artist management firm, to launch EA Recordings, 'a groundbreaking digital distribution label'.[39] The initiative aims to deliver music from EA video game titles as ringtones and MP3 files for download from retail websites like iTunes, MSN, Yahoo! Music, AOL Music and Rhapsody. This latest EA collaboration raises a number of key questions about the role of music in this lifestyle/digital/content paradigm. At its heart, EA Recordings expands thinking about how video game music, and potentially all music, can be monetized. For instance, consumers utilizing EA Recordings can download new and back-catalogue tracks licensed for use in a game. But they can also download new musical compositions and orchestral works scored specifically for a game title. Remixes by artists like Paul Oakenfold, and even in-game hip-hop beats produced by acts like Da Riffs and Just Blaze, are also added to the roster of available digital music which can be imported to computer hard drives, portable music players and also to mobile phones.

Indeed, in this push towards a range of new distribution opportunities, EA, and to a lesser degree competitors like Activision and Rockstar, have continued to develop and exploit new distribution channels for music where the music industry itself has failed to uncover them. In the same way that Napster and iTunes demonstrated to the major labels the mass-market potential for online music, EA Recordings is pioneering a process for the hybridization of content and technology. Platform providers, mobile phone manufacturers and consumer hardware creators are all watching the gaming

---

36 Giancarlo Varinini, 'The soundtrack for EA Sports' latest basketball game is the first video game soundtrack to go platinum' (2003), http://videogames.yahoo.com/newsarticle?eid =360530&page=0 (accessed 12 May 2007).

37 Stephen Kline, Nick Dyer-Witheford and Greig de Peuter, *Digital Games: The Interaction of Technology, Culture, and Marketing* (Montreal, 2003), p. 234.

38 Kline et al., *Digital Games: The Interaction of Technology, Culture, and Marketing*, p. 235.

39 Electronic Arts, 'EA and Nettwerk Music Ground Announce 'EA Recordings'' (2005), http://www.info.ea.com/news/pr/pr705.htm (accessed 12 May 2007).

industry with an eye towards moving closer to a 'one-click purchasing' model which will bring together a holistic entertainment and gaming lifestyle. Frost reports Sony Computer Entertainment and Microsoft are both exploring the feasibility of developing gaming consoles which will let players download music tracks or albums directly to portable devices like MP3 players or mobile phones.[40] As Weiss writes, '"Computer" companies such as Apple and video game companies like Electronic Arts smell opportunity – ultimately, to end-run around the content producers entirely. First they built the tools with which to create and distribute media – but next they'll make (and sell) the media itself.'[41]

The new MTV?

It is clear that EA, through its EA Trax, Next Level Music and EA Recordings deals, has aggressively pursued a vast array of music industry relationships, from dealing with artists to music publishing to establishing their own record company, and, most recently, venturing into digital distribution and online sales of video game music. All of these partnerships lend credence to Schnur's belief that music is no longer listened to, or even watched, but instead, *played* on mobile phones, on computers and websites, on media players, but especially on video game consoles as part of an overall gaming experience. But is it reasonable to conclude that video games are the new MTV? And if so, what has become of the 'old' MTV in this new world vision?

It is important to note that EA's ventures into the music industry are not without precedent. Nearly a decade earlier, Sega embraced the relationship between music and gaming with the founding of Twitch Records 'which specialized exclusively in video game music' with its own rosters of record pluggers, bands, recording studios and executive producers.[42] An idea likely ahead of its time, Twitch Records eventually folded, but was clearly a precedent for EA's more contemporary efforts. Its demise indicated music and video are not, as Schnur would like us to believe, equal partners. Instead, despite some shared benefit and mutual promotion, music is still a 'value-added' commodity and not a core product essential to the *oeuvre* of video games (except, perhaps, karaoke and other 'sing-along'/'dance-along'/'play-along' titles).

Questions of the 'market logic' and of the durability of popular music then lie beneath Schnur's assertion. That is to say, Schnur has made much of the fact labels and acts have benefited from early exposure through placement in video games. Clearly, this arrangement underscores the cultural power of music: if music did not have value, commercial and/or creative, it would serve no practicable purpose in being placed in video games. Yet this seemingly comfortable relationship between music and video games begs examination of the production and development schedules of each. Some artists are commissioned to write new songs for a specific

---

40 Laurence Frost, 'Video games drive music sales', *USA Today*, 26 January 2006, http://www.usatoday.com/tech/gaming/2006-01-26-music-stars_x.htm (accessed 12 May 2007).

41 Weiss, 'From Bits to Hits', p. 24.

42 Kline et al., *Digital Games: The Interaction of Technology, Culture, and Marketing*, p. 233.

video game title. But what of the other soundtrack inclusions? Will a video game's market release be postponed if a given act is dropped from its label? If the band breaks up? If the album's release is pushed back by the label?

Sergio Pimentel, music licensing and A&R manager for Sony Computer Entertainment Europe, speaking at the 2007 Game Developers' Conference, repeatedly stressed the tight deadlines for the production and release of new game titles, as well as the inevitable disappointment when faced with inability to license a particularly suitable track. Licensing fees for video games are generally at a rate that is less than in other media uses, like television commercials or film soundtracks, usually accounting for just one to two per cent of a video game's overall budget.[43] But is that an appropriate rate for the contribution of music to the gaming experience? Ultimately, it must be argued that virtually all licensed video game music remains a substitutable quantity. If the copyright holders want too much money, if the master recordings are lost, if there is an unavoidable delay in completing the track, game publishers will often either find an alternative song for the soundtrack, or simply do without it. In this regard, video games publishers hold a far greater amount of power than do labels or acts. That is not to say, however, that EA's business strategies should be summarily dismissed as opportunistic or unimportant rhetoric. EA, along with other industry innovators like Apple and Sony, have understood and created a new market for entertainment and youth culture. It is undeniable that video games and music are at the hub of these new uses and exploitation of intellectual property. Yet while on the surface the future looks promising for a video game-driven entertainment economy, there are still further considerations which should be evaluated.

Chief amongst these further considerations is the question of the role of music as intellectual property. In Schnur's view of the future of gaming, music is still at its heart. But what are the creative and commercial implications for musicians, composers and lyricists in a model where music is a value-added commodity and not the primary product? While EA and record labels have been quick to publicize the success of artists who have benefited from promotion in video games, there have also been criticisms levelled at game publishers who feature music as a prominent element of their titles. In a 2003 *Music Week* editorial, Catherine Bell lobbied that EA's policy of 'not paying royalties for the use of our [European] music in their games means they are at present unable to use all the music they want'.[44] Ironically, Bell drew her own parallel between EA and MTV saying, 'MTV entered the market a couple of decades ago, achieving incredible success by convincing record companies they should give its rights to use videos they had made, at considerable expense, for free because it was "promotion". What a great business plan: get your content free and then charge the viewer for seeing it.'[45] Schnur countered Bell's allegations in a letter to *Music Week* where he defended EA's practice of one-time, lump-sum

---

43 High, 'Industries in tune to woo young fans', p. 14; Frost, 'Video games drive music sales'.

44 Catherine Bell, 'Electronic Arts boss just wants our music for free', *Music Week*, 15 November 2003, p. 16.

45 Bell, 'Electronic Arts boss just wants our music for free'.

compensation to artists and labels for music used in games (called 'buyouts') as an alternative to the payment of royalties as being typical to the industry.[46] Supporting Schnur's position are comments from Sergio Pimentel, who concurs that buyouts are a standard practice.[47] Moreover, in his text *Game Design* author Bob Bates summarizes, 'A common compromise is for you to make a one-time payment to acquire all the rights you need for the life of the game, while the musician retains the rights for "non-interactive" use so that he can sell the music again in other arenas.'[48] Bates's phrase 'non-interactive' brings to light further issues surrounding the broader value of music in video games. Whether financial payments are in buyout or royalty form (or even signed away for 'promotional consideration'), the concept that the value of music can be divided in this new bifurcated way – interactive and non-interactive – necessitates a new, holistic way of considering music in video games based on how consumers utilize it in relation to the medium in which it is presented.

In the wake of MTV, video channel competitors like The Box offered viewers the opportunity to 'interact' with music video by phoning in to request certain songs. MTV chased this trend towards interactivity first through shows like *Total Request Live* and then, eventually, by broadcasting from glass-fronted Times Square studios before live audiences and spectators. Yet through all of these 'interactive' developments, the emphasis was still on the music video itself; ostensibly viewers were focusing on the music and visuals they voted to see. Once the videos aired, audience interaction ended. The same assumption cannot be made about the role of music in video games, where players' attention is never fully focused on the music. This realization leads on to a broader query regarding the artists and genres of music which exist outside the easy fit of the shared demographics between video games and popular music consumption. Jack Banks notes how in the 1980s talented but perhaps less photogenic acts, as well as entire musical genres that fell beyond the mainstream and popular, received less attention by both record labels and MTV, which favoured artists with a more provocative, aesthetically and/or visually appealing image.[49] Yet, as the medium of video music matured, rival and format-specific music channels filled the gaps left by MTV. BET (Black Entertainment Television), CMT (Country Music Television) and VH1 (music for an older demographic) are all examples of how video truly has become integrated into the music industry, through its ability to grow and adapt to changing market conditions. Because video games rely on active engagement, they cannot become 'background' entertainment that can be listened to while performing other tasks, unlike television.

While EA's ventures into popular music have been generally successful, it is still too early to tell whether their accomplishments are leading a developing market, or

---

46   Steve Schnur, 'Electronic Arts is happy to pay for its music', *Music Week*, 6 December 2003, p. 15.

47   Sergio Pimentel, '7 Deadly Sins of Music Licensing', *Game Developers Conference 2007*, 5–9 March 2007.

48   Bob Bates, *Games Design* (Boston, 2004), p. 190.

49   Banks, 'Video in the Machine: The Incorporation of Music Video into the Recording Industry'.

are just one company's benefit of hiring an executive who is a seasoned veteran of the music industry. Not everyone in the gaming industry shares Schnur's enthusiasm and vision. For instance, Adrian Strain, spokesman for the IFPI,[50] has said that video games are 'a small but very interesting growth area' of the $21 billion worldwide music industry.[51] Indeed, synching music to video games is not always a 'slam dunk' marketing coup for musicians and/or labels. For instance, despite high volumes of sales for both the game and the initial soundtrack for *Grand Theft Auto*, a sequel title, *Grand Theft Auto: Vice City*, followed a similar game–soundtrack release model, but the 1980s collection of music managed only 30,135 units sold whereas the game itself sold approximately 8.5 million units worldwide.[52] Moreover, the vice-president of marketing for rival video game publisher NCsoft seems less than enthusiastic about partnering with record labels: 'The music stands on its own ... I don't know if any of it will end up in the top 10 of the *Billboard* charts, but you never know.'[53]

Ultimately, while it is indisputable that video game publishers and the music industry have become inextricably intertwined, I would assert that it is still video games that are benefiting more from the arrangement. Schnur is furthering a long-standing tradition at EA, begun by company founder Trip Hawkins in 1982, to maximize the cultural cache surrounding video games by emulating music industry marketing techniques, like packaging its games with 'album-like artwork and liner notes', and promoting its developers like rock stars in game magazines'.[54] But what of MTV itself in this new interactive age? Schnur's comment that video games are the new MTV implies the 'old' MTV is somehow irrelevant or extraneous to the EA world-view of the entertainment industry. Yet MTV is not quite the relic Schnur would have the public believe it is. In 2005 the video music channel collaborated with Midway Games to launch MTV Games, in a move that could be seen as an attempt to maintain/re-establish a cultural link to gamers. Its first release was the street-racing game *LA Rush*. In a direct challenge to the video game–music pairing promoted by Schnur and EA, MTV and Midway are pioneering a music video/video game partnership which launched with the game *Pimp My Ride*, based on the MTV lifestyle show of the same name. In an entirely differently cross-promotional strategy, MTV broadcast a special about the game in October 2005 to a worldwide audience of people who, evidently, still watch music as well as 'play' it.[55]

---

50 IFPI is the International Federation of the Phonographic Industry.

51 Cited in Frost, 'Video games drive music sales'.

52 Klepek, 'Frag to the music: Record labels, games publishers see licensed music as booming biz', p. 33.

53 High, 'Industries in tune to woo young fans', *Financial Times*, 6 September 2005, p. 14.

54 Kline et al., *Digital Games: The Interaction of Technology, Culture, and Marketing*, p. 97.

55 High, 'Industries in tune to woo young fans', p. 14.

Conclusion

Are video games the new MTV? According to EA worldwide executive of music Steve Schnur, the answer is a resounding 'yes'. And on first glance, it is an exciting idea. As technologies advance and as corporations become increasingly global in scope, video games as a central hub linking mobile technologies, gaming platforms, hardware, software, digital distribution and content is a compelling argument. More than just promotional positioning, EA has followed through on Schnur's vision with three innovative music industry deals: EA Trax, Next Level Music and EA Recordings. While not without precedent, these ventures clearly put EA at the fore of a new business model where music and gaming share cross-promotional space with an aim of attracting the same consumers.

But has EA, and by extension the whole of the video game market, become the same kind of cultural and industrial force that MTV became in the early 1980s? Video games clearly share a number of the same production, promotional and distribution practices that video music pioneered 25 years earlier. Schnur has inarguably carved out a niche in an intensely crowded marketplace, and in doing so, developed new and legitimate channels for the promotion of popular music. And to his credit, MTV was operating on a far less technologically dense playing field. Video music was at the hub of a society coming to grips with cable (or satellite) television, video recorders and a music industry seeking to find its way out of the doldrums left by disco and punk. Video games today face far more competition: mobile technologies and ringtones, digital television technologies like TiVo, satellite and subscription digital radio, online and digital downloading, in addition to traditional television, film and print media. So the fact that EA has managed to find new and successful ways of promoting music and gaming that ties together hardware, software and content in such an elegant and seemingly natural fashion is nothing less than remarkable. Schnur has made partners of companies and industries that would in lesser hands be perceived as competitors. Therefore, EA, I would argue, is, for all these reasons, *a* new MTV, if not necessarily *the* new MTV.

What EA has demonstrated is that there is a clear way forward to exploit intellectual property effectively in the mobile age, both creatively and commercially. But the EA model is not the only way forward. And it is certainly not one that places a premium on the creative value inherent in music. Instead, EA and MTV, along with their competitors and compatriots, are ultimately hawking popular culture, youth culture in particular, which just happens to utilize music as a secondary selling point. And, as Jimmy Iovine, President of Interscope/Geffen/A&M Records (owned by Universal Music Group) has said, 'When you create popular culture, you should benefit by it ... We will start to pick up revenues from the coattail that we create. If we're involved in creating popular culture ... we're going to be paid around our music. The other people are.'[56]

---

56 Donaton, *Madison and Vine: Why the Entertainment and Advertising Industries Must Converge to Survive*, p. 156.

Chapter 2

Marketing music through computer games: the casc of Poets of the Fall and *Max Payne 2*

Antti-Ville Kärjä

On 19 January 2005 the Finnish pop charts were bewildered. The reason behind the excitement was the new number one album, namely *Signs of Life* by the group Poets of the Fall. There was nothing particularly novel or extraordinary in the album's contents, as indie rock sung in English is arguably one of the main trends in contemporary Finnish popular music, but what made the situation peculiar was the fact that the group did not have either a recording or publishing deal with any music company; in other words, *Signs of Life* was issued as a custom, or self-released, album on the group members' own label. For this reason, there was no marketing campaign promoting the release of the album. 'Late Goodbye', a song from the album, had been released as a single in June 2004, and it had been well received in radio stations, thus reaching top positions in radio play charts. While the success of the single release may explain (at least to some extent) the popularity of the album, is there anything else that might account for the ascendancy of the single?

According to numerous comments and reviews, the answer to this question is the first person shooter (FPS) computer game *Max Payne 2: The Fall of Max Payne* (PS, PS2, Xbox), produced by the Finnish game development company Remedy Entertainment Ltd and released in October 2003. The song 'Late Goodbye' can be heard during the end credits in its entirety, and there are also modified snippets of it audible amidst some of the actual gaming sequences. The song and the group were awarded first prize at the annual GANG (Game Audio Network Guild) ceremony, which was televised on MTV and on the US G4TV channel. According to the group's agent, '[r]adio stations in many countries have placed Late Goodbye on their playlist, and mp3 files of the song have spread all over the internet like a virus.'[1] Thus, with the game the song was spread 'to millions of homes throughout the world' and the group had fans all over 'even before the release of the first single'.[2] Furthermore, reaching the pole position in the album charts after only three gigs was, for some, 'in the contemporary culture of attention economy and the crossfire of *Popstars* and

---

[1]   Sam Agency, 'POTF bio in English' (2006), at http://www.samagency.fi/ (accessed 3 January 2007).

[2]   *Curly-Zine*, 'Poets of the Fall' (2005), at http://www.curly.fi/ (accessed 3 January 2007). My translation.

Idolses ... an incredible accomplishment'.[3] To be sure, even in 2005 using computer games as an outlet for breaking new bands was by no means a new phenomenon,[4] but the results of this particular combination and its relationship to conventional marketing practices within the popular music industry have proven to be somewhat extraordinary.

The juxtaposition of the group's success with *Pop Stars* and *American Idol* is instructive when it comes to examining the ways in which the practices of music production, dissemination and marketing have changed in recent years. Apparently, because of allegedly increased losses caused by thriving piracy, aided in turn by continually more efficient and effortless digital copying methods, new forms and structures of production and marketing have been adopted within the recording industry. While especially within the realm of rock (with which Poets of the Fall are most often associated), ideas about hard work and a long career on a grass-roots level have been persistent. Elsewhere the aid of audio-visual media, in particular in marketing and promoting (and, as the derogatory rock proverb goes, 'selling out') acts, has been welcomed without significant suspicions. Indeed it should be remembered that there is nothing exceptionally new in the general principles behind the use of either media or competitions for A&R and promotion purposes, virtually simultaneously. For example, in Finland the annual Tango Royals competition (held since 1985) is televised live, and in 1959 the first Rock King of Finland, Rock-Jerry (born Kaj Järnström), was likewise crowned in a live television show, namely *Music, Music, Music* (yes, originally in English).

The more recent A&R television programmes such as the *Pop Stars* or *American Idol* series may very well demonstrate a shift in the practices within the recording industry. As Catherine Moore writes about the outcomes of *Pop Stars*, the eventual records are not '"made for TV" but records "made on TV"', just as the record deals for the winners are 'the reward for success in front of a TV camera' instead of 'honing [their] skills in an unseen suburban garage, and learning to perform by playing in tiny clubs'.[5] The case of 'Late Goodbye' gives substantial reason to suspect that computer games might also play a role in all this, and it is this line of inquiry that I will follow. In other words, I will investigate the changes implied here with respect to popular music production and marketing, as well as to the production context of computer game music. I will lay a particular emphasis on conceptualizations of synergy and practices associated with it, with a separate stress on copyright issues.

Conglomeration

The interrelations between music and media have not passed unnoticed within scholarly activities, particularly the study of film music, which now has a long history.

---

3   Jocka Träskbäck, 'Poets of the Fall' (2005), *Stara.fi*, at http://www.stara.fi/ (accessed 3 January 2007). My translation.

4   See Karen Collins, 'Grand Theft Audio? Popular Music and Intellectual Property in Video Games', *Music and the Moving Image*, 1/1 (working draft, forthcoming in 2008).

5   Catherine Moore, 'A Picture is Worth 1000 CDs: Can the Music Industry Survive as a Stand-Alone Business?', *American Music*, 22/1 (2004), p. 181.

While much of this research has been carried out in music(ology) departments with a tendency to emphasize the 'masterpiece tradition' by concentrating on classical film scoring and thus overvaluing human agency and aesthetic concerns at the expense of social, cultural, economic or technological circumstances,[6] in accounts on popular music production the latter aspects have been readily accepted with respect to the interconnectedness of music and media. Here, examinations of the music industry are paramount, as it is in these that the web of connections between music, media, legislation and consumption transpire clearly.[7] It should be borne in mind, however, that while these studies in many cases are centred on various forms of popular music, the essential principles outlined in them are applicable to all kinds of music that is produced, disseminated and consumed within an industrial context. Just as Robert Burnett states, 'for the music industry, popular music consists of whichever musical styles sell sufficient numbers to be deemed successful or representative of an audience.'[8]

Conglomeration turns out to be a key issue here. Following David Hesmondhalgh, conglomeration can be defined as the process of formation of corporations that consist of 'a group of companies, dealing in different products or services'.[9] For example, in the current situation (that is, early 2008), the world music market is dominated by the 'Big Four' companies, each of which operates not only in the music business, but most notably in various other media. One of these companies is Sony BMG, with apparent links to the production of, for instance, the Sony PlayStation video game console.

Despite this kind of more than obvious connection between music and computer games, scholarly accounts on the topic are virtually non-existent, whether focusing on aesthetics, production or any other aspect. As is the case with the majority of analyses of audio-visual media, questions concerning aesthetics and interpretations tend to be questions about visual representations and narrative. Still, as can be suggested on the basis of a quotation from a review of the recent *Lara Croft Tomb Raider: Legend* game, game audio aesthetics could be worth consideration too:

> As for the game's sound, the game's soundtrack, voice acting and sound effects make this a satisfying cinematic experience. The eclectic score, for one, changes with each situation and area. In Peru, for instance, the score mixes in pan flutes fitting of the region's music.[10]

The reference to cinematic experience is of primary importance here, and a number of established film music scholars have in fact turned their attention towards game music aesthetics, for instance emphasizing 'iterative narration' with a resemblance to techno music aesthetics, or the 'nonlinear' nature of computer game music which

---

6 Jeff Smith, *The Sounds of Commerce* (New York, 1998), p. 3.

7 See for instance Robert Burnett, *The Global Jukebox* (London, 1996), and Geoffrey Hull, *The Recording Industry* (Boston, 1998).

8 Burnett, *The Global Jukebox*, p. 37.

9 David Hesmondhalgh, *The Cultural Industries* (London, 2002), p. 59.

10 N. Valentino, 'Lara Croft Tomb Raider: Legend Review' (2006), *GameZone Xbox*, at http://xbox.gamezone.com/ (accessed 5 January 2007).

'allows the composer to develop dynamic scores that are constantly changing'.[11] Yet the case of Poets of the Fall and 'Late Goodbye' does not fit in with this schema, as the song does exist in a relatively immutable linear form – audible in the end credit sequence of *Max Payne 2*, for example. Although some commentators have found the song meaningful in terms of the plot, its melody and other structural features remain recognizable even when sung in the shower by one character or played on the piano by another.[12] Although it is up to the player's choices whether or not these short pieces of incidental (or 'diegetic', to borrow the term from film theory) music will be encountered, they are hardly meaningful examples of dynamic audio. Rather, they can be interpreted as a sort of teaser, in that they exist in part in order to awaken interest in the music in its own right and not just as a part of the game.

Thus it is clear that narrative functions are not the only, or even the predominant, reason for computer game music to exist. Based on Gorbman's probe, there is music in the games in order to provide 'dynamism, tension, genre identity, and occasionally mood in the manner of movie underscoring',[13] but this does not account for such games as *Guitar Hero*, *Sing Star*, *Wii Music Orchestra Hands-On* or *Dance Dance Revolution* in which there is no game without music, whether or not controlled by a 'guitar', microphone, baton or feet, respectively. Furthermore, there is no reason to forsake conglomeration, as the mutual cross-promotion of music and audio-visual media is a long-lived convention by now. In other words, it may be argued that 'Late Goodbye' is there as much in order to promote *Max Payne 2* as vice versa. Within film and music industries, this is generally termed 'synergy'; in the words of Lee Barron, what one has here is 'a practice by which media products can be utilized to advertise or support other media products'.[14]

Synergy

The term 'synergy' derives originally from medical science, where it refers to the '[c]ombined or correlated action of a group of bodily organs (as nerve-centres, muscles, etc.)' producing results greater than the sum of the elements, so to speak. The term is used also in a more general sense when referring to any kind of joint working, but it has a special ring to it as emphasizing '[i]ncreased effectiveness, achievement, etc., produced as a result of combined action or co-operation.'[15] Within

---

11 Anahid Kassabian, 'The Sound of a New Film Form', in Ian Inglis (ed.), *Popular Music and Film* (London, 2003); Claudia Gorbman, 'Aesthetics and Rhetoric', *American Music* 22/1 (2004), pp. 24–6.

12 Silja Hakulinen, 'Salakavalat listaykköset' (2005), *Skenet.fi*, at http://www.skenet.fi/ (accessed 5 January 2007); Jonathan Mander, 'Poets of the Fall: Oopperaakin on laulettu', *Plaza – Kaista*, 15 February 2005, http://plaza.fi/kaista/musiikki/haastattelut/poets-of-the-fall-oopperaakin-on-laulettu (accessed 5 June 2007).

13 Gorbman, 'Aesthetics and Rhetoric', p. 16.

14 Lee Barron, '"Music Inspired By ...": The Curious Case of the Missing Soundtrack', in Ian Inglis (ed.), *Popular Music and Film* (London, 2003), p. 150.

15 *Oxford English Dictionary*, at http://dictionary.oed.com/ (accessed 11 February 2007).

political economy, synergy is furthermore a widespread concept and mostly used in analyses of corporate mergers and takeovers.[16] In addition, it has been found useful within anthropology when referring to the ways in which the social structure 'provides for acts that are mutually opposed and counteractive [or] mutually reinforcing' and renders possibilities for people to join together for common action, resulting in mutual benefits and advantages.[17]

According to Jeff Smith, synergy is more than mere cross-promotion, since at the core of the issue there is an intent to create several commodities out of one intellectual property, first and foremost in order to spread financial risks. He also stresses the importance of conglomerate interests, especially in the form of more efficient management of human resources. Thus the larger context of economic motivations should be taken into account when investigating this kind of synergy, as it is 'a strategy that not only creates multiple profit centers but also serves to spread risk and maximize resources' and covers 'a whole system of cross-promotional practices designed to reinforce the conglomerate structure both vertically and horizontally'.[18]

Smith himself centres on the 'packages' that are formed by films, music and music videos, but he does refer in passing to video games as a part of this totality. According to Smith, the games have two functions in this aggregate: first, they help in pre-selling the other products, most notably films; second, they offer ready-made narrative elements and imagery, once more predominantly for films. For Smith, a prime example of these practices is provided by Disney, with its films, cartoons, comics, theme parks and various paraphernalia created on the basis of one extremely large set of intellectual properties.[19] Yet in the case of computer game music it is questionable as to whether one can talk about just one set of intellectual properties, particularly when dealing with separately released popular music. Undoubtedly the game in question will have an impact on the way in which the music is made meaningful and vice versa, especially in relation to genre conventions.[20]

An indication of the ways in which the role of music in computer games has changed is provided by the FIFA football game series, produced by the leading computer game company Electronic Arts. On the back cover of the *FIFA 99*'s manual is the following: '"The Rockafella Skank" (The Funk Soul Brother) performed by Fatboy Slim is available on the album You've Come a Long Way, Baby.'[21] Indeed, there is the possibility of listening to the song while playing, but only that one song. When compared to the following year's version, the difference is notable: there are

16 See for example Hao Zhang, 'US Evidence on Bank Takeover Motives: A Note', *Journal of Business Finance & Accounting*, 25/7&8 (1998), pp. 1025–32, and Zsuzsanna Fluck and Anthony W. Lynch, 'Why Do Firms Merge and Then Divest? A Theory of Financial Synergy', *The Journal of Business*, 72/3 (1999), pp. 319–46.

17 Ruth Benedict in Abraham H. Maslow and John J. Honigmann, 'Synergy: Some Notes of Ruth Benedict', *American Anthropologist*, New Series, 72/2 (1970), p. 326.

18 Jeff Smith, *The Sounds of Commerce* (New York, 1998), pp. 188–91. See also Simone Murray, 'Brand loyalties: rethinking content within global corporate media', *Media, Culture & Society*, 27/3 (2005), pp. 415–35.

19 Smith, *The Sounds of Commerce*, pp. 189, 192.

20 Gorbman, 'Aesthetics and Rhetoric', p. 16.

21 *EA Sports FIFA 99 PlayStation* (1998), SLES 01584.

an even dozen songs in *FIFA 2000*. To compare further, on the website of *FIFA 07* there are a total of 40 songs in the 'EA Trax' section.[22] Thus, it would appear that the turn of the millennium is something of a transition phase with respect to the synergy equation between popular music and computer games. This suspicion is supported by Karen Collins, as she credits the release of the PlayStation 2 console in the year 2000 as an turning point after which 'it would be unusual for a hit game to be released by a major developer that does not have a popular artist involved in its soundtrack'. Yet the evidence is hardly substantial; Collins herself points, with a particular emphasis on the changes in game audio technology, also to the mid 1990s as a phase in which 'it became far more popular to license material already available, even releasing the games soundtracks as separate CDs'. Whether or not this constitutes 'a long history between the music and video games industries', there is no denying that 'there exists a symbiotic relationship between the music industry and the game industry – the games are being used to promote artists, or the artists are being used to sell games.'[23]

The local and the global

When assessing the importance of synergy, especially conceptualized as a practice driven by conglomerate interests, different production contexts and circumstances should be borne in mind. In other words, it is hardly meaningful to compare EA with a small-scale national production company such as Remedy. It may be that both are driven by a desire to acquire financial profit, but in terms of risk management, the difference between the two is crucial. In other words, there is no possibility for Remedy to build their production on blockbuster ideology, while in the case of EA this is more than probable. Of course, the success of *Max Payne* and its sequel has created a certain amount of fame for Remedy, but it may very well create certain expectations – and if these are not met, the sales expectations will not be met either, and the consequences for the company may be lethal. With small companies working within a field where the degree of product differentiation is low, the logics of 'only the latest merits count' constitutes a significant risk factor.

   Understandably, this is where a successful band or artist can be of aid. As Collins points out, games can be aimed primarily at specific fans, and the stars can be used as key elements in marketing the games. She further mentions Britney Spears, Pink and Kylie Minogue as the type of 'pop idols' who have been promoted in this manner, and eventually gives the ultimate credit to the game *50 Cent: Bulletproof* (2005) for taking the procedure one step further with exclusive tracks, several videos and a 'sound studio mode', (that is, the possibility to remix tracks).[24] The list can be easily continued: in September of 2005 EA announced a deal with Jay Kay, the vocalist of Jamiroquai, according to which he participated in the launching and

---

22 *EA – FIFA 07*, http://fifa07.ea.com/home.asp?lang=en (accessed 11 February 2007)

23 Collins, 'Grand Theft Audio? Popular Music and Intellectual Property in Video Games'.

24 Collins, 'Grand Theft Audio? Popular Music and Intellectual Property in Video Games'.

promotion of *Need for Speed Most Wanted* by linking it to Jamiroquai's concert tour. In addition, Jamiroquai's song 'Feels Just Like it Should' 'will feature exclusively in the forthcoming *Need For Speed Most Wanted*', and there are also 'other exciting collaborations around the *Need for Speed* franchise' to be seen.[25]

Yet the collaboration of Remedy with Poets of the Fall is significantly more complicated in this respect. As has been commented repeatedly, it was *Max Payne 2* which acted predominantly as a springboard to fame for the band, and not vice versa. However, this does not mean that the music would be an irrelevant factor in promoting the game, or that the choice of music would have been a random one. As the leader and singer Marko Saaresto puts it, at first the game was instrumental in promoting the band, but gradually the configuration became more reciprocal.[26] The arrangement can be approached also from the point of departure provided by genre theories, as a certain type of music will immediately imply certain kinds of consumers,[27] and thus it is possible to argue that the choice of music per se is by no means insignificant when thinking about a game's target audience. As Collins puts it, 'the game becomes about the music', at least partially.[28]

Furthermore, the role of Poets of the Fall is somewhat unusual with respect to the predominant ways of uniting music and games. According to Collins, there are three major categories when it comes to including popular music in games: 'popular music or musicians as the subject or narrative component of game, popular musicians as composers for games, and the use of licensed popular music in games'.[29] As 'Late Goodbye' was written for the game in the manner of a theme song, it could be argued that Poets of the Fall acted as composers. At the same time, however, in its linear form, the song can be thought of as an independent or at least supplementary element in the game, just like any pre-existing licensed piece of music. As Collins points out, 'the placement of this music in a game is generally limited (cut-scenes, title themes, credits, etc.), as is the type of game where such music may be appropriate.'[30] Also the fact that the song obeys the conventions of 'western' popular music in its strophic form and centrality of lyrics suggests that it can be interpreted more or less as a separate entity within the game. This is not to say that it would not have any effect on the ways in which the game sequences are interpreted or vice versa, especially in terms of mood and affect, or that instrumental music could not be interpreted likewise, but because of the more symbolic and less convention-laden nature of musical communication than those of imagery and language, songs with

---

25 'EA and Jay Kay in Need for Speed™ Showdown', *EA News* (2005), http://www. electronicarts.co.uk/news/4823/ (accessed 5 March 2007).

26 Jussi Tolonen, 'Pelimaailman pelimannit', *Nyt*, 44 (2006), p. 45.

27 See for example Simon Frith, *Performing Rites: On the Value of Popular Music* (Oxford, 1996).

28 Collins, 'Grand Theft Audio? Popular Music and Intellectual Property in Video Games'.

29 Collins, 'Grand Theft Audio? Popular Music and Intellectual Property in Video Games'.

30 Collins, 'Grand Theft Audio? Popular Music and Intellectual Property in Video Games'.

words are ostensibly more directly taken as 'meaning' or 'telling' something than mere instrumental music.

Issues of authenticity and innovation

Interestingly, fame as computer game musicians is not without its downside. While Saaresto admits that the game has been 'a very good accelerator', on the basis of various magazine and newspaper interviews he has nevertheless been keen to point out that their success in the album charts should be attributed to radio play and 'a couple of gigs' (they had three before the release of the album) too.[31] Furthermore, in another interview he doubted that making music for more games would be 'too labelling', but that providing songs for films or television would be quite alright;[32] and yet according to the Poets of the Fall's agent they are to be heard 'in the jet selling *Half Life 2* PC game modification: *Half Life 2 Counter-Strike: Source Realism*', as well as in British and Australian films with their adjacent music videos.[33] In addition, Saaresto has elsewhere commented that there have also been conversations about future collaborations with Remedy.[34]

Also for other commentators the pole position in the charts has been difficult to accept without 'a belief in the might of music' and without denigrating 'television's headhunting programmes and multinational record compan[ies] with [their] marketing machinery'.[35] Dimensions of aesthetic unity very much in the sense of 'traditional' ways of judging film music have been juxtaposed with 'purposeless' background music too, at least by implication: 'One reason why the effect has been positive at least in Finland is the way in which the piece presents itself in the game. It really is a theme song.'[36] Thus it is possible to find an intriguing tension between the ostensibly transcendent 'might of music' and the exploiting, inhumane conglomeration of media and music industry here as well – debates concerning popular music's authenticity especially in relation to commercialism and audio-visual media have a long history.

For some, synergy represents in fact a threat for the survival of the music industry as a stand-alone business. Moore, for instance, writes that if the music industry wants to stay alive as an independent area of activity, the only solution is to break 'the bonds of synergy'. In her opinion, '[s]ynergy demands cliché and conformity, crossover genres that are not genres any longer, and a subordination [of music] to TV, film, DVD, CD-ROM, and other audiovisual constructions.'[37] It is not clear on the basis of her account, however, why it is necessary for the music industry to survive as a stand-alone business. Furthermore, her argument appears to

---

31 Mander, 'Poets of the Fall: Oopperaakin on laulettu'.

32 Tiia Öhman, 'Poets of the Fall – fanit odottelevat Uudessa-Seelannissa', *Tuhma* 2 (2005), pp. 36–7.

33 Sam Agency, 'POTF bio in English'.

34 Tolonen, 'Pelimaailman pelimannit'.

35 Hakulinen, 'Salakavalat listaykköset'; my translation.

36 Mander, 'Poets of the Fall: Oopperaakin on laulettu'; my translation.

37 Moore, 'A Picture is Worth 1000 CDs: Can the Music Industry Survive as a Stand-Alone Business?', p. 183.

be founded on a very a-historical interpretation of the interrelations between music and 'audiovisual constructions'. As Smith demonstrates, it is extremely difficult to separate the histories of sound recordings and moving images – even in the earliest forms of cinema (as the term is understood today) film clips and various sound carriers were in many cases a part of the same package and used to promote each other in the sense that both could act as attractions leading to mutual exposure.[38] In the end, it is likely that behind Moore's concerns about synergy in the music industry are two sets of larger issues: economic and ideological. The latter is in fact used as a justification for the former; in times of declining record sales and associated alleged financial uncertainty, arguments in favour of the autonomy of musical production and marketing represent one form of a cry for help, which in turn is easily defended by referring to age-old and deeply established modes of thinking about musical autonomy and authenticity. Of course, as Moore herself is a professor of music industry, her concerns can be interpreted as deeply personal too.

Thus, there appears to be a significant tension within the synergistic practices of music and entertainment industries. On the one hand, decline in music sales has been attributed to competition from other media and the availability of free music on the Internet, among other things.[39] On the other, however, potential mutual benefits are clearly acknowledged, especially with respect to rising talents; hit games reach an audience measured in hundreds of millions of people, and not-too-famous artists are probably cheaper than superstars, whose publicity is not necessarily so dependent on new forms of promotion.[40] Nevertheless, for Moore there is something deeply disturbing in this selling of music in a 'synergistic' situation, as music 'is almost always secondary to other products or services', and subsequently the business and leadership is in effect beyond the control of the music industry. Yet she herself points out that 'the music industry does not have to pay for new technological R&D or infrastructure construction', which according to my logics at least constitutes a major advantage, and indeed provides the basis for being 'the sales beneficiary of successful cross-promotions'.[41]

It is furthermore worth noting that the collaboration of Remedy and Poets of the Fall is not the only possible synergy equation within digital media. In the case of Remedy, in May of 2006 it was announced that Microsoft Game Studios would publish *Alan Wake*, 'the highly anticipated psychological action thriller' developed by the company. Not surprisingly, the deal means that the game will be published exclusively for the new Windows Vista PC operating system and the Xbox 360 game console.[42] Here, previews of 'the highly anticipated' game have been used in order

---

38 Smith, *The Sounds of Commerce*. See also Rick Altman, 'Silence of the Silents', *Musical Quarterly* 80/4 (1997), pp. 648–718.

39 Mark Fox, 'E-commerce Business Models for the Music Industry', *Popular Music and Society* 27/2 (2004), p. 201.

40 Collins, 'Grand Theft Audio? Popular Music and Intellectual Property in Video Games'.

41 Moore, 'A Picture is Worth 1000 CDs: Can the Music Industry Survive as a Stand-Alone Business?', p. 178.

42 Remedy, 'Microsoft Game Studios and Remedy partner in delivering "Alan Wake"', *Remedy Entertainment – Press Info* (2006), http://www.remedygames.com/contact_info/press_info.html

to demonstrate the gaming features of Vista, thus hopefully aiding in spreading the new OS, while the dominant market share of Windows will provide a basis for wide dissemination of the game – assuming that PC owners will eventually find Vista worth updating to. Despite the virtual monopoly of Windows there are nonetheless significant risk factors here; in late February 2007 it was reported that the sales of Vista had not reached the goals set by Microsoft.[43] But then again, at that time *Alan Wake* had not been released, nor was there any certainty about the music, which for its part would elevate these products to fame.

And of course, not only games can be used as a platform for promotional purposes for music. According to a biography provided by the agent of Poets of the Fall, their second single, 'Lift', released in September 2006, had 'considerable exposure as the song is appearing on a new benchmark software', eventually reaching more than ten million downloads.[44] While there is no indication in the biography whether or not this groundbreaking software has anything to do with Remedy or gaming in the first place, the deal may be taken as an indication of yet more versatile synergistic practices mobilized in different areas of the cultural industries. In fact, one can only wonder why this is still relatively rare, since who could survive without computer software in the world nowadays? Well, half of the population, to be frank, but then again, for that half the question of surviving is more urgent than the latest hit of Poets of the Fall. That notwithstanding, when pondering possible future forms of synergistic combinations of music and digital media, analysts should be cautious of models that emphasize the role of conglomerate structures. Instead, it may very well be that various activities associated with fandom are the most 'innovative', like in the case of 'freestyling' the moves of the *Dance Dance Revolution* dancing game and even hacking into the game and making personal edits of it.[45]

Production structure

Assuming that the production structure of the majors constitute the 'traditional' way of producing music, the traditional process goes something like this: a talent is picked up by a major's A&R people, a contract is signed with her or him to ensure that her or his artwork cannot be exploited by anyone (else), songs are selected or manufactured for upcoming releases, a producer is hired, possibly session musicians too, studio time booked, the songs are recorded, mixed and mastered, and finally released and marketed as singles or albums or both. The scale of this traditional

---

(accessed 7 March 2007); and Olavi Koistinen, 'Suomalainen pelitalo saa Vistasta nostetta', *Helsingin Sanomat*, 3 February 2007, p. B5. See also Mia Consalvo, 'Console Video Games and Global Corporations: Creating a hybrid culture', *New Media & Society* 8/1 (2006), pp. 117–37.

43 See for example Nick Farrell, 'Ballmer blames pirates for poor Vista sales', *The Inquirer*, 19 February 2007, http://www.theinquirer.net/default.aspx?article=37721 (accessed 7 March 2007).

44 Sam Agency, 'POTF bio in English'.

45 Jacob Smith, 'I Can See Tomorrow In Your Dance: A Study of Dance Dance Revolution and Music Video Games', *Journal of Popular Music Studies* 16/1 (2004), pp. 58–84.

framework is big, to say the least, as there are usually lots of talents and songs to be evaluated, lots of pages in the contracts to be signed, lots of money to be spent on the costs of producers, musicians, studios and marketing campaigns. Thus it is not unusual at all if the total process takes up to a year to be completed.[46] Even with ostensibly new ways of 'talent scouting' or 'manufacturing stars' such as the *Pop Idol* competition, the process is hardly less time-consuming; in the 2007 Finnish *Idols* the first auditions were organized on 28 October 2006, with the winner announced on 6 April 2007. Here of course the way in which television is implicated in the process is also a significant factor.[47]

However, according to many a commentator, the spread of digital technology, especially since the latter half of the 1990s, has indeed revolutionized the processes of music production. Steve Jones, for one, referring back to the last years of the twentieth century, points out how 'in addition to the ability to record high-quality digital audio in the home, the ability to press CDs at home, and print colour inserts for CD jewel boxes, thus creating not only home studios but home pressing plants, have become a reality'.[48] Also Robert Burnett and Patrick Wikström claim that '[d]igital technology has been partially responsible for lowering the cost of both producing and distributing music', and that 'the beginning of this new century will almost certainly be remembered as one of the most turbulent and important times in the evolving history of the music industry.'[49]

Poets of the Fall are a case in point in this respect. The album *Signs of Life* was released on the band members' own label, Insomniac. In terms of production, what happened before this was that 'Marko sold everything he had to invest in pursuing the love of his life, music, with his buddies Olli and Captain. He moved into his folks' basement, when he couldn't keep a place of his own any longer. The guys then built a little studio of their own in Captain's living room for the recording and producing sessions, and kept an office in Olli's beat up old car.'[50] Whether or not there is more than one romantic enhancement in this story, it serves to point to the ways in which the importance of so-called home studios in particular has increased in recent years, and for some it may constitute an aesthetic as well as ideological criterion in its own right.

It has been pointed out repeatedly that small labels are dependent on the majors' distribution networks, and most music industry observers concur that to get the products marketed and sold is really what counts.[51] For custom labels such as Insomniac, distribution may indeed become a problem – new acts always constitute a higher risk both for production and distribution companies. But this is where the

---

46 See for example Burnett, *The Global Jukebox*, and Hull, *The Recording Industry*.

47 See Tim Wall, *Studying Popular Music Culture* (London, 2003), and Robert Burnett and Patrick Wikström, 'Music Production in Times of Monopoly: The Example of Sweden', *Popular Music and Society* 29/5 (2006), p. 581.

48 Steve Jones, 'Music and the Internet', *Popular Music* 19/2 (2000), p. 217.

49 Burnett and Wikström, 'Music Production in Times of Monopoly: The Example of Sweden', p. 575.

50 POTF, 'Without silence there can be no music', *POTF – Poets of the Fall*, http://poetsofthefall.com/aboutpoets/ (accessed 2 March 2007).

51 See for example Burnett, *The Global Jukebox*, and Hull, *The Recording Industry*.

importance of *Max Payne 2* has been paramount. With two million copies of the game sold and thousands of inquiries for the release of the song 'Late Goodbye', a demand is already in place. In the words of Olli Tukiainen, the guitarist: 'An incredible chance for us. It's really a pretty good situation to issue an album when millions of people around the world have already heard us.' Saaresto in turn states that a song in a game – and, at least implicitly, the success of the package – represents 'a nice way of jumping over a couple of phases when starting off a band'.[52] In any case, it is more than doubtful that a distribution company would decline a deal involving the song in question, unless there are some conglomerate-inflicted, exclusive deals to be taken into account. And, even the conglomerate distribution companies might be interested in such deals, if not solely to boost the sales of the release in question, to ensure and 'protect' the sales of other competing releases.

Yet digital technology itself has not put this particular song and this particular game together. This is where aspects of agency are crucial. In his study of the Finnish popular music sound recording production from 1945 to 1990, Jari Muikku contends that the level of 'personality' has been remarkably high. What he means by this is that the production has been in the hands of very few individuals, and that interpersonal relations have thus played a key role behind production decisions.[53] Apparently, not much has changed in 20 years, as in numerous accounts on the success of *Max Payne 2* and 'Late Goodbye' it is stressed that Remedy scriptwriter Sami Järvi and Saaresto have been friends a long time, and all began when the former asked the latter to write a song for a new game.[54] In an interview for the webzine *Stara*, Saaresto tells that they had considered the possibility of making music for a game many times. 'Once on a rainy night, while sitting in a car, we decided that I will make a song ... Originally it was supposed to be a hit song in the game's world, but the producers wanted to have a final version too.'[55]

It should nevertheless be remembered that digital technology has only aided in the way in which custom production or self-releases have become more common, and mainly so because of economic reasons. In other words, 'unofficial' recordings have been made and issued long before the alleged digital revolution; the bottom line is that recording studios and pressing – or perhaps better to say copying – plants are essentially commercial enterprises, and thus they will accept almost any kind of commissions. They will of course charge for it. It may also be that a band without a deal with a record company find themselves in the studio between two and six a.m. more often than not, with relatively unenthusiastic engineers who are inclined to label the product a 'demo' rather than a 'song' or 'album'.

---

52 Curly, 'Poets of the Fall' (2005), *Curly-Zine*, http://www.curly.fi/content/view/47/42 (accessed 3 January 2007); my translation.

53 Jari Muikku, *Musiikkia kaikkiruokaisille: suomalaisen populaarimusiikin äänitetuotanto 1945–1990* (Helsinki, 2001), p. 330.

54 See Sam Agency, 'POTF bio in English', and Hakulinen, 'Salakavalat listaykköset'.

55 Jocka Träskbäck, 'Poets of the Fall', *Stara.fi*, 4 March 2005, http://www.stara.fi/?p=165 (accessed 3 January 2007); my translation.

Copyrights

As is suggested by defining synergy in terms of creating multiple commodities out of one set of intellectual property,[56] intellectual property rights constitute one of the most important issues with respect to computer gaming. Yet there is an important distinction to be made between the intellectual property rights per se and the compensations based on them. In fact, it may be argued that the recent – and also even more ancient – debates surrounding copyright issues do not really concern the rights, but instead the money that is allegedly lost because of various 'infringements'.

For argument's sake, let us look briefly into the ways in which Teosto, the Finnish Composers' Copyright Society (also representing lyric writers, arrangers and publishers), aims to control and administer the various ways of using published music. On Teosto's website, there are 116 different categories listed under the rubric of 'Fees and Instructions', including such uses as music on the Internet, music on mobile devices, music on water buses, and even music at *hirvipeijaiset* (a feast after moose-hunting). There is no entry for computer or video games; CD-ROMs as storage media come closest. There is also a separate listing of the fees for 'music in audiovisual productions'. According to the latter, the amount to be paid in terms of synchronization rights is €0.91 per second. In other words, if there is a total of three minutes of published music on the audio-visual production in question, the producer owes €164 to the rights owner. In terms of mechanical rights the fee is €0.007 per second per copy – taken that there were two million copies made by the producer, the total amount of mechanical rights compensations would be roughly €2.5 million. Furthermore, the royalties to be paid on the basis of sales are, according to Teosto's guidelines, €0.59 per minute divided by 80. In other words, if two million 'legal' copies were sold, the amount of royalties would result in €44,250.[57]

Whether or not the fees for music in audio-visual productions would be used as the basis for agreements over the use of music in computer games, the case of 'Late Goodbye' in *Max Payne 2* falls outside of this schema. This is so because of a simple reason: as the song was not published anywhere else before the release of the game, and because the band had not released any other recordings or even performed in public, and thus they had no reason to be Teosto's clients, there was in practice nothing to license. Instead, one can think of the arrangement more plausibly in terms of 'work for hire',[58] whereby an author is hired to compose music for a particular audio-visual product on the basis of a fixed remuneration. In addition, it is entirely dependent on the details of the agreement in question who owns the rights to the work (although according to the Finnish Copyright Act, the rights owner has to be a natural person). There is no indication that the song would be owned by Remedy, but there is no indication either that €44,250 royalties would have been transferred to the bank accounts of the members of Poets of the Fall, not to mention the €2.5 million compensations on the basis of mechanical rights. But, as the album *Signs of Life*

---

56 Smith, *The Sounds of Commerce*.

57 Teosto, 'Hinnat ja ohjeet', http://www.teosto.fi/ (accessed 13 March 2007).

58 See Hull, *The Recording Industry*.

has gone platinum (that is, 30,000 copies) in Finland, there has been a reasonable amount of monetary traffic between various retailers and the Insomniac label.

In general, it appears that the practices associated with licensing and composing music for computer games in Finland are based on a 'work for hire' principle and thus on bilateral agreements between game companies and authors of music. This is regardless of possible agreements between the authors and Teosto, especially with respect to licensing the authors' works. According to Jari Muikku, the director of the media department of Teosto, the disorderly situation was quickly realized in the copyright organization, and instead of 'clubbing' their clients, they decided to withdraw from licensing music for games altogether, and even from providing advisory services. This new guideline has been effective since the beginning of 2007. In addition to the 'sorrowless' agreement violations, Muikku points to two other factors behind the decision: on the one hand, the magnitude of computer game music licensing in Finland is such that it deems the area rather poor in terms of mass licensing, also taking into account the fact that the agreements are fairly complicated; on the other hand, the relationship between incomes and expenses, especially from the point of departure of the copyright organization, is out of balance. In the end, he feels, it is nonetheless up to the authors as to what kind of agreements they are willing to sign and what kind of risks they are willing to accept.[59]

There is indeed some indication that not all participants have been happy as a result of their involvement in computer game music. While in many cases the mutual benefits are clear, that is to say the game company gets the music relatively cheap and the author of the music gets valuable promotion for her or his work, the amount of work and the compensation acquired may be taken as incongruous, especially if and when the game proves to be a success. For instance, in the case of the 'original' *Max Payne* (2001), the opinions expressed by the authors of the music are openly divided. The two musicians in question are Kari 'Kärtsy' Hatakka, the leader of the 'cross-over metal' band Waltari, and keyboardist, electro-percussionist Kimmo Kajasto. Hatakka has obviously been quite happy with games as a promotion and marketing vehicle, and claims that he was able to live off the money he got from making the music for two years while Waltari was not active. Kajasto in contrast complained that as game music is sold with one-time compensations and that there are no royalties to be earned, even five-digit sums do not sufficiently cover the hours spent making the music.[60]

It should also be noted that while €2.5 million is a tidy sum, it is estimated that licensing accounts for only five per cent of the total retail price of a given game. Almost half of the expenses go into programming and design, and roughly a quarter to marketing and distribution.[61] Yet it should be remembered that it may not be so easy to cut down the programming and design expenses; instead, creative solutions

---

59 Jari Muikku, telephone discussion with the author, minidisc recording, Turku, 13 March 2007.

60 Tolonen, 'Pelimaailman pelimannit'.

61 Rachel Rosmarin, 'Why Gears Of War Costs $60', *Forbes.com*, 12 December 2006, http://www.forbes.com/technology/2006/12/19/ps3-xbox360-costs-tech-cx_rr_game06_1219expensivegames.html (accessed 13 March 2007).

within marketing and licensing may prove to be more lucrative. To begin with, for original-concept games licensing fees are zero, but then again, belonging to a well-known franchise (including films) can result in significantly lower marketing costs. In other words, marketing and licensing expenses are, to a considerable extent, reversely proportional to each other. And, in the end, for small companies like Remedy profitable products are virtually the only alternative, whereupon evading disbursing millions of euros is nothing more than smart risk management. While the calculated amount of €2.5 million in the form of various compensations constitutes 'only' one quarter of Remedy's total profits in 2002, the year after the release of the 'original' *Max Payne*, there are no guarantees that the next endeavour will yield the same. Furthermore, as the size of the company means that there cannot be too many – if any – concurrent productions underway, there are no guarantees either that one product will cover the losses possibly caused by another. In the case of Remedy, the bottom line has indeed been fluctuating; in 2004 the company's financial statement indicated losses of €812,000. This notwithstanding, the company's equity ratio since 2003 has been very good (over 80 per cent), which indicates a high level of risk tolerance.[62]

Conclusion: let us play (with) music!

In recent years, the international success of certain Finnish popular music acts – most notably HIM, The Rasmus, Bomfunk MC's and Darude – has been a much discussed topic in Finland. Arguably, it has finally been proven that Finnish music can be sold across national and cultural borders, and thus a 30-year-old dream has finally come true. Interestingly, in this discussion nationalist discourses intermingle with economic ones; on the one hand, participants are happy because 'our culture' is demonstrating its vitality and spreading to different parts of the world, and, on the other, they are happy because of the financial 'export potential' of the music, that is, the various remunerations accruing to Finland on the basis of international sales and media exposure. In terms of international copyright compensations, Finnish music is no longer just Jean Sibelius. This was proven by The Rasmus' hit 'In the Shadows' (2004), as it was the first recording ever to surpass Sibelius's works in the annual statistics of Teosto (in 2004, Sibelius still held six of the top ten positions). Also, in December 2005, HIM made a 'historical' breakthrough with their 'love metal' into the US charts by reaching number 18 with their album *Dark Light*.

Despite the worldwide dissemination of 'Late Goodbye' through *Max Payne 2*, Poets of the Fall do not appear in these statistics. In comparison, the music of The Rasmus or HIM has not been promoted through computer games. Instead, these bands have achieved their breakthroughs by 'traditional' means, that is, by persistent touring and million-euro marketing campaigns. These campaigns include the making of several music videos, which each in their turn compete for the title of the most expensive Finnish music video ever, even if the tendency is that as the budgets rise,

62 'Remedy Entertainment Oy – Taloustiedot', *Inoa*, http://www.inoa.fi/showFinancialInformation.do?company=172754 (accessed 14 March 2007).

videos are made outside Finland and by non-Finnish (which apparently is a synonym for 'more professional') personnel. At the same time music industry executives and state officials are emphasizing the importance of copyright compensations and the cultural industry in general as a profession (that is, a source of taxes) for the national economy.

Nevertheless, new ways of promotion are constantly sought out within the 'traditional' music industry too. Here also the value of computer games is recognized; HIM's manager Seppo Vesterinen, in order to keep the band in the US Top 200 as long as possible, was pondering the possibilities of getting HIM's music in feature films and computer games in early 2006.[63] There has not been any news that this has happened, but other bands have been lucky in this respect. For example, the music of the metal band Lullacry from Helsinki can be heard in the game *The Sopranos: Road to Respect*. According to guitarist Sami Vauhkonen, the value of the game deal is most importantly in promotion, as the band was at the same time looking for a new record company.[64] Clearly, the issue is once more the relationship between a band's market value and a game company. What is the price tag on a given band's 'brand', and will selling it to a computer game also mean 'selling out'?

Continuously re-emerging discussions over this issue demonstrate that the ideology of authenticity is a vital component in the ways in which music, among other cultural phenomena, is made meaningful in public discourse, despite all the arguments in favour of a 'post-modern', value-relativist social condition. With respect to this, it should not be forgotten that it is not just any kind of music's 'might' that saves Poets of the Fall from the curse of inauthenticity, but that of indie rock, or to be a bit more precise, 'a novel blend of pop, rock, metal and industrial sounds'. Yes, it is made with machines (although so is all instrumental music!) and the sounds are elaborately synthesized, but their style has been characterized as 'poetic' and 'alternative', with the addition that as they allegedly release only 'the select few' songs of 'well over one hundred' that are ready, each album 'seem[s] like a compilation rather than using "filler songs" like some other bands today'.[65] An indication of their approval is the awarding of two Emma Awards (the Finnish equivalent of the Grammy) by IFPI Finland in 2005: one as the Best Newcomer of the Year, and another for the Best Debut Album of the Year.

Apparently, there are not many changes in the attitudes towards the interconnections of music and audio-visual media either. According to Collins, 'licensing existing pre-composed music has become a mainstay of the gaming industry today',[66] and yet there obviously is something highly bothersome in connecting music and various forms of audio-visual media to each other. For instance, a recent article in a leading Finnish PC magazine on social gaming was entitled 'Who's the Grisliest of Them All?';

---

63 Jussi Ahlroth, 'Stadin kundi Ville Valo palasi kotiin', *Helsingin Sanomat*, 29 December 2005, p. C1.

64 Tolonen, 'Pelimaailman pelimannit'.

65 POTF, 'Without silence there can be no music'. See also *Wikipedia*, 'Poets of the Fall', http://en.wikipedia.org/wiki/Poets_of_the_Fall (accessed 16 March 2007).

66 Collins, 'Grand Theft Audio? Popular Music and Intellectual Property in Video Games'.

in the article the role of singing, dancing and drumming was heavily emphasized, and it included numerous judgemental comments about karaoke games in particular by reference to 'horribly wonderful 80s hits', 'most horrible and most beautiful pop' and to a 'similarly shame-free' attitude as in the 'norm-karaoke'.[67] The implication is that outside of social gaming there would be something shameful in these kinds of performances or practices. And this is nothing more than a question of prevalent cultural values, reinforced most prominently by institutions involved in education, critique and legislation. Following Jacob Smith's comments on 'free-styling' and 'hacking' *Dance Dance Revolution*,[68] it might be argued that there is always a more bottom-up line of action which, if nothing else, deems top-down authorial voices and claims for authenticity relational and ambiguous.

Discussion and claims around authenticity can be further related to the idea of 'media panics', recurrent with the emergence of any 'new' media technology, be it moving image, sound cinema, television, music video or computer games. This in turns raises questions concerning 'media literacy' and media education in general. It has been argued that the younger generations may very well be more competent in interpreting media content than the older are willing to believe and, more importantly, that instead of finger-shaking, parental guidance is what yields critical thinking and evaluative abilities. Of course, public organizations and institutions play a key role in this too, since opinions expressed from either in school or the House of Parliament, or in national broadcasts and newspapers, have a significant amount of authority. In some cases, this may have direct bearing on economic state support as well. For example, instead of supporting, say, the Finnish porn film industry, the State of Finland reportedly invests €130,000 through its investment company Finnish Industry Investment Ltd in Virtual Air Guitar, a company developing an air guitar game.[69] In addition, in a Ministry of Education committee report released in March 2007 it was suggested that the amount of state support to cultural exports would be increased by €64 million between 2007 and 2011, the total amount of support being €228 million and the overall value of cultural exports reaching €500 million by 2011. The 'vision' of this 'Programme for Cultural Export Promotion' reads as follows:

> Cultural exports will have grown into an acknowledged part of Finnish exports. The value of cultural exports will have at least tripled and the creative sectors will have made the structure of industry and commerce more varied. They will also have created new jobst [*sic*]. Culture will form a distinctively more pronounced part of Finland's country image and brand. The economic well fare [*sic*] of individuals and groups working in cultural sectors will have improved through cultural exports.[70]

---

67 Tapio Berschewsky, 'Ken on heistä kaikkein kauhein', *MikroBitti*, January 2006, p. 59.

68 Smith, 'I Can See Tomorrow in Your Dance: A Study of Dance Dance Revolution and Music Video Games'.

69 Jyrki Alkio, 'Valtion riskirahaa ilmakitarapeliin', *Helsingin Sanomat*, 7 February 2007, p. B5.

70 Ministry of Education, 'Do Finnish Cultural Exports Have Staying Power? YES! Proposal for Finland's Cultural Exports Promotion Programme', http://www.minedu.fi/OPM/

In *Helsingin Sanomat*, the leading Finnish newspaper, it was suspected that the areas benefiting most from this kind of programme would be music, film and games.[71] The State of Finland has increased its involvement in music exports crucially since the turn of the millennium through financing Musex (Music Export Finland), an association consisting of 'members on a broad front from Finnish music industry organisations', including IFPI Finland, Teosto, the Finnish Musicians' Union and The Finnish Music Publishers' Association. The main source of funding for Musex is the Ministry of Trade and Industry, covering up to 60 per cent of the total expenditure.[72] Within attempts to export Finnish music, there are pieces of evidence about synergistic practices, as the Finnish Music Information Centre (that is, FIMIC; a subdivision of Teosto) has released a couple of promotional CDs under the rubrics *Finnish Music for Your Films* (about 2000) and *Music for Moving Pictures* (2005). It remains to be seen and heard whether the new exports programme will result in the emergence of compilations with titles such as *Playing with Finnish Moosic*.

Amidst all of the hyping of cultural and creative industries and the export potential, it should be remembered that the scale of game production in Finland is nonetheless rather small, and one cannot but wonder whether this kind of activity is really exhorted by threats expressed by executives of ICT companies like Nokia to move their operation to less-taxed countries. Well, one can always sell one's game company to another conglomerate after the first big hit. Meanwhile, however, creative solutions – especially in terms of cost-effectiveness – are worth their weight in gold. Approached from the stance of the game developers and producers, it appears that while in earlier years of computer game production 'the one who owned a keyboard got to make the music', now 'the one who knows a band without a publishing deal gets them to make the music'. And, as the change in the workings of Teosto demonstrates, in certain circumstances even the personnel of copyright organizations may be willing to interpret agreements and laws more according to their spirit than their letters.

Julkaisut/2007/esitys_kulttuuriviennin_kehittamisohjelmaksi.html?lang=en (accessed 16 March 2007).

71 Teemu Luukka, 'Työryhmä esittää kulttuuriviennille kymmeniä miljoonia lisää tukea', *Helsingin Sanomat*, 2 March 2007, p. C1.

72 Musex, 'New Export Association for Finnish Music Launched' (2004), *Musex.fi* > *News Archive*, http://musex.fi/ (accessed 16 March 2007).

PART 2
Ringtones and mobile phones

Chapter 3

Could ringtones *be* more annoying?[1]

Peter Drescher

Like games in the 1980s and the Web in the 1990s, the mobile audio industry is the new Wild West. And as in the Old West, companies large and small are trying to stake a claim because 'there's gold in them there hills!' Of course, a lot of people got shot and killed in the Old West, so my chapter is intended, in some small way, to help those of you getting into mobile audio to survive the experience. My background is as a piano player who got lucky, because I got into the multimedia audio business after I got too old to be a road-dog blues musician. I currently hold the position of sound designer at a very cool start-up in Palo Alto, California, called Danger, Inc. We produce a mobile Internet device called the Hiptop, available for purchase at a T-Mobile store near you (T-Mobile sells it under the name Sidekick). This device is an excellent example of what is known as 'convergent technologies'. Basically, it is a cellphone, but it is also a web browser, an instant messenger, an email client, an SMS text messenger, an address book, a calendar, a camera, a mobile blogger and a game platform ... and more! Of course, it also includes an online catalogue of downloadable ringtones, which is what I would like to discuss.

My own involvement with ringtones began about twelve years ago, when I was hired by Sprint PCS to program their brand-new line of cellphones with a series of time-and-frequency modulations (basically, 'this frequency for that long') so that the little piezo ringer, a square of plastic and ceramic the size of a thumbtack and the smallest speaker I have ever designed for, would trigger a wimpy-sounding *Für Elise*. At the time, I remember thinking very clearly, 'Are you kidding me? What an incredibly stupid idea! Who is going to want that to play every time their phone rings? Could you *be* more annoying?' OK, so, I was wrong. This is why I like to say that I do not have my finger on the pulse of the American public. Apparently, *everybody* wants their phone to play a melody instead of just the standard ding-a-ling-a-ling. OK, maybe not absolutely everybody. I know many people's phones just chirp, and a friend of mine was complaining to me just the other day that he could not find a ringer on his new cellphone that just sounded like a regular phone.

---

1 Editor's note: This is an edited transcript of Peter Drescher's speech, 'Sound Design for Really Small Speakers' presented at the 2004 Texas Interactive Music Conference and Barbecue. Every October since 1996, the conference, better known as Project Bar-B-Q, has assembled 50 of the top minds in computer audio to brainstorm the future of music on computers. Project Bar-B-Q is hosted by George Alistair Sanger (also known as the Fat Man), a prolific video game composer who grew frustrated with the disappointing MIDI playback on computer sound cards in the 1990s and decided to do something about it.

Nevertheless, millions and millions of people, all over the planet, currently have their phones set to make a wide variety of sounds to alert them to the fact that somebody wants to talk to them. As Richard Dreyfuss says in *Close Encounters of the Third Kind* while sculpting a giant mound of mashed potatoes, 'This means something. This is important!'

The use of mobile ringtones is a worldwide phenomenon that shows no sign of letting up any time soon. In fact, it is only going to get bigger and bigger until personalized ringtones become absolutely ubiquitous, if they aren't already. You will hear them everywhere you go. You will hear them all the time. You will hear them in the streets, in restaurants, in cinemas, at concerts, at weddings, at funerals. You will even hear them in your own pocket. And let's face it: ringtones are really annoying. And yet, the consumer has spoken: People absolutely love annoying ringtones and the annoying effect that they have on everybody else around them; otherwise, they would not spend so much money on them, would they? But every time I hear your cellphone ring, it annoys me, and I'll tell you why: First, because you have a phone call and I don't. Second, because the ringtone is inevitably followed by one side of a conversation I don't want to hear. And third – and most important – because when the phone rang, it played a really horrible rendition of Britney Spears's 'Oops, I Did It Again' that tells me things about you I really wish I did not know.

A familiar ring

At the same time, ringtones can be a lot of fun if you are the guy with the cool tone. For example, I'm at the first showing of the latest *Harry Potter* film, there's a big crowd, everybody's all excited and restless, and as we wait for the lights to come down and the previews to start, I pull out my trusty Hiptop and play the *Harry Potter* theme. And ... bam! Suddenly it's a party and I am the centre of attention. Some people laughed, some people were irritated, some didn't recognize the song as the Harry Potter theme and so were wondering what the hell that annoying noise was, but everybody around me had some sort of reaction, and that was kind of fun. And then the cute girls sitting in the row in front of us turned around, pulled out their cellphones and started showing off their ringtones. So I played a few more of mine, and they played a few more of theirs ... By now, we are really annoying everybody around us, because it is as if they have been forced to attend a party they were not invited to. But what can I say? It's a social phenomenon that is not going away any time soon, so you had better get used to it.

So, what is the deal, really? Why are ringtones so popular? Do people really take so much pleasure from annoying everybody around them? Are people in general really that uncaring and impolite? No, that's not it; that's just a side effect. Ringtones are popular because they are a direct expression of that most egregious of the seven deadly sins: vanity. And as Al Pacino says in *The Devil's Advocate*, 'Vanity: definitely my favourite sin!' People are so hungry for ringtones because they are a cheap and easy solution to a problem that they actually have. And the problem is, 'How do I show off how cool I am? How do I attract attention? How do I make a statement about *my* individuality and *my* personal preferences and *my* taste in music and *me*?'

To paraphrase P.T. Barnum, 'Nobody ever went broke overestimating the vanity of the American public.'

Now, this is really good news for those of us in the audio business. This is cause for rejoicing and celebration and throwing hats in the air – and I will tell you why. Think about it: Here we have an audio product that consumers are absolutely crazy about! They will shell out huge amounts of cold, hard cash to have this product installed on their phones. They will talk about ringtones for hours. They will post amazingly long and impassioned threads on Internet bulletin boards about their favourite ringtones. They will demand that more and more ringtones be made available every day. They even will get incredibly upset when they can't get the ringtone they want. Now, when was the last time you saw someone get upset about audio on a web page, or start jumping up and down about the soundtrack to some new video game?

Most importantly, consumers will buy ringtones in unbelievable numbers. For example, at Danger we started offering a limited number of ringtones for sale on the Hiptop and within six months we had over one million downloads. Now, we do not even have that many subscribers (yet), so multiply our experience by the number of people out there who own cellphones, and you start to get an idea of the amounts of money we are talking about here. This is a whole different ball of wax from so many 'wouldn't it be cool if ...' Internet audio schemes that always seemed to me to be solutions to problems that nobody had. This is more like the fashion industry, where the product is designed to make a personal statement about the owner. And in the same way that you don't want to show up at a Halloween party wearing the exact same costume as somebody else, there's nothing cooler than having a unique ringtone, a sound that nobody else has got.

Roll your own

Fortunately, anybody with a computer and half a brain can 'roll their own' ringtone. On the Hiptop it is very easy. Here is how you do it:

- Step 1: Take any audio clip, off any CD, in any format, at any resolution, up to 17 seconds long.
- Step 2: Email it to your Hiptop.

And basically, that is all there is to it. Now, at Danger, we do a number of things to make this possible and easy. Any data transmitted over the airwaves is first formatted and compressed specifically for our device by the Danger servers. That way, nicely formatted web pages and pictures get downloaded quickly and efficiently and show up on the Hiptop looking the way you want them to. For audio, the service takes whatever type of file you throw at it and transcodes it into the preferred format for playback on our device, which is currently a 16-bit, 11kHz, IMA 4:1-compressed WAV file. Then the service attaches the transcoded file to your email and sends it on down the wire (or wireless, as the case may be). Bing! Your email appears with a file attachment. The attachment contains the name of the audio file and two buttons, one marked 'play' and the other marked 'install as ringtone'. I can then assign the ringtone I just made to play only when a specific person in my address book calls.

That way I can have the phone play 'our song' when my girlfriend calls, or even a recording of the Fat Man saying 'Hey, it's the Fat Man' when he calls me.

But more than likely, given that I'm so vain and I want to show off to all my friends just how cool I am, I'm going to forward that email to my buddy: 'Hey man, check out this cool ringtone I just pulled off the new Beyoncé CD.' Now, if he's got a Hiptop – badda-bing, badda-boom, no problemo – he can install the ringtone on his device and then pass it on to his friends. If he's on some other type of phone, it's not always so easy, but it can be done, using either email or MMS [Multimedia Messaging Service] or some other software. And given that the market for this kind of thing is usually technically savvy college kids, you can bet that it will be done, one way or the other.

OK, wait a minute; back up there a second. Did I hear that one right? A system that allows users to share audio files over a network for free?! Oh my God! It's Napster all over again! You can bet that the big record companies are absolutely shaking in terror at the concept of Napster for cellphones. They have been burned that way before, and they do not want to see the ringtone cash cow run out of the barnyard like it did for MP3s. And we are talking big business here: There was a very interesting statistic in an article on the front page of the Wall Street Journal reporting sales of the ringtone of 'In Da Club' by 50 Cent had outsold online downloads of the song.[2] Think about that for a second. Here is a cut off of a multi-platinum album making more money as a ringtone than as an iTunes selection! You can understand why the record companies do not want to let it be given away for free. Unfortunately, there does not seem to be much they can do about it, since this kind of functionality is already built into the system in various ways.

In addition, because the data is transferred over cellphone networks, the cellphone carriers get a piece of the action too. Now, they have been making money on ringtones over the past few years by charging customers for the SMS text messaging and the WAP browser downloads that are used to transfer monophonic and polyphonic ringtones to phones. But beep-tones and MIDI ringtones are of limited appeal and are quickly becoming extinct. The real money is in real music, meaning digital audio clips of recognizable songs. And since pay-by-the-megabyte accounting is also quickly being superseded by flat-rate all-you-can-eat data plans, the carriers are in danger of losing out on ringtones as well.

Putting music on hold

This issue has become very apparent to the major cell phone carriers in the United States. At least one carrier's solution to the ringtone problem has been to require Danger to disable the 'install ringtone from e-mail' functionality on their version of the Hiptop operating system. This means that you can only install ringtones from their built-in catalogue, thereby ensuring that everybody in the food chain gets paid – the carrier, the record companies and Danger. We also set a copyright-protection

---

2   See Rob Walker, '50 Cent Is Calling: Rap's biggest star is now appearing on cell phones near you', *Slate*, 24 June 2003, http://www.slate.com/id/2084756 (accessed 15 May 2007).

bit, so that ringtones installed from the catalogue cannot be forwarded off the device, via email or anything else. Once you download a ringtone from the catalogue, that's it, end of story. It stays on your device until you delete it. Sure, you can still attach audio files to an email; you can even play them. But that's all. It seems kind of pointless, doesn't it? Let me tell you, it has been a *huge* bone of contention with our users, who complain about it endlessly and bitterly, start petitions, write threatening letters, jump up and down and get all red in the face. I have never seen so many people get so emotional about any other audio product with which I have ever been involved. The reason they get so upset is that they are being prevented from doing something they really, really want to do: express themselves using audio.

Carriers who disable the 'install as ringtone' button are missing a very important point here, which is that no matter how extensive a catalogue is, it will not – it cannot – address this issue of individual expression. Sure, clips of the latest hip-hop tunes are great, and they sell like ice cream on a hot day, but people also want sound effects, film quotes, recordings of their own voice, recordings of their kids' voices, or their dog barking, or the song they wrote themselves, or that song they like that nobody else has ever even heard of and so on. No catalogue can contain all things for all people, and if I have learned anything lately, it is that there are as many ideas about what makes a 'good' ringtone as there are people with cellphones. Now obviously, this is a digital rights management issue that is better left to more qualified brains than mine. But the demand for ringtones is already gigantic; there is lots of money to be made, and everybody is scrambling to come up with some good answers, but there are still many other issues to be addressed.

Ring in the future

The current situation, with multiple proprietary ringtone formats and everybody trying to get a little piece of the action, is guaranteed to be temporary. Five years from now the whole issue of 'How do I make money selling ringtones' is going to be completely obsolete, eliminated by advances in telephone technology. All of the scrambling and legal issues and technical limitations and consumer aggravation will be totally passé, unimportant; yesterday's news. The reason for this is convergence. Convergence may be an over-inflated buzzword, but it really does describe an interesting trend. For example, five years ago putting a camera in your cellphone seemed like a silly idea, but now you can get megapixel camera phones on Amazon for free when you sign up for service. And it turns out that this is a very popular way to go, because again, it addresses a problem that people actually have – namely, 'How do I conveniently carry a camera around with me everywhere I go and send those spur-of-the-moment snapshots to all of my friends and family?'

There is another device that is really popular at the moment; in fact, I will bet many of you have one – it's called an iPod. Now imagine, if you will, an iPod with a cellphone built in: a mobile Internet device with a fast connection and 40 gigabytes of memory that lets you talk on the phone and plays all your music, all in one small, well-designed little package. It is such an obviously good idea, I'm surprised they are not on the market already, but I guarantee you, somebody out there is working on this concept right now. It's kind of a no-brainer, and given the popularity of all things convergent, I've got to figure it is only a matter of time before cellphone-plus-iPod-plus-camera-plus-Internet devices are fairly commonplace. When they are, the ringtone game is over! No more monophonic/polyphonic tunes for sale at inflated prices. No more hassles over who owns what on whose phone. No more limitations on what ringtone you want to play. You will simply assign whatever song you like from your over-600-hours-of-music to everybody and anybody in your address book. You will even be able to set a marker so that it starts playing at whatever point in the song you would like (probably at the hook). It will be so easy and fun and convenient that everybody will want to do it, and you will be able to have your phone play whatever music you like, whenever you like.

But that is at least five years from now. In the meantime, the ringtone market is exploding because there are more and more cellphones out there every day. I like to think of cellphone carriers like AT&T and T-Mobile – and hardware manufacturers like Nokia and Samsung – as big ships moving through a sea of money, harvesting profits as they go. Like any big ship, they frequently leave total chaos in their wakes in the form of multiple incompatible platforms, confusing file formats and arcane legal complications. This is natural and normal, and we have all been there before, with games and on the Web, but it sure makes for a bumpy ride and makes it harder for us audio people to turn a profit. Usually, there are no monetary resources to make our lives easier, because, as we all know, sound is always considered secondary to the actual product. But this time it's different: This time it's way better. This time, the good ship 'Audio' gets to ride up right alongside the battle cruiser 'USS Cellphone', because we have something they need: fuel and ammunition, in the form of ringtones.

Cellphones are a product where the audio is not secondary, a product that does not work without the audio. Here is a product that's already in the pocket of practically every single person on the planet. And since ringtones provide a nice constant flow of currency to the carriers, it changes the way their businesspeople look at us. Now, they need us; now we can make them money. So the next time you hear an annoying ringtone go off at an inappropriate time, don't get mad; get happy. That is the sound of money in your pocket.

Addendum: two and a half years later

Well, I'm not going to say, 'I told you so', since the development of cellphones with built-in MP3 players seems fairly obvious, particularly in retrospect. But I am a little surprised by the lack of customer backlash against the outrageous, exorbitant and unnecessary gouging they are getting on ringtones from the cellphone carriers. Sales of all types of ringtones have done nothing but increase exponentially since this presentation was originally given at BBQ in October 2004, and there is no end in sight to that trend. This seems to me to be a triumph of marketing. Somehow, the carriers have managed to convince the public at large that there is a fundamental difference between 'music I listen to on my iPod' and 'music that plays when my phone rings', even when the two items are sitting side by side on the same device.

The main difference in the mind of the consumer seems to be 'iPod music sounds good, ringtones sound bad!' Of course, that was true when mobile phone CPUs were not powerful enough to play 'real' music (that is, digital audio files, as opposed to MIDI renditions or monophonic beep-tones). But current mobile devices are significantly more powerful than the laptop computers of just a few years ago, and most support high-quality audio/video players and stereo headsets, plus gigabyte removable storage cards. The latest version of the T-Mobile Sidekick features an MP3 player application that lives right next door to the ringtone catalogue, which sells nothing but MP3 ringtones.

This means that our customers can shell out $15 for a Justin Timberlake *FutureSex/LoveSounds* CD, rip the songs to high-resolution stereo MP3, load them onto an SD card and listen to them on their Sidekicks. But if they want to assign 'Sexy Back' from that same album to someone in their address book, they have to go to the ringtone catalogue and spend another $2.50 to download a 15-second, low-resolution mono MP3 clip that gets installed in the device's RAM (not on the SD card). If they were to do that for every song on the album (even if they were available), they would end up spending more for the ringtones than they did for the CD!

This seems completely insane to me, since I know for a fact that the ringtone file contains exactly the same data as the CD cut (just less of it), and there is no technical reason why you could not play an MP3 file from your SD card, starting at a specified place, when the phone rings. Granted our audio system is not really set up to do that, but the real reason we have not updated the software to allow this feature (which would delight our users immensely) is because no carrier on the planet has any interest in supporting it. Quite the opposite, in fact: no carrier would sell our device if we enabled that kind of custom ringtone functionality, since it would basically eliminate their ringtone catalogue sales.

Nevertheless, I still believe that the current ringtone market is ripe for obsolescence, and the (as of writing this, 5 May 2007) imminent release of Apple's iPhone only bolsters my confidence in that statement. Here we have the ultimate rendition of the 'Pod + cellphone' device described in my original presentation, completely integrated with iTunes, a music download service that features 30-second preview files for every one of its five million songs; preview files that just happen to be perfectly formatted for use as ringtones. It will be very interesting to see what Apple does with this enormous potential revenue stream.

Chapter 4

Indeterminate adaptive digital audio for games on mobiles

Agnès Guerraz and Jacques Lemordant

Audio and games on mobiles

A mobile game is a video game played on a mobile phone. The game market for mobiles is clearly regarded as a market with a future,[1] as the multiple investments carried out in this segment testify. Mobiles are true platforms for large and general-public games. Mobile games can be downloaded via the mobile operator's radio network, WLAN, Bluetooth or a USB connection. Mobiles phones give game developers a unique set of tools and behaviours and with a little creativity, game developers can make some really great games for this platform. The challenges posed by portable devices are numerous, but the biggest complaint of many in the industry is the lack of standards. It is necessary to adapt each game to the various models of existing terminals, which do not offer the same features (memory, processing power, keys and so on). Consequently, the number of different versions of a game rises to several hundred. As we will see, Java Micro Edition (J2ME) attempts with some success to solve these problems.

The market for mobile audio products is exploding, creating opportunities for sound designers and content providers. With the mobile phone firmly established as a credible digital music player, mobile music-related applications are becoming an increasingly important component of each mobile phone supplier's product offering. As end-users want access to digital entertainment on the move, building as much functionality as possible into the mobile phone is logical. No game will be complete without sounds.

Audio is a participatory medium, which actively engages the listener in the ongoing processing of aural information. Audio constitutes an essential part of any game, especially in helping to create a feeling of immersion. A convincing combination of sound and image is a key aspect in producing games. Spatialized sound sources, audio special effects, interactive audio and animated digital signal processing (DSP) parameters are the main ingredients for building such environments. However, their successful combination can only be achieved if they are correctly synchronized with the visual world: any interaction with one of the media must be immediately and relevantly associated with a corresponding interaction by the

---

1   Trip Hawkins (CEO, Digital Chocolate), 'Making Mobile Phones the Ultimate Game Platform', *Games Developers Conference*, 2007.

other. Audio technologies for mobile devices are being developed and deployed at an astonishing rate: sophisticated mixers for digital audio have begun to appear on the last generation of mobiles, opening the way to new kinds of audio applications. DJ-style applications are now possible and the music experience on the phone is then much more than just playing music tracks. Audio technologies and interactive applications on mobiles will change the way music is conceived, designed, created, transmitted and experienced. We shall see in the following how game audio designers can now build complex interactive soundtracks for games on mobiles.

Digital audio on mobiles

Digital audio is the method of representing audio in digital form. An analogue signal is converted to a digital signal at a given sampling rate and bit resolution; it may contain multiple channels (two channels for stereo or more for surround sound). The digital signal is then compressed into a standard format like MP3, AAC or 3GPP. Digital audio is not the only way to represent audio on mobiles: MIDI is a communication protocol where music is represented as digital data 'event messages' such as the pitch and intensity of musical notes to play, control signals for parameters such as volume, vibrato and panning, cues and clock signals to set the tempo. MIDI is notable for its success, both in its widespread adoption throughout the industry, and in remaining essentially unchanged in the face of technological developments since its introduction in 1983.

Generating music by using digital audio chunks is a quite new way to build a soundtrack, which has started to be used for games on consoles and is now possible on mobiles due to the presence of powerful mixers for digital audio. First experiences in generating music from digital audio chunks can be traced back to early 2004 when Kenneth Kirschner, a New York-based composer, used Flash to compose ever-changing pieces of digital music.[2] These compositions generally consist of a number of digital audio files that are randomly layered simultaneously, and can play for as long as the listener desires. A piece of music that is indeterminate has no inherent end and is therefore well suited for games, which can drive it to give the appearance that no matter what the player does, the music is appropriately supporting the action. Indeterminate adaptive digital audio meets the requirements of mobile phones with limited memory and digital audio mixer. We believe that the experiences of minimalism and contemporary musical forms will be fundamental in building rich audio for multimedia graphics applications (games, navigation and guidance applications and so on) that can be developed on mobiles.

Most mobile phones are now shipped with a Java virtual machine and a Java programming environment called Java Micro Edition (J2ME). The Java Community Process or JCP, established in 1998, is a formalized process, which allows interested parties to be involved in the definition of future versions and features of the Java platform. The JCP involves the use of Java Specification Requests (JSR), which

---

2   Marc Weidenbaum, 'Musique for Shuffling', http://www.disquiet.com/kirschner.html (accessed 5 June 2007).

are formal documents that describe proposed specifications and technologies to be added to the Java platform. Formal public reviews of JSRs are conducted before the JSR becomes final and are voted on by the JCP Executive Committee. A final JSR provides a reference implementation, which provides an implementation of the technology in source code. There are over 300 JSRs; the more visible JSRs that concern us are:

- Java Advanced Multimedia Supplements API called JSR 234;
- Java Mobile Media API (MMAPI) for Java ME called JSR 135;
- Scalable 2D Vector Graphics API for J2ME called JSR 226;
- Mobile 3D Graphics API for Java ME 1.0 and 1.1 called JSR 184.

An application programming interface (API) is a code interface that a program library provides in order to support requests for services asked by a computer program. The software that provides the functionality described by an API is said to be an implementation of the API. The API itself is abstract, in that it specifies an interface and does not get involved with implementation details. An API that is particularly interesting for audio has been defined in a JSR. This API is called Advanced Multimedia Supplements or Java Specification Request (JSR-234). The audio part of JSR-234 is a well-designed object-oriented framework which enhances the audio support on mobile devices by adding rendering features like 3D audio, special audio effects and virtual acoustics. We will explain how this API can be used to drive the game's music at runtime, according to a set of rules established by the composer/editor. As there is no specific support in JSR-234 for interactive audio, we will have to define new objects to manage time, synchronization and animation of DSP parameters.

Content development for games

Content development is the process of designing, writing, gathering, organizing and editing content that may consist of graphics, pictures, recordings or other media assets that could be used on mobile devices. Content development is the responsibility of audio designers, visual designers and software developers. Audio content development for games must take into account the non-linear nature of games, which means that game-play length is indeterminate. In a recent article Collins discusses in depth the implications of the non-linearity of game audio and music on their aesthetics and functions in the context of games.[3] In addition to spatial acoustics helping to create an environment, the music, dialogue and sound effects help to represent and reinforce a sense of location in terms of cultural, physical, social or historical environments.

At this stage we can make an analogy between the Web at its beginning in the 1980s and today's mobile applications, especially mobile gaming. When the World

---

3   Karen Collins, 'An Introduction to the Participatory and Non-Linear Aspects of Video Games Audio', Stan Hawkins and John Richardson, (eds), *Essays on Sound and Vision*, (Helsinki, 2007).

Wide Web began, Web developers either generated content themselves or took existing documents and coded them into hypertext mark-up language (HTML). In time, the field of website development came to encompass many technologies, so it became difficult for website developers to maintain so many different skills. Content developers are specialized website developers who have mastered content generation skills. They can integrate content into new or existing websites, but they may not have skills such as script language programming, database programming and graphic design. As shown in Figure 4.1, a usual approach to game development takes into account the visual content with animated graphic objects, the audio content with 3D audio sources and sound effects, and the software development linking the audio and graphical objects with game events and rules. Letting the audio designers produce animated audio sources and sound effects and giving them tools to construct these animations is one of the key motivations for designing formats for interactive audios.

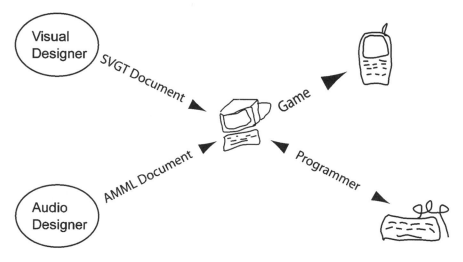

Figure 4.1   Content development

Audio designers

By audio designers we mean composers and/or sound designers, depending on the application and the content to be built. In the case of game development, both are needed to achieve a complete audio rendering in the game. Audio designers maintain direct control over the composition and presentation of an interactive game soundtrack. The audio designer recognizes the limitations of the medium and strives to engage interaction between the sound stimulus and the listener's interpretive ability. Frequently, the perception of a message is greatly influenced by the listener's ability to create multisensory imagery within the mind. These mental images are formed in response to an analysis of the signal received, and the personal experience the listener has with the subject or content. In effect, each individual fills in details beyond the limited audio information provided. The ultimate objective of all games is to reproduce specific conditions so as to make users feel as if they are in as real a situation as is possible. Sound immersion, especially using headphones, is truly amazing. The sound really appears to emanate from all over, from right to left, back to front.

Visual designers

Visual designers conceive and create assets, and refine their look and feel for the application. This includes, but is not limited to, the components of the application, user interface controls, iconography and so forth. The visual designer is responsible for providing the conceptual design including typography, colour, branding and graphics. While visual designers may relay concepts through documents, mood boards and other artefacts, graphic assets are their primary contribution to the development process.

Software developers

Software developers work with the live tree obtained by parsing the documents produced by audio and visual designers. They have to write the logic of the application, detect collision between visual objects, get input from the user and actualize the graph of audio and visual objects inside the main loop at the right frequency.

Audio formats and API

There are numerous formats available to make audio content with more or fewer music and sound functionalities. A series of documents regarding existing and potential formats for audio content are developed by groups such as the Interactive Audio special interest group (IAsig).[4] In 1999 the IAsig published an Interactive 3D Audio Rendering Guideline Level 2.0 (I3DL2), and in 2005 the Synchronized Multimedia Activity of the World Wide Web Consortium (W3C) designed the Synchronized Multimedia Integration Language version 2.0 (SMIL 2.0) for choreographing multimedia presentations where audio, video, text and graphics are combined in real time.[5] As a result, there have been a series of important advances and suggestions for overcoming the difficulties involved in creating multimedia content for games. SMIL and I3DL2 can be joined as shown by Kari Pihkala and Tapio Lokki.[6] In their approach, visual and audio elements are defined in the same SMIL document.

In 2007, eight years after the completion of the I3DL2 guidelines, IAsig announced the completion of a new interactive audio file format to complement I3DL2. This new format, based on the open-standard XMF file format, is called

---

4 'Interactive 3D Audio Rendering Guidelines Level 2', Interactive Audio SIG, http://www.iasig.org (accessed 5 June 2007).

5 'W3C, Synchronized Multimedia Integration Language (SMIL2.0)', http://www.w3.org/TR/2005/REC-SMIL2-20050107/ (accessed 5 June 2007).

6 K. Pihkala and T. Lokki, 'Extending SMIL with 3D Audio', in *Proceedings of the 2003 International Conference on Auditory Display* (Boston, 6–9 July 2003), pp. 95–8.

Interactive XMF (iXMF). The goal of the IAsig in designing this format is to put artistic control into the hands of the artists, to keep programmers from having to make artistic decisions, to eliminate rework for porting to new platforms, and to reduce production time, cost and stress. The main objects in iXMF are cue events. A cue can be defined as a symbolic name associated to a graph of audio elements producing a continuous soundtrack from discrete media chunks. Clearly, iXMF with its four-level hierarchical model for mixing and muting (track, chunk, cue and mix groups) is a complex low-level file format, which has not been designed with mobiles in mind.

The Synchronized Multimedia Integration Language (SMIL) has been recommended by W3C and allows time-based multimedia delivery on the Web. It offers a way to synchronize media, text, video, graphics, audio and vector-based animation based on a timeline. SMIL-based timing and synchronization and SMIL-based declarative animation have not been used by the IAsig to define the iXMF format. We think that for mobiles (and probably not only for mobiles) a format for interactive audio can be defined by extending SMIL modules with the audio object-oriented format (close to I3DL2) specified in JSR-234: SMIL-based timing and synchronization and SMIL-based declarative animation for DSP parameters can be joined with the audio part of JSR-234 to give something with capabilities similar to iXMF and easier to implement on mobile phones.

3D audio and JSR-234

If we want audio to be a participatory medium, we have to make sounds appear to be located in a three-dimensional space around the user, and we have to produce audio effects such as hard sound effects, background sound effects and collision sound effects. The presence of 3D audio on a device can expand the user's experience beyond the physical dimensions of the device. 3D audio allows the user to hear sounds not just way beyond the left and right sides of the device, but in front and behind the user, and even above and below him or her.

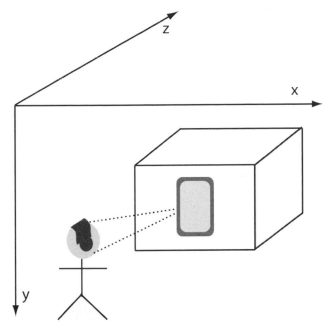

Figure 4.2   3D audio rendering

A mobile device can support both stereo microspeakers and stereo headphones, as in Figure 4.2, so that the users can choose how they listen to their spatialized audio (the way the microspeakers are mounted in a mobile device is critical to ensuring a good quality 3D audio).[7] JSR-234, Advanced Multimedia Supplements,[8] extends the Mobile Media API (MMAPI, JSR-135) with additional controls for three-dimensional sound and audio effects. This API allows for a kind of effects network of a limited complexity to be built from Java, allowing real-time submixing (with various effects being applied to each input before the submix and after the submix). JSR-234 has been designed in a modular fashion and is based on JSR-135's principle of creating a player for a particular piece of media, adding the player to a group or module and then obtaining controls from that module. The JSR-135 is the Mobile Media API. This specifies a multimedia API for Java Micro Edition (J2ME), allowing simple, easy access and control of basic audio and multimedia resources while also addressing scalability and support of more sophisticated features.

3D effects are accomplished via SoundSource3D objects, which specify a 3D position and other spatial properties. Adding a player to a SoundSource3D object causes its audio content to be spatialized accordingly. Sequences of insert effects and submix groups all require processing power, which at present is still limited on mobile devices. Applications such as mixing, karaoke software and immersive games with dynamic 3D sounds will be opened up with JSR-234 API. The content

---

7   Porter Hayden, 'Sonaptic discusses JSR-234 3D Audio', http://sonify.org/tutorials/interviews/jsr234 (accessed 5 June 2007).

8   Pihkala and Lokki, 'Extending SMIL with 3D audio'.

would usually be prepared as a standard monophonic format file (MP3, AAC, 3GPP and so on) and the positioning applied at run-time under programmatic control from Java.

Interactive audio and iXMF

iXMF is a public standard structured audio file format that supports cross-platform interchange of advanced interactive audio soundtracks. It uses a queue-oriented model, is programming-neutral and can be used without licence agreements or royalty payments. iXMF was released to the public by IAsig in 2007. The main concept in iXMF is that of a cue, shown in Figure 4.3.

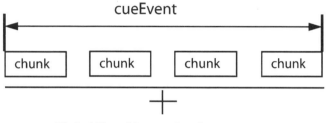

Figure 4.3   iXMF model

Some terms that are used in conjunction with iXMF should be defined. These are 'media chunk', 'cue request' and 'cue'. A media chunk is any piece of playable media data. It can be an entire audio file (or a defined contiguous region of an audio file), or either an entire MIDI file or a defined contiguous region within a MIDI file. The continuous soundtrack is built by stringing media chunks together, and sometimes by layering them. A cue request is an event that the game signals to the soundtrack manager, and to which the soundtrack manager responds with a corresponding action designed by the audio artist at the time of authoring. That action is called a cue. A cue can contain any combination of services or operations that the soundtrack manager can perform. In most cases a cue will contain a playable soundtrack element, but it may also be used to perform other soundtrack manager functions that do not result in something audible, such as setting a variable, loading media or executing a callback to the game.

Synchronization and DSP animation with SMIL

SMIL is an XML-based language and is a recommendation of the W3C consortium.[9] SMIL does not embed media objects (images, video/audio clips, text and so on); instead, a SMIL presentation consists of at least one XML file and some external media files (which can be distant or available locally). SMIL is composed of many

---

9   W3C, 'Synchronized Multimedia Integration Language (SMIL 2.0)'.

modules; the following two are of particular interest: timing + synchronization, and animation. SMIL is a complex language and requires editing tools that can handle various aspects of the authoring process: layout design, timing specification, encoding support, document preview and so on. An authoring application for SMIL, called LimSee, has been developed by the WAM (Web Adaptation Multimedia) team at INRIA (l'Institut National de Recherche en Informatique et en Automatique.[10]

AMML: a format for 3D and interactive audio

The advantage of using an XML format to specify 3D and interactive audio is that we have many tools to transform and edit XML documents. Moreover, an XML format can be used as a generic design format as we can generate from it Java code for JSR-234 or C code for another interactive audio API like Fmod.[11] Another advantage is that a graphical editor for music composers and its associated soundtrack manager can be constructed more easily by using an XML format as a serialization mechanism. A soundtrack manager will control the audio playback and will provide the following functionality in response to cue requests:

- Responding to game sound requests by playing appropriate sound media, sometimes influenced by game state;
- Constructing continuous soundtrack elements from discrete media chunks, whether via static play lists or dynamic rules;
- Dynamically ordering or selecting which media chunks get played, sometimes influenced by game state, sometimes to reduce repetition;
- Mixing and/or muting parallel tracks within media chunks;
- Providing continuous, dynamic control of DSP parameters such as volume, pan and 3D spatial position, sometimes influenced by game state, sometimes to reduce repetition.

In this section, we will show how an XML format for 3D and interactive audio on mobiles can be designed. This format will be called AMML for Advanced/Audio Multimedia Markup Language and the grammar of the format will be controlled by an XML-Schema. If mobiles are the main target, it is best to have a format the closest possible to the JSR-234 Advanced Multimedia API for 3D audio and the closest possible to SMIL timing and synchronization modules for its interactive audio capabilities.

---

10 R. Deltour and C. Roisin, 'The LimSee3 Multimedia Authoring Model', *DocEng 2006*, ACM Symposium on Document Engineering (Amsterdam, 10–13 October 2006), pp. 173–5.

11 Fmod, sound designer middleware tools, http://www.fmod.org/ (accessed 5 June 2007).

AMML and 3D audio

The best way to derive a format for 3D audio from the JSR-234 is through an XML serialization of the JSR-234 API objects. This will have two advantages:

- It will be easier to build a graphical authoring system allowing an audio-designer to produce AMML documents by embedding the JSR-234 engine in the authoring system.
- It will be easier for an application programmer to parse an AMML instance document and map it on the JSR-234 API's objects.

In Figure 4.4 we have a Unified Modelling Language (UML) view with inheritance of the AMML XML-Schema driving the AMML format. The light grey part of the schema corresponds to the serialization of the JSR-234 API and consequently to 3D audio. A cueEvent is the main object of the AMML format. CueEvents are of two types as in JSR-234: *SoundSources3D* for 3D audio rendering and *EffectModule* for audio special effects. The position of the spectator is controlled in a 3D-space and is detained by the AMML root object. Global environment parameters are also under control of the AMML root object.

AMML and interactive audio

Structuration

The lower right part of the schema, shown in Figure 4.4, supports the interactive capabilities of the format and is borrowed from the SMIL timing and synchronization modules. We have defined three new types of objects: layer, chunk and chunkExcl (see Figure 4.5). These three objects are containers helping to structure the data: a cueEvent aggregates layers, and a layer aggregate of audio chunks of type chunk or chunkExcl. A ChunkExcl is itself a container playing its audio chunks in random order. This brings into the API a six-level hierarchical model for mixing, muting and rendering composed of the following objects: AMML, cueEvent, layer, chunk or chunkExcl, player and tracks.

Synchronization

In the AMML model for interactive audio, the component synchronization is made as in SMIL, with the help of sequential compositions, parallel compositions and timing attributes (*begin, end, dur, repeatCount, repeatDur*).

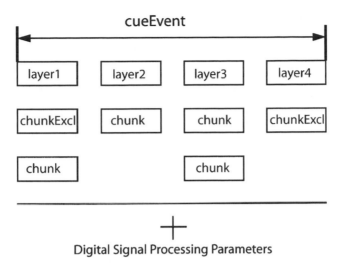

Figure 4.4   AMML interactive audio model

The temporal relationships among media elements are determined by time elements, which are of three kinds:

- *CueEvent* elements execute their children in parallel.
- *Layer* elements execute their children in sequence.
- *Chunk* elements of type *ChunkExcl* execute one child at a time like an iPod in shuffle mode. In fact, an object of type *ChunkExcl* is more than a state machine: although only one child may play at a time, several other children may be queued. SMIL offers an attractive conceptual framework called *priority classes* for doing so. Each priority class is characterized by a *peers* attribute to determine how members of the class would interrupt each other. The possible values are *defer* (don't interrupt, but put the interrupting peer into the queue), *pause*, *never* (don't start the interrupting peer), and *stop* (stop the current peer right away).

Animation of DSP parameters

In order to keep the diagram (Figure 4.4) readable, we have not shown the important part corresponding to the animation of the DSP parameters. Animation of the DSP parameters is done using XML elements and attributes defined in the SMIL animation module. The example given below shows how the animation of the reverberation time is specified in the AMML language:

```
<reverbControl>
  <animate attributeName="reverbTime" begin="1" end="3" from="120"
  to="412"/>
</reverbControl>
```

AMML schema

An XML-schema can be defined to control and validate AMML documents. The hierarchy of the types comprising this schema is shown using an UML diagram (Figure 4.5). One part of the schema is dedicated to 3D audio and the other part (lower right) is dedicated to interactive audio. Extra types, not shown on the figure, are needed to control the animation of DSP parameters.

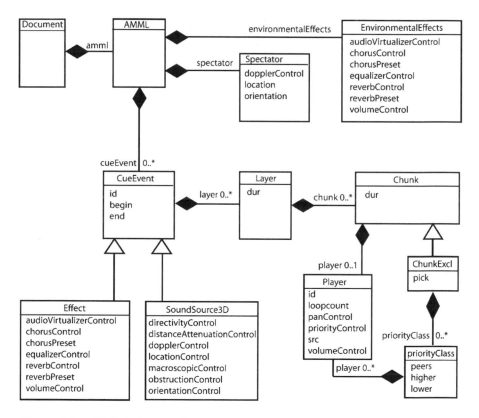

Figure 4.5   AMML XML-schema

An example: Breakout

A detailed example will help to clarify the basic idea. We chose to develop a 'Breakout' game for mobile phone with 3D interactive audio. A 'Breakout' game is a well-known example for mobile gaming; see for example a Scalable 2D Vector Graphics (SVGT) implementation of this game on mobile by Vincent Hardy et al.[12] We have tested our implementation on a Nokia N95 phone with Scalable 2D Vector Graphics for the visual part and with Java Advanced Multimedia Supplements for 3D interactive audio. It was found to run very satisfactorily both for the visual part and the audio part.

A layer of 'bricks' lines the top third of the screen as shown in Figure 4.6. A ball travels across the screen, bouncing off the top and side walls of the screen. When the ball hits a brick, the ball bounces off and the brick disappears. The player loses a life when the ball touches the bottom of the screen, and to prevent this from happening, the player has a movable paddle to bounce the ball back into play.

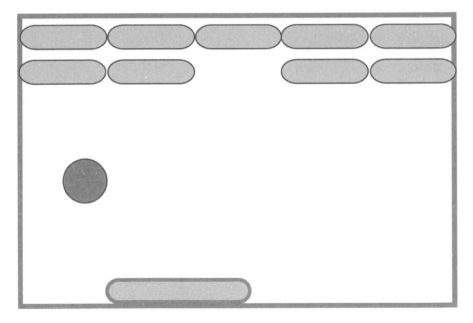

Figure 4.6   Breakout game screenshot

12 Deltour and Roisin, 'The LimSee3 Multimedia Authoring Model'.

SVGT and JSR-226

SVG is a language for describing a two-dimensional graphics in XML. SVG allows for three types of graphic objects: vector graphic shapes (such as paths consisting of straight lines and curves), multimedia (such as raster images and video) and text. SVG drawings can be interactive and dynamic. Animations can be defined and triggered either declaratively (that is, by embedding SVG animation elements in SVG content) or via scripting. Industry demand and requests from the SVG developer community has established the need for some form of SVG suited to displaying vector graphics on small devices. In order to meet these demands the SVG Working Group created a profile specification that was suitable for use on mobile devices as well as on desktops. The SVG Mobile 1.1 specifications defined SVG Tiny (SVGT) 1.1 suitable for mobile devices, but the absence of scripting in SVG Tiny prompted a second look at the use of programming languages and scripting. In conjunction with the Java JSR-226 group, a lightweight interface called the microDOM, or uDOM, was developed. With this advance, lightweight programmatic control of SVGT (in Java in the case of JSR-226) became feasible on the whole range of platforms from cellphones through to desktops.

Visual description of the game

The following SVGT document, whose rendering is shown in Figure 4.6, illustrates the visual part of the game. It contains the game layout, the ball, the brick lines (only one to keep the document simpler to read) and a visual special effect whose id is *collisionFX*:

Example: breakout.svg document
```
<svg width="176" height="208" xmlns="http://www.w3.org/2000/svg"
version="1.2" baseProfile="tiny">
<defs>
<rect id="brick" x="0" y="0" rx="7" ry="7" width="33" height="16"
     fill="rgb(0,255,0)"/>
</defs>
<!--FX-->
<circle id="collisionFX" r="1" cx="80" cy="80" fill="rgb(140,140,0)">
    <animate attributeName="r" begin="collisionFX.focusin" dur="0.8s"
    from="1" to="3"/>
</circle>
<!--background-->
<rect id="clear" x="0" y="0" width="176" height="144" fill="white"/>
<!-- Game Layout -->
<rect id="top" x="0" y="0" width="176" height="5" fill="rgb(200,200,200)"/>
<rect id="bottom" x="0" y="138" width="176" height="5" fill="rgb(200,200,
     200)"/>
<rect id="left" x="0" y="5" width="5" height="133" fill="rgb(200,200,200)"/>
```

```
<rect id="right" x="171" y="5" width="5" height="133" fill="rgb(200,200,
    200)"/>
<rect id="perimeter" x="5" y="5" width="166" height="133" fill="none"
    stroke="red"/>
<!-- lines of bricks -->
<use xlink:href="#brick" x="5" y="6" id="brick1"/>
<use xlink:href="#brick" x="38" y="6" id="brick2"/>
<use xlink:href="#brick" x="71" y="6" id="brick3"/>
<!-- paddle -->
<rect id="paddle" x="30" y="126" rx="5" ry="5" width="40" height="12"
    fill="rgb(0, 0, 255)"/>
<!-- ball -->
<circle id="ball" cx="80" cy="80" r="10" fill="rgb(255, 0, 0)"/>
</svg>
```

Audio description of the game

The following AMML document illustrates the audio part of the 'Breakout' game. We have one link with the breakout.svg document, contained in the LocationControl element: breakout.svg#ball. This link instructs the system to use the location of the ball for the cueEvent whose id is source3D0. The user position is specified in the spectator element. In this game the audio design is built from two cues, one corresponding to the sound of the ball and the other corresponding to the sound effect associated with the collision between the ball and the paddle. The audio associated with the ball is composed of two layers, one playing music in a shuffle (random) mode. The sound is spatialized according to the position of the ball. The audio associated to the collision has only one layer composed of two chunks, which are played sequentially, and to enhance the effect, the DSP parameters are animated using an animate element inside a reverbControl element (animation of graphics parameters is done the same way in SVGT).

Example: Breakout.aml document

```
<p:amml xmlns:p="amml">
<spectator location="-1 0.5 0.5" />
    <environmentalEffects reverbPreset="arena" chorusPreset="flanger">
            <equalizerControl wetLevel="13" modulationDepth="20"/>
    </environmentalEffects>
    <cueEvent xsi:type="SoundSource3D" id="source3D0" begin="0">
        <locationControl location="breakout.svg#ball"/>
                <layer>
                    <chunk>
                        <player src="ball0.aac" loopCount="-1"/>
                    </chunk>
                </layer>
            <layer>
                <chunk xsi:type="excl" pick="random">
                    <priorityclass peers="stop">
                        <player src="ball1.aac" loopCount="-1"/>
                        <player src="ball2.aac" loopCount="-1"/>
                        <player src="ball3.aac" loopCount="-1"/>
                    </priorityclass>
                </chunk>
            </layer>
    </cueEvent>
    <cueEvent xsi:type="Effect" id="effect0">
        <volumeControl level="24"/>
        <reverbControl>
        <animate attributeName="reverbTime" begin="1" end="3" from="120"
to="412"/>
        </reverbControl>
        <layer>
                <chunk dur="0.4s">
                    <player src="collision0.aac"/>
                </chunk>
                <chunk dur="0.6s">
                    <player src="collision1.aac"/>
                </chunk>
        </layer>
    </cueEvent>
</p:amml>
```

Programmatic control

The application follows the Model-View-Controller paradigm as shown in Figure 4.7 where we have the presentation layer composed of four modules (3DSound

Source, Audio effects, Visual Objects and Visual FX), the model composed of two modules (Game and Effects objects) and the control composed of three modules (Game Canvas, Input and Collision Detection).

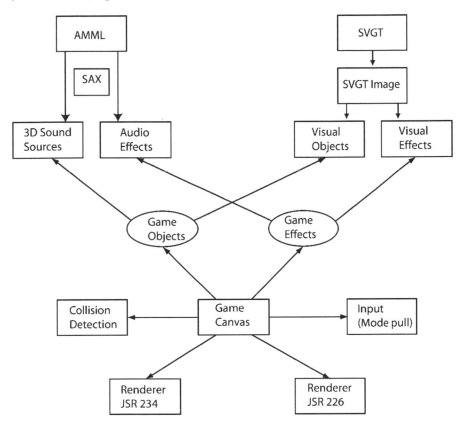

Figure 4.7   Programmatic control

The application accesses the SVGT document through the JSR-226 type called SVGImage. We use a simplified SAX parser to read the AAML document and map the elements and attributes onto Effects and 3DSoundSources modules of the JSR-234. The Game Canvas is a central object, which has access to all the necessary information in order to control the game. It has a main rendering loop which accesses player input in a pull mode, detects collision, modifies accordingly game and effects objects and activates the audio and graphic rendering at an appropriate frequency.

Conclusions

Currently, the history of audio for games is repeating itself on mobile platforms. It began as simple beeps, and then progressed to high quality sounds. Indeed, while only a few years ago mobile games produced simple beeps, they are now catching up to the level of audio on console or computer video games. We have presented an architecture for games on mobile devices separating content creation (audio and graphics) from content manipulation. The development of several 2D and 3D games for mobiles showed us that a format for 3D interactive audio was missing and this evidence was the motivation for creating the AMML format. In order to describe sound sources, special effects and environment properties, the Advanced/Audio Multimedia Markup Language (AMML) format uses an object-oriented approach, which follows rather closely the advanced multimedia API for mobiles described in the JSR-234. For describing interactive audio aspects, time and synchronization, animation of Digital Signal Processing (DSP) parameters, we have used the corresponding multimedia SMIL-based modules and embedded them in our markup language. We have also show how to link the audio presentation layer with the visual presentation layer. Having a format using XML is a big advantage as it is easy to parse and generate code from it: it should be possible to use this format to reach other interesting devices like game consoles. It is also possible to use this format to build an authoring system for interactive and spatialized audio. This authoring system will allow artistic control to be put in the hands of a sound designer, in the same way as SVGT (M2G) or Mobile 3D graphics (M3G) allows artistic control to be put in the hands of a visual designer using an authoring system such as Adobe Illustrator or 3DSMax.

PART 3
Instruments and interactions

Chapter 5

Theoretical approaches to composing dynamic music for video games

Jesper Kaae

Composing dynamic music for computer games involves many aspects that would normally not need to be taken into consideration in traditional composing. These include technical considerations regarding computer power/technology, composing tools and implementation, functional considerations regarding aesthetics and user experience, and not least the compositional requirements of dynamic music, which often require a completely new way of thinking about music. In this chapter I will focus mainly on the compositional aspect of dynamic music, as it is easily forgotten in the technical hype and the tendency to transfer the theories and practice of linear film and popular music into computer games without paying attention to the non-linear nature of the media.

Dynamic music in this case refers to music which is in some way able to react to game-play, and/or is in some way composed or put together in real time by the computer. I focus here on elements like time, structure and the experience of dynamic music, as well as make suggestions regarding how to deal with these elements compositionally. There are of course no exact answers as to how to compose dynamic music, so please consider these suggestions as possibilities for exploration, rather than actual solutions.

I will begin by taking a philosophical/theoretical point of view in looking at the elements of dynamic music, and then will examine dynamic music from a more technological/practical point of view. Later I will argue that despite the fact that this is a relatively new area of composition, there might be lessons to be learned from the past when dealing with the problems of dynamic music. Finally I will make suggestions as to why and how to use musical parameters as compositional effects when creating dynamic music.

Time

Lübcke noted, 'Time is something that you cannot escape, but what time actually is, remains dim.'[1] The following is not an attempt to solve the mystery of what remains dim, but an invitation to dig into what cannot be escaped. Time plays a significant

---

1   Poul Lübcke, *Tidsbegrebet* (Copenhagen, 1981), p. 10. Original: 'Tiden er noget, som vi ikke kan komme udenom, men hvad tiden egentlig er, forbliver dunkelt.'

role in music and particularly in dynamic music. Time is present in music or music is present in time: Normally we accept that fact without even thinking about it, but time often becomes a problem when we want to integrate music in computer games, which can have variable approaches to time.

Based on the ideas of people like J.M.E. McTaggert, modern philosophy distinguishes between A-series and B-series of time, which can also be seen as a dynamic understanding of time and a static understanding of time respectively,[2] and both understandings of time are present in our everyday life. Static time is represented by metaphors like the timeline. In static time we see events as arranged on a line where a certain event comes before, after or simultaneous with other events. When we use phrases like 'a long time ago' or 'time is short' we speak with the timeline in the back of our heads. To see the time as static is like seeing the time from the outside.[3] Dynamic time is represented by metaphors like the time stream. In dynamic time we see events as moving. Things that were in the future an hour ago are now present and will soon be past. When we use phrases such as 'as time goes by' or 'time stands still', we speak with this time stream in the back of our heads. To see the time as dynamic is like seeing the time from the inside.[4]

Philosophers also make a distinction between events and processes in time.[5] The difference is that processes – unlike events – take time. Thus a person's birth and death are events, while the person's life is a process. A journey by train from New York to Boston is a process while departure from New York and arrival in Boston are events. Events do not take time, but rather function as borders between processes. The train arrival in Boston (an event) marks the ending of the train fare (a process) at the same time as it marks the beginning of a holiday in Boston (a process). Processes can overlap each other, while events are characterized by being before, after or simultaneous with other events. Processes can be partly before, partly after or partly simultaneous with other processes. A person's journey from New York to Boston can take place at the same time as another person starts the same journey. The first person's journey is thereby partly before and partly simultaneous with the other person's journey. I shall return to these philosophical terms later.

There can be a great inconsistency between the actual time and how we experience the time. We may talk of an objective time represented by the ticking watch on our arm and a subjective time represented by our inner clock which is highly influenced by our thoughts and emotions. The objective time can be seen as a structural view of time, whereas the subjective time is a more phenomenological view of time. In the following I make a distinction between these two views of time, looking first at time and structure in dynamic music, and then at the experience of time in dynamic music.

---

2   See Jan Faye, 'Den gådefulde tid', in David Farverholdt (ed.), *Hvad er tid?* (Copenhagen, 1999), p. 17; Lübcke, *Tidsbegrebet*, pp. 17–48.

3   Peter Øhrstrøm, *Tidens gang i tidens løb* (Århus, 1995), p. 12.

4   Øhrstrøm, *Tidens gang i tidens løb*, p. 12.

5   Lübcke, *Tidsbegrebet*, p. 18.

Multi-linearity: time and structure in dynamic music

With time in mind we can make an interesting comparison between the philosophical understanding of events and processes on the one hand and the structure of links and notes in the hypertext on the other. 'A hypertext is a text which is organized as nodes and links understood as information units and mutual (non-linear) links between these nodes.'[6] The hypertext is thus often mentioned as a non-sequential or non-linear text contrary to the conventional linear text in, for example, a book. This is, however, an improper simplification of the two types of text, since non-linear texts will always contain linearity to some extent.[7] For example, it does not make any sense to jump randomly from word to word in a sentence in a hypertext. At the same time even the most linear text is open for non-linearity. A page can be skimmed or skipped, or the last page in a crime novel could be read before starting from the beginning. Ironically, the hyperstructure in, for example, an adventure game makes it possible to dictate a certain line that the user has to follow. It is possible to prevent the user from reading the last page in the book so to speak. In this case the writer actually has more control over the reader in a hypertext than in a conventional text.

In principle the hypertext does not have any certain duration, just as a book cannot be said to last for a certain time. It is, however, obvious that it will take some time to read. From the reader's point of view the text does have duration, therefore, and this brings us back to our comparison of the philosophical terms of events and processes and the nodes and links of the hypertext. Just as the event does not have any duration and functions as a border between processes, the link can be said to function as a border between two nodes. The nodes are carriers of content as well as the fact that it is processes that make any kind of experience clear to us. And just like processes can overlap each other, many nodes can be present at the same time or partly at the same time.

Music can also be seen as a course of events and processes. A piece of music can be split into smaller pieces, for example a verse and a refrain. The verse will then consist of phrases or sequences and so on. A phrase, a verse, a refrain or the whole piece of music are all to be considered as processes, while the transitions between them are to be considered as events. It should also now be easy to see the correspondence between phrases, verses, refrains and so on in music and the nodes in a hypertext, and this is exactly how dynamic music is often built. Small pieces of music are put together to form a hyperstructure, and one of the challenges of composing dynamic game music is thus to get the events and processes of the music to fit the events and processes of the game.

From the listener's point of view, music will always be linear, since music exists in a length of time. This is of course provided that we still use the timeline

---

6   Jens F. Jensen, 'Multimedier, Hypermedier, Interaktive Medier', in Jens F. Jensen (ed.), *Multimedier, Hypermedier, Interaktive Medier* (Ålborg, 1998), p. 32. Original: 'E hypertekst er en tekst, der er organiseret som en struktur af nodes og links, forstået som informationsenheder og indbydes (ikke-lineære) sammenkædninger mellem disse enheder.'

7   Jørgen Riber Christensen, 'Multimedier og det postmoderne', in Jens F. Jensen (ed.), *Internet, World Wide Web, Netværks-kommunikation* (Ålborg, 1999), p. 165.

as a metaphor and see time as linear. This means that no matter how the music is organized, it will always appear to be linear to the listener in a structural sense, but this is not necessarily the case to the composer or the practising musician, as the manuscript for the music may very well be non-linear.[8] The score can be written in a way that instructs the musician to read and play the music in a non-linear way.

In 1956 Karlheinz Stockhausen composed *Klavierstück XI* as one of the first classical examples of so-called mobile form. The score for *Klavierstück XI* consists of a note sheet with nineteen separated segments, which are to be played at random, decided by the player. Information in regards to tempo and dynamics for the next segment is stated at the end of each segment, and the whole piece is finished when one of the segments has been repeated twice.

The fundamental idea for this kind of music is far older than Stockhausen, however. *Ars combinatoria* was the name of a game used at private parties in the eighteenth century, in which simple pieces of music were composed by putting together small musical fragments. An example is Mozart's *Musikalisches Würfelspiel* from 1787, a dice game in which the player could put together a small 16-bar minuet. The manuscript for all these pieces of music are, as mentioned, not linear, but because of the fact that readings, writings and music listening will always be linear, we probably should not describe them as non-linear. Inspired by George P. Landow's writings, Petter Dyndahl uses the term multi-linearity for 'courses which are organized in a way that the elements or sequences of elements can vary from time to time'.[9] Stockhausen's *Klavierstück XI* is thus a multi-linear piece of music. So multi-linearity in this case has to do with the structure of music, whereas non-linearity has to do with the experience of time and motion in music.

Before composing any music for a game, it is worth knowing the structure of the game at all levels. If the game or a part of the game has a tree structure or a hub-and-spoke structure as shown earlier, we would probably be able to compose a more goal-directed music and thereby a more linear music for this particular part of the game than if the part has a point-to-point structure. With a tree structure the game or the game parts have many goals, whereas the hub-and-spoke structure has one single goal with small detours.

Non-linearity: time and experience in dynamic music

We are now moving from a structural point of view to a more phenomenological point of view of dynamic music. Jonathan D. Kramer has made a significant contribution to the discussion of time in music with his book *The Time of Music*, in which he defines linearity and non-linearity as follows:

> Let us identify linearity as the determination of some characteristic(s) of music in accordance with implications that arise from earlier events of the piece. Thus linearity is

---

8   Petter Dyndahl, 'Hypertekst og musikalsk spatio-temporalitet', in S. Furuseth (ed.), *Kunstens rytmer i tid og rom* (Trondheim, 2005).

9   Dyndahl, 'Hypertekst og musikalsk spatio-temporalitet'. Original: 'Forløb som er organisert slikt at elementene eller sekvenser av elementer kan variere fra gang til gang.'

processive. Nonlinearity, on the other hand, is nonprocessive. It is the determination of some characteristic(s) of music in accordance with implications that arise from principles or tendencies governing an entire piece or section. Let us also define linear time as the temporal continuum created by a succession events in which earlier events imply later ones and later ones are consequences of earlier ones. Nonlinear time is the temporal continuum that results from principles permanently governing a section or piece.[10]

To Kramer, linear music is characterized by a cause–consequence relationship between the individual parts of the music. The progression in the music is a consequence of what has happened earlier in the music. Thus linearity is typical for tonal music. Non-linear music is characterized by a missing cause–consequence relationship between the individual parts of the music. The progression in the music does not depend on what has happened earlier. Thus non-linearity is more typical for atonal music. But it is important to note that according to Kramer, linearity and non-linearity are present to some extent in almost every kind of music. It is also worth noting that Kramer only focuses on classical music in his analyses, but his ideas can also be of use in analysing popular music.

Along with a phenomenological explanation of time in music, Kramer uses the mathematical model of Markov chains to describe the degree of linearity in music:

A Markov chain is, loosely speaking, a series of antecedents contributing to the probability of a consequent event. In a first order Markov chain, an event is understood as 'chosen' on the basis of probabilities suggested by the immediately preceding event. For example the chances that a C will follow a B in a passage in C major are decidedly different from the probability of encountering a C after a B in F-sharp major. In a second order Markov chain the probability of each event depends on the two preceding events. There is, for example, a specific probability in an A minor of hearing a C after we have heard a B following an A.[11]

Thus the higher the Markov order, the greater the linearity. To specify the terms of linearity and non-linearity Kramer operates with five types of time in music: goal-directed linear time, non-directed linear time, multiply-directed linear time, moment time and vertical time. Goal-directed linear time is the most linear temporal mode, whereas vertical time is the most non-linear. The other types of time mediate between these two extremes.[12] Before going into detail on the five types of time, it is important to remember that almost all music contains both linearity and non-linearity to some degree, and that music can be linear in one voice or instrument while being non-linear in other voices. Linearity and non-linearity are complementary forces, which are often in constant change in the music.

Goal-directed linear time is the most linear of the types of musical time, and it can be seen as a symbol of the Western way of thought for centuries. This type of time is primarily present in tonal music where the notes exist in a hierarchical system, which means that some notes have greater importance than others. It is a kind of music that moves towards a goal, while the goal is a recurrence of the tonic.

---

10 Jonathan D. Kramer, *The Time of Music* (New York, 1988), p. 20.

11 Kramer, *The Time of Music*, p. 22.

12 Kramer, *The Time of Music*, p. 58.

In reality the music does not move anywhere, but that is how we experience tonal music because of its constant changing between tension and relaxation. The music is built with Markov chains of high order.[13] According to Kramer, tonal music sounds natural to Westerners because it conforms to Western culture, and we tend to believe that the recognition of the tonal hierarchy is an intuitive law of nature. But Kramer thinks that it is a learned ability as the existence of more non-linear cultures might show.[14]

By the end of the nineteenth century, music was so rich with chromatics that the tonal continuity was blurred and the sense of the tonic disappeared. For some composers this tendency ended in a regular atonal music, which Kramer characterizes as being non-directed linear time. Atonal music can be linear, but because of the weak or missing sense of a tonic, this kind of linearity does not particularly lead towards a goal, or the goal is achieved by other means, such as changes in rhythm, timbre or texture. The music can still be experienced as moving but the movement is created by other musical elements that normally play a secondary role in tonal music. The experience is such that the listener does not realize where the music is moving towards before actually reaching the goal. This time-sense in music is made with Markov chains of low order.[15]

Multiply-directed time is characterized by discontinuity. The music still contains linear forces, but the movement in the music often points in so many directions that the linearity is disturbed. As opposed to non-directed linearity, which has no clear goal, there is a great deal of goal-direction in multiply-directed music, but it points towards many goals. Kramer uses the following hypothetical example:

> Passage A grows softer. Passage B, which is pianissimo, can function as the goal of passage A even if B does not follow A immediately. Suppose furthermore that A is also becoming more dense texturally. Then either passage B (soft and, let us assume, sparse) or some passage C (load and dense) can serve as a goal of A. Passage A progresses in two directions at once, either of which may or may not lead immediately to a goal.[16]

The experience of multiply-directed linear time is dependent on the listeners' ability to recognize an underlying linearity, even if it is not presented in a linear structure.

Kramer's term 'moment time' is inspired by Stockhausen's moment or 'mobile' forms, to which the *Klavierstück XI* mentioned earlier is related. The mobile form represented by *Klavierstück XI* can be seen as a more extreme version of moment form since here the component moments are not just experienced as being random; they actually are random. Even though there is not any fundamental linearity in this kind of music, it is still experienced as being continual. Where the three linear types of music mentioned above most often have a clear beginning and a clear ending, music in moment time just starts and stops. Moments are independent sections which might

---

13 Kramer uses the first movement of Beethoven's String Quartet No. 7 in F Major (opus 59, no. 1, 1807) as an example of goal-directed music. Kramer, *The Time of Music*, p. 26.

14 Kramer, *The Time of Music*, pp. 22–5.

15 Kramer uses the first movement of Alban Berg's Chamber Concerto of 1925 as example of non-directed music. Kramer, *The Time of Music*, pp. 32–40.

16 Kramer, *The Time of Music*, p. 46.

relate to each other but they are not connected to each other through transitions. The way the sections seem to be related is through other musical elements like texture and timbre. If a section seems to lead towards another section, the music is no longer in moment time.[17]

When the present or the moment becomes the whole essence of the musical work, the discontinuity disappears in favour of an unchanging consistency. No events are dependent on earlier events, just as no events are the cause of other events later in the music. Vertical time is the most non-linear type of time, and music containing vertical time lacks any progression, movement or direction. It is static. It often lacks basic things like phrases, which will normally be found in music containing any of the other types of time. As in music in moment time, this kind of music does not really begin or end; it merely starts and stops. It does not build to a climax or fulfil any expectations from the listener. The music approaches zeroth-order Markov chains.[18] As Kramer puts it, music in vertical time gives the listeners a choice of either giving up their expectations and entering vertical time, or becoming bored. Because this type of time is far from the general understanding of time in Western culture, most people will do the latter according to Kramer.[19] It is, however, worth noting again that Kramer focuses on classical music and his examples of music containing vertical time are limited to avant-garde and minimalist composers like John Cage, Terry Riley, Yannis Xenakis, Steve Reich and others. The fact is that much of the popular music of today also seems to contain some element of vertical time. 'Techno' dance music seems to have much in common with the 1950s avant-garde when it comes to time. The often monotonous rhythm and the sparse melodic movement mean that, in a sense, 'Techno has no linear direction' as Blokhus and Molde write.[20]

Musical linearity

I will now take a deeper look at linearity in music and discuss why it can be difficult to deal with in dynamic music. Lars Bisgaard argues that most Western music has a structure that he describes as a cyclic-hierarchic form in four states. That the form is cyclic means that 'the musical stream is led through a certain order of states each with its own characteristics and its own function in the whole.'[21] That the form is

---

17 Kramer uses Stravinsky's Symphonies for wind instruments as an example of music in moment time. Kramer, *The Time of Music*, pp. 221–85.

18 Kramer uses John Cage and Lejaren Hiller's HPSCHD from 1969 as example of music in vertical time. Kramer, *The Time of Music*, pp. 55–6.

19 Kramer, *The Time of Music*, p. 56.

20 Cited in Dyndahl, 'Hypertekst og musikalsk spatio-temporalitet'. Original: 'Techno har ingen lineær retning.'

21 Lars Bisgaard, 'Musikalsk hermeneutik på hierarkisk grundlag – bidrag til en musikalsk Fænomenologi' in *Dansk Årbog for musikforskning* nr. 16 (Copenhagen, 1985). Original: 'Den musikalske strøm ledes igennem en ganske bestemt række af faser eller tilstande med hver sit særpræg og hver sin funktion i helheden', p. 77.

hierarchic means that 'it manifests itself at many levels in the same piece of music.'[22] The following description is highly influenced by Bisgaard's model even though some changes and additions have been made:

1. Exposition: In the first state of the form a musical statement is presented. This could be a motif, a phrase, a theme and so on. This statement will normally be experienced as the primary idea in the music piece.
2. Re-exposition: The second state emphasises the primary musical idea from the first state by presenting it again in a recognisable form. The re-exposition is not necessarily a repetition of the first state. It will often vary more or less from the original statement. Even if the notes are totally identical it may be problematic to speak of a repetition from a phenomenological point of view, since our memory of the first statement will influence our experience of the second.
3. Polarisation: The third state introduces some kind of musical contrast. Whereas the second state can be seen as a confirmation of the first state, this state can be seen as a denying of the two previous states. The polarisation creates a psychological tension, which in some ways makes us uncomfortable, but at the same time we will often be longing for some kind of variation at this point.
4. Finalisation: The fourth state forces the music back to the original idea from state one, which is now often intensified. We have been in deep water during the polarisation and have a strong urge to feel at home so to speak. In tonal music this often means the expectance of getting back to the tonic in the music. We will in this state often see strong allusions to the primary musical idea.

Just like Kramer's observations, this model is created with reference to classical music, but can be transferred to popular music as well. As mentioned, this cyclic form often takes place at many levels in the music from the overall form of the musical piece down to each individual phrase. At the highest level the cyclic form is known as the AABA form, or the AAB form since polarization and finalization often merge. Let us see how the form looks from a very low level in music. Figure 5.1 shows the cyclic-hieratic form as a rhythmic pattern. It is a well-known rhythmic sequence, which is often clapped by people at larger sports events:

---

22 Lars Bisgaard, 'Musikalsk hermeneutik på hierarkisk grundlag – bidrag til en musikalsk Fænomenologi', p. 77. Original: 'Den manifesterer sig på mange tempoplaner samtidigt i løbet af et givet musikstykke.'

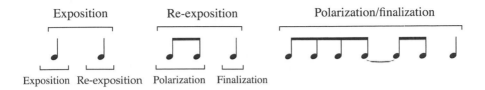

Figure 5.1   Cyclic-hieratic form as rhythmic pattern

When clapping this rhythmic sequence twice we will probably feel an urge to clap something different, and thereby we are automatically starting the cyclic-hierarchic form at a new level. Whether the hierarchic level is high or low, it will always take time to run through the cyclic form, and it is obvious that the higher the level the longer the time it will take. This is actually the essence of the problem of linearity in music. Linearity can also have other forms, but the cyclic-hierarchic form is a way to illustrate the problem of a cause–consequence relationship in music when we want to make the music dynamic. Linear music is constantly moving towards a goal, and when used in a game it might not be able to change course quickly enough to keep up with the events in the game or the acts of the player.

Variability and adaptability

When composing dynamic music, we work with both the static and the dynamic understanding of time. As Kramer describes, music actually provides a special context for understanding the paradox of these types of time, since music can 'divorce the past-present-future from the earlier-simultaneous-later'.[23] Music offers the possibility to present endings, transitions, introductions and so on, in places contrary to the conventions of these elements. This becomes even more clear when working with dynamic music. Static time is used when composing blocks or segments of music corresponding to the nodes of a hypertext, whereas dynamic time is used when deciding how and when these pieces of music should interrelate corresponding to the links of a hypertext. In software for composing dynamic music the static understanding of time is often represented by a timeline similar to the track view of traditional recording software, whereas the dynamic understanding of time is often represented by a scripting environment with conditions like if/then, do/while and so on.[24]

From a technological point of view, dynamic music can be dynamic in two different ways, namely through variability or through adaptability.[25] The variability

---

23 Kramer, *The Time of Music*, p. 161.

24 This kind of division characterizes software like Microsoft's DirectMusic Producer and Creative Lab's ISACT.

25 Scott Selfon, 'DirectMusic Concepts', in Todd M. Fay, *DirectX 9 Audio Exposed: Interactive audio development* (Plano, TX, 2004), pp. 4–7. The terms of variability and adaptability come from the book *DirectX 9 Audio Exposed*, which is mainly about developing

in dynamic music for games is often built on the same principle as Stockhausen's *Klavierstück XI*.[26] Segments of musical material are constantly chosen at random and put together to form a piece of music. Instead of a practising musician, the computer is now the interpreter. It is here a task for the music engine in the game to choose between a set of segments at random to make variation. The elements chosen by the computer could be anything from the velocity of a single note to the order of long precomposed musical pieces, and theoretically the technology behind it could be anything from simple random number generation to complex artificial intelligence. Most often the music system will at least offer some kind of weighted probability. In any case the music is in some way generated by the computer itself and the concept is therefore what we would call generative music.

Adaptability is reflected in the ability of the music to react to the game-play. This is done by sending events from the game engine to the music engine where it is decided when to respond to the events. Theoretically the response could occur at any point in the music, but normally the response is set to occur immediately, at the next beat, at the next bar, or at the next marker if the system offers possibilities for creating markers in the music. This is what I call adaptive music.

It appears that variability tends to have less focus in games than adaptability. At least it would probably be the adaptive aspect of dynamic music that most people would think of first. The thought of making music capable of adapting to the game events is probably more promising to many people than to just vary the music, but variability plays a significant role in dynamic game music both as a way to save computer memory and as a way to keep the music sound new and 'fresh'.[27] After all, computer games are most often designed to last for many hours, and so should the music. On the other hand it is also the adaptability which is most often criticized for not working properly. In cases where the adaptability fails, the music draws attention to itself in an unfortunate way.

Learning from the past

Game music composers are not the first to deal with the problems of musical linearity. We also find non-linear attempts in early Western film music which traditionally and generally has a passion for late nineteenth century orchestral music like Wagner and Strauss – in other words, music which sounds big and grandiose and has linear memorizable themes. When Hollywood composers in the first half of the twentieth century laid the foundation for what could be called the classical film music aesthetic,

---

interactive audio with the tool *DirectMusic Producer*. In the original user's manual of *DirectMusic Producer* the term responsiveness is used instead of adaptability. Responsiveness is a broader and somehow more adequate term, but since, as mentioned in the beginning, I have chosen to see reactive music as mainly adaptive music in this article, I will stick with the term of adaptability.

26 This is especially the case in systems which are based on audio instead of MIDI. When using MIDI the possibilities for variation are much wider, because you are able control each individual note. This is normally not the case when using audio.

27 Selfon, 'DirectMusic Concepts', p. 5.

they seemed to struggle with the same problems as today's composers of dynamic music, particularly the problem of not knowing when things happen. The reason was that the composers were often told to finish their music before the cutting of the film was completed. This meant that it had to be possible to quickly lengthen or shorten the music without leading to incoherent music. The composer had to compose an elastic music, as the writer and composer Leonid Sabaneev expresses himself in his book *Music for the Films*. Here he specifies a complete set of rules for composing film music. Among several suggestions regarding time, tempo and tonality, Sabaneev stresses that 'musical phrases should be short, because a long phrase must be completed without fail, and cannot be abbreviated.'[28] 'Sequences, and progressions in the form of sequences are very useful; their links may be repeated *ad libitum*, or, conversely, may be cut short. For this purpose, modulator sequences progressing (shifting) by a semitone, a tone or a third, are convenient, particularly the last named, as it very quickly brings us back to the original key.'[29] He also writes that 'where the background is neutral and dynamic, the music had better be chromatic and without a clearly expressed tonality, because it can more easily be lengthened or shortened without appreciable aesthetic detriment.'[30] Sabaneev even mentions what today is normally known as stingers when he writes that 'notes, or even chords, may conveniently be inserted here and there in the musical texture.'[31]

Sabaneev's text could as well have been written 70 years later as an overall instruction in how to compose dynamic music for computer games.[32] Again, there is no exact answer on how to compose dynamic music, but the suggestions of Sabaneev are worth bearing in mind. It is clear, however, that Sabaneev sees film music from a somewhat conservative point of view, focusing on fundamental elements in music like melody, harmony and rhythm. In film music these elements are traditionally used as the main elements for creating tension and relaxation in the music. But as we have already seen, these elements can be tricky to work with in dynamic music because of their linearity, and I will therefore later describe the possible forces of using other musical elements when composing dynamic music.

As discussed earlier, there were also composers of non-linear music in the 1950s avant-garde and minimalist styles, even though their interest and reasons for working with these forms of music were quite different from those of the composers of classical Hollywood film music or the composers of today's computer game music. We also find non-linear music in non-Western cultures, particularly in East Asia, which was of course a great inspiration to many Western composers in and before the 1950s.

---

28 Leonid Sabaneev, *Music for the Films* (London, 1935), p. 45.

29 Sabaneev, *Music for the Films*, p. 45.

30 Sabaneev, *Music for the Films*, p. 46.

31 Sabaneev, *Music for the Films*, p. 46.

32 Sabaneev is not the only one to describe how film music sometimes aims at non-linearity, despite of the linear nature of film. See Claudia Gorbman, 'Aesthetics and Rhetoric', *American Music* 22:1 (2004): 14–26; David Bessell, 'What's that funny noise?' in Geoff King and Tanya Krzywinska (eds), *Screenplay: Cinema/Videogames/Interfaces* (London, 2002).

Another spokesperson for finding solutions for dynamic game music in the avant-garde has been David Bessell, who throws composers like Boulez and Lutoslawski into context:

> In game terms, Boulez has introduced interactivity into musical form while managing to maintain a common identity between different readings of the piece. This new Boulezian model of musical structure has not generally been taken up by Hollywood film composers precisely because of its incompatibility with linear narrative, but its usefulness to game programmers struggling with non-linear forms seems self-evident.[33]

In the article Bessell analyses the music of three different games: two games in the horror genre and a snowboarding game. Roughly speaking the music for the horror game is linear in a more or less traditional filmic style, whereas the soundtrack for the snowboarding game is popular loop-based rhythmic music. He concludes that the loop-based music for the snowboarding game is the best functioning music of the examples he examines because of its non-linear elements. What Bessell seems to pass lightly over, however, is that not only the music, but also the games themselves, are probably very different when it comes to linearity. Sports games like the snowboarding game are often more linear because they are directed towards a clear goal. They may have a tree structure or a hub-and-spoke structure. Moreover, the fast tempo, the lack of any great variations and the lack of sudden frights and rises in human emotions are replaced by a more constant feeling of tension and excitement. This makes popular rhythmic music more appropriate to these games. Thus Bessell might be right in his argument for a more non-linear music in computer games in general, but there may be good reasons why the non-linear music for the snowboarding game works, and linear music might have worked as well because of the game type. This does not mean that appropriate music cannot be made for horror games. In fact non-linear music, or vertical-time music, is quite often used in this genre for films. A well-known example is the soundtrack from Stanley Kubrick's *The Shining*, which included composers like Penderecki, Ligeti and others. Moreover, this film genre is very dominant in the computer game industry, which should speak for a more non-linear music in these games.

Musical changes and transitions

'As a general rule, transitions are best executed on or slightly before a cut or hit. Those placed even a fraction of a second afterward tend to look and sound late',[34] Jeff Rona writes about transitions in music in films, but it is likely that the same rule applies to computer games, and this is indeed one of the big challenges when composing for games. In principle it will never be possible to execute a transition before a game event occurs, and most often one would not even be able to execute the transition exactly on the game event without interrupting the musical flow. In her article 'An Introduction to the Participatory and Non-Linear Aspects of Video Games Audio',

---

33 David Bessell, 'What's that funny noise?'.
34 Jeff Rona, *The Reel World: Scoring for Pictures* (San Francisco, 2000), p. 9.

Karen Collins gives a detailed description of transition types in games in which she distinguishes between cue-to-cue transition, cross-fade transition, transitions based on instrument layering and so on.[35] In the following sections I will describe these types of transitions in another way, distinguishing between horizontal and vertical changes in music and discrete and continuous changes in music.

Horizontal and vertical changes in music

To see music as horizontal and vertical is related to our understanding of the manuscript paper as representation of the music. Vertical changes in music are therefore changes that happen at the vertical level of the manuscript paper, that is to say, changes in the instrumentation or the amount of simultaneously sounding notes. Horizontal changes are changes that happen at the horizontal level of the manuscript paper, that is to say, changes that happen over time like, for example, a melody line. All music can be seen as both horizontal and vertical, but some music seems to be either vertically or horizontally orientated. To illustrate the difference, we can use two of the great periods in music history as examples. Baroque music is said to be polyphonic music as opposed to the music of the Classic era, which is more homophonic. Polyphonic is not seen here as the opposite to monophonic, as both polyphonic and homophonic music can have many simultaneous voices, but music of the Classic era often has a leading voice with adapting harmonic voices, whereas Baroque music is often made of many individual voices which wind into each other. The fugue is a good example of this. These differences make the music of the Classic era a more vertical kind of music than Baroque music because it is more orientated towards the musical sound in the present moment, whereas Baroque music is more orientated towards the musical movement in time.

The distinction between vertical and horizontal is not unimportant when composing for games, since vertical changes in music like changes in instrumentation are more independent of time than horizontal changes. Theoretically it is possible to add a doubling voice to an existing voice at any time in music without destroying it, even though it might sound better if the voice was doubled at a specific beat or bar. Changes in the time signature of music must also be categorized as horizontal since a certain amount of time must pass before the listener realizes that the metre has changed. Changes in metre are often a convenient way to blur the linearity in music when composing for games. The listener loses the focus of any fixed points in the music without getting the feeling that the music is interrupted. When the listener does not know where he or she is in the music, changes become more acceptable.

---

35 Karen Collins, 'An Introduction to the Participatory and Non-Linear Aspects of Video Game Audio', Stan Hawkins and John Richardson (eds), *Essays on Sound and Vision* (Helsinki, 2007).

Discrete and continuous changes in music

It has been discussed whether music should be described as build-up of discrete or continuous events or both. These terms have a certain resemblance to the philosophical terms of events and processes. In my earlier comparison between music and hypertext, I argue in some way for the latter, that music can be seen as both events (meaning discrete events) and processes. This discussion is also reflected in the representation of music in music software, and 'in these systems, the distinction between continuous and discrete is normally between sound generation and the discrete events which describe the sound in several attributes, or, in other words, between the instrument and the score.'[36] It is, however, obvious that, for example, changes in dynamics and tempo in the score are often best explained as continuous changes.

When determining values for the changes in dynamic music, the composer will often get two types of messages to work with from the game engine. These could also be considered discrete and continuous messages. In software for composing dynamic music, the discrete messages are often referred to as events or routines and the continuous messages are often referred to as RPCs (runtime parameter controls) or variables. Events are, for example, on/off messages sent when a game avatar enters a trigger box, whereas RPCs are continuously changing values indicating, for example, the health reserves of an avatar or the acceleration of a car. Events are often used for playing one-shot sounds or for telling the music to change on the next marker, bar, beat and so on. RPCs, however, offer possibilities for a more continuous change of the music, but quite often the RPCs are used by the composers as if they were discrete events.

Using musical parameters

Imagine a situation in a game where a heroic character is fighting his way upwards in a high tower trying to beat a series of obstinate monsters. In the top of the tower the princess is waiting for him. We have no idea how long it will take to get to the top, or if he will ever make it at all. What we would probably like to have here is a kind of music that on the one hand is moving towards a goal, but on the other hand does not tell us when or if that goal is ever reached. So the music has to create tension, but at the same time it must be able to keep the tension up as long as needed.

The Shepard Scale is a useful way to theoretically illustrate what we would like to do musically in this situation, and in some cases it might even be a usable solution.

The Shepard Scale is an auditory illusion invented by Roger Shepard. The scale actually consists of a series of overlapping ascending or descending scales that fade in and out, thereby creating an illusion of a scale rising or falling indefinitely. It has its graphical analogy in the illusion of the endlessly ascending or descending stairs drawn by people like Roger Penrose and M.C. Escher. Because of the way the scale works, it is most convincing when made in a digital environment using

---

36 Henkjan Honing, 'Issues in the Representation of Time and Structure in Music', *Contemporary Music Review* 9, (London, 1993), p. 9.

electronic instrument sounds instead of acoustic instruments. The scale uses the volume parameter as a way of creating the illusion of infinity. Many researchers have made interesting discoveries on musical parameters such as volume, timbre, pitch and tempo when it comes to the ways in which people experience these elements. Among these discoveries are the so-called quasi-synaesthetic connections, which have to do with the visual images sometimes 'seen' when hearing sound. So let us take a deeper look at how, when and why musical parameters might sometimes be a solution when composing dynamic music.

Synaesthesia is a phenomenon where sense perceptions from one sense area evoke impressions from another sense area, for example that the experience of a specific tone can be joined by the experience of a specific colour in a person's mind. Synaesthesia is only experienced by a few people, but in the book *Unity of the Senses*, Lawrence Marks describes some other audio-visual relations that tend towards synaesthesia, but which most of us can experience. Two of the most elaborate examples have to do with brightness and size.[37] Most people will experience the sound of a flute as being brighter than the sound of a tuba, and at the same time most people will experience the sound of a tuba as being bigger that the sound of a flute. These phenomena are what Nicholas Cook describes as quasi-synaesthesia in the book *Analyzing Musical Multimedia*[38]. He uses the term quasi-synaesthesia because people do not necessarily see a dark colour when they hear a tuba, but they will probably have this experience if they are told to describe what they hear. We know these quasi-synaesthetic connections from our everyday language where we for example talk about high or low notes, and they are often used in film or cartoon music in what is called mickey-mousing. An example is to play a descending glissando when somebody falls down a staircase.

Pitch, timbre and volume

Linguistic research has shown that vowels with high pitch are described as being small, sharp, bright, fast and active, whereas vowels with low pitch are described as being big, dull, dark, slow and passive.[39] Other research shows that when people have been told to associate visual figures with two nonsense words, they drew a figure with round and soft curves to the word *maluma* and a more hard-edged figure to the word *takete*.[40]

Research such as this is interesting, as it seems to be likely that parameters like pitch, timbre and volume are able to affect people in ways which are normally achieved through other musical elements. Parameters[41] like pitch, timbre and volume are in principle indefinitely variable, although nothing is really indefinitely variable when working in the digital domain. The parameter of timbre actually covers a

---

37 Lawrence E. Marks, *Unity of the Senses* (New York, 1978), p. 92.

38 Nicholas Cook, *Analysing Musical Multimedia* (Oxford, 1998).

39 Marks, *Unity of the Senses*, p. 80.

40 Marks, *Unity of the Senses*, p. 77.

41 When working with MIDI, parameters like these are called continuous controllers.

whole range of specific parameters or filters like equalization, distortion, flanging, reverberation and so on.

There are two interesting advances in using these parameters in the composition of dynamic music for games. Firstly, they can be connected to RPCs and thereby follow game actions at a very detailed level because of their indefinite variability. Secondly, they do not affect musical elements like melody, harmony and rhythm, meaning that they are more time-independent. They can be manipulated in real time without disturbing the musical flow.

Tempo

Research has also shown that when people are told to associate visual pictures when they listen to a piece of music, the faster the tempo, the more sharp and awkward the pictures.[42] In the 1980s other interesting research was undertaken by Marshall and Cohen regarding temporal aspects of film music.[43] In short, a group of people were shown a short animated film with three geometric figures: a large triangle, a small triangle and a small circle, which were all moving in and out of a rectangle. The film was shown with two types of music, one of which was characterized as strong, and one characterized as weak. The film was also shown without any music. The people were then told to judge the music within three categories:

1. Evaluative (good/bad, nice/awful, beautiful/ugly, pleasant/unpleasant);
2. Potency (weak/strong, powerless/powerful, submissive/aggressive, small/large);
3. Activity (calm/agitated, passive/active, quiet/restless, fast/slow).

As expected, the two pieces of music were judged most differently in the potency category when they were listened to without the film. What was surprising was that when the music was played to the film, the two pieces were judged almost similarly in this category, suggesting that the potency category had very little effect on the construction of meaning in the film. The geometric figures were ascribed almost the same personality to the two pieces of music. What was even more surprising was that the activity level of the small triangle was judged as much higher with the strong piece of music than with the weak piece of music. What seemed to happen was coherence between the rhythm in the small triangle and the rhythm in the strong piece of music. This coherence made the small triangle more visible, so to speak. The research by Marshall and Cohen suggests that a parameter like the tempo in music can sometimes have a significant influence on how people experience certain aspects of moving pictures. Like timbre, pitch and volume, tempo is also an indefinite variable parameter in music. By using tempo changes as a compositional effect, it is possible to evoke associations or connotations that may point to specific things in the game.

---

42   Marks, *Unity of the Senses*, p. 93.

43   Sandra K. Marshall and Annabel J. Cohen, 'Effects of musical soundtracks on attitudes toward animated geometric figures', *Music Perception* 6/1, (Berkeley, CA, 1988), p. 108.

Conclusion

The fact that music exists in time is an essential problem when composing music for computer games. The terms multi-linearity and non-linearity cover directions for which composers might aim, in an attempt to escape the linearity of music. Loosely speaking, multi-linearity represents a structural view of time in music, whereas non-linearity represents a phenomenological view of time in music. Besides the different understanding of time in many non-Western cultures, lessons might be learned from Western composers of the twentieth century, especially composers of the avant-garde and minimalism, and composers of early film music. In other words, there might be ways to compose music that is better integrated with the game. By using multi-linear and non-linear techniques, we create music that is less dependent on time. By using musical parameters like timbre, pitch, volume and tempo as compositional effects, it is possible to make continuous changes in music that follow game events in real time.

Chapter 6

Realizing groundbreaking adaptive music

Tim van Geelen

Imagine this: You take a quick last sip from your drink before clutching the game controller in your hands, hearing the engines of all the cars on the track ready to go. The crowd cheers, the announcer names your opponents. There it is, the light goes from red to green, you hit the drive button as fast as you can, and a powerful energized rock beat pumps through your speakers. You are filled with adrenaline when you take the first turn and with that, take the lead. The music roars, your engine roars, your adrenaline peaks, you are totally immersed and you feel like a winner.

Now imagine this: You are playing an adventure game. You are exploring a part of a level that you have been to many times. The music is haunting and spooky, as if a monster could jump out and grab you all of a sudden. Very fitting music for this level indeed, had it not been the case that you have been here many times, and know that there is not going to be a monster around the corner. You know that the monster is further into the level. When you meet it and grab your weapon to strike at just the right time, the music keeps on being spooky, just like the last ten times. The impact is gone.

Both of these scenarios are very common in computer games. Yet in the first, the feeling of immersion is much greater, because all of the elements of the game – not in the least the music and sound effects – work together to suck you into the game world. In the second scenario, however, the music is completely detached from what is actually happening, draining much of the feeling and impact of the game.

Does that mean that music is simply not a possible way of lifting the second scenario to a higher level of immersion? Not at all. Imagine this: Your mind is set on one thing, getting to the bad guy in one piece and taking him on the right way. You enter the level, check your ammunition and make your way towards the enemy. You hear a pulsating bass, pounding like a heartbeat. You take a left turn, start running and focus on spotting the enemy. A high, fast rhythm joins the beat. You hear the roar of the monster, jump sideways, grab your gun in mid-air and land a first bullet right in the arm of the monster. At the moment of impact, a heavy drum and bass beat pounds through the speakers. The heat is on, you are stoked and completely hooked on the game.

The creative side of games audio

The above example is just one way of increasing the value of music in games. Let us take a look at what would work well to increase immersion into the game through music. We can learn from lots of methods used in film. We all know that the use of high tremolo violins typically means that the 'bad guy' is right around the corner, or big drums signal the start of a big battle, and this increases the sense of tension in the scene. These are things we could copy one-on-one into the game, but we can also do much more. One aspect that can be greatly exploited, and works extremely well in some cases, is game-play rhythm. This can mean many things, from the rhythm with which the player character runs, to the speed with which the player clicks icons on the screen, to the rhythm with which the player lands an impressive combination of moves and so on.

For example, in the game *Metal Gear Solid* the player is often required to judge precisely when to move in a slow and stealthy fashion and when to blast forward with both guns blazing. The player must avoid detection by guards, otherwise an adrenaline-pumped show-down of co-ordinated moves takes place, aiming to take down the enemy. If the composer were able to somehow track what kind of tactic the player had in mind, the score could greatly follow his/her moves. The drawing of a weapon coupled with the proximity of the enemy (and the change in proximity) could, for instance, be conditions to load in a 'confrontation imminent' piece, which could start playing at the first sixteenth note after the player has started charging towards the enemy.

If we look at the adventure scenario described in the beginning of this chapter, these 'guesstimate' conditions could also be used. If a player has met a certain enemy at a certain place before, and is running directly toward that area, than chances are significant that he or she is going to attack the moment the enemy comes in sight, which means the audio engine can load in the appropriate piece beforehand, and even prepare a transition piece to enable the new piece to start in perfect sync with the player's moves.

To make the game-play fit the rhythm of the music (rather than vice versa), small delays in reaction to the player's input could be used to make the player's character do his/her thing exactly on the beat of the music. This device is already used in dance games, where a combination of keys has to be pressed in a certain order, after which a dancer busts out his or her moves in sync with the music.

Koji Kondo, composer of game music for the *Mario* and *Zelda* series, is a big believer of matching music with on-screen action, by using rhythm placement, density and arrangement. For instance, in *The Legend of Zelda: The Wind Waker* (Nintendo 2003), a small series of notes are played each time the player subsequently slashes a sword successfully, creating a short, optimistic-sounding melody. Kondo also implements instruments in the stereo field relating to the location of an enemy. He uses many of these techniques with relatively simple-sounding music to make the interactivity really obvious and effective. He seems to try to tell the story with these interactive features, rather than trying to make the music itself more complex.

There is also another way to approach game music: the diegetic way. Diegetic music is music that is played 'from within' the game world.[1] Most sound effects fall

---

1   For a discussion of levels of diegesis in a game, see Karen Collins, 'An Introduction to the Participatory and Non-Linear Aspects of Video Games Audio', in Stan Hawkins and John Richardson (eds), *Essays on Sound and Vision* (Helsinki, 2007).

into this category, but more recently there have been some games that have also used music in a diegetic way. The *Grand Theft Auto* (*GTA*) line of games has used diegetic music since the first game in the series. In the first *GTA* game, every car option had a different radio station, giving every car a different musical style. In *GTA3* this idea was expanded upon. Here, radio stations could be tuned in, with each offering everything that a real radio station would also offer, including corny (and in the case of *GTA*, often very humorous) commercials, DJs answering callers' questions and so on. This function added a whole new dimension to the game, because it allowed for a greater sense of immersion. It also provided the player with an easy way to make the music fit the game situation, because each radio station had a different style of music. Getting into a hot-rod sports car, high-energy electronic music seemed very fitting, while the dub station K-Jah was much more suited for a relaxed ride through the neighbourhood. Another example of diegetic music was found in the game *Black & White*, in which a group of carpenters building a boat sing a sea shanty in which they ask for the player's help. In my opinion, this was a fresh departure from traditional game music. While not significantly explored in games, diegetic music works to varying degrees in immersing the gamer in the game-play. However, it is not always easy to create music to so tightly follow a game's narrative and image. There are many obstacles that must be overcome.

The difficulties of adaptive music

There are several reasons why creating adaptive music (that is, music that adapts to the game-play) can be difficult. Until recently, music has typically been composed in a linear fashion, to be played from beginning to end, without intervention. This linear approach works well for nearly every form of music except for game music. Let us look at the production process as it exists for linear music:

- Step One – The composition: The composer writes a part of a composition, be it a melody on a guitar, some chords on a piano, a short rhythm on drums, and so on. The end result is always linear.
- Step Two – The arrangement: The composer adds more parts to the composition, bringing together rhythms, melodies, harmonies, bass notes and so on.
- Step Three – The recording: The music is played by musicians (or with the help of computers) and is recorded. It is then mixed, mastered and finally distributed on the radio, placed underneath a film, performed for grandparents on weekends and so on.

Interactive and adaptive music, on the other hand, require a non-linear approach. First of all, the composer has to learn how to compose music that can develop from one emotion to many different emotions at any given time. This process can be learned if we look at how music for film is composed: Here, the music also often moves from one emotion to another in a short amount of time. However, the moments at which these transitions happen are predetermined, and the music can be composed to synchronize perfectly with the on-screen changes. A game composer doesn't know when a gamer chooses to attack, or to run away, or to call for help, or to try a different tactic and so on. In terms of the technology, there are also many difficulties. Sequencers (the software programs into which composers record music) are nearly always linear in the way they have been designed to function. *ProTools*, the market leader of audio recording software, works much like a tape machine, recording from beginning to end in a linear fashion. Other popular programs such as *Cubase*, *Nuendo*, *Logic*, *Digital Performer* and *Sonar* are also linear in their workflow. One exception is *Ableton Live*, which allows composers quickly and neatly to jump or transition from one piece of music to another. A final difficulty is implementing the music into the game, designing the music to react to different elements in the game-play.

Realizing adaptive composition

It is evident that it is no small task to create effective adaptive music, and that it takes a different workflow from that of linear music. However, some effective adaptive music techniques have been created, some of which have become more or less standard when trying to create adaptive music for games. These include branching, layering, transitions and generative music. Branching is a method in which a linear musical piece is divided into different layers ('branches'), for instance two percussive layers (one heavy and one light sounding), the bass line, the harmonies and the melody. When a change in game-play occurs, one or more branches are either muted or exchanged for different versions. For instance, if the tension increases, a branch with long, steady bass notes could be exchanged for more aggressive short repeating notes, creating a sense of danger. This can happen smoothly, because the other branches remain the same. Of course, the composer must check all of the branches with each other to ensure that they sound good together. This can make branching very time-consuming, especially if multiple versions of all the branches are needed. It is also resource-heavy in terms of computer memory, because instead of one stereo music track, there must now be multiple tracks in near-perfect sync.

Layering is related to the branching technique, but is based on the idea that more music means more tension or action. A good example is found in the game *Tomb Raider Legend*, in which certain parts of the game have a heavy guitar track added to an ambient layer upon the encountering of enemies. It is questionable whether or not this actually provides more immersion, however, because the effect often becomes very predictable, and the individual layers cannot offer much depth on their own.

A composer can also compose several pieces of music, and then a small transition piece for every possible jump from one track to another, offering a fluent way of going from one emotion to another. This is also very time-consuming, because for every new track, multiple new transitions have to be composed. There are also a very small number of composers who use generative and algorithmic composition methods to create and play back music. The computer can be 'taught' to create variations on certain themes at random. Here, individual notes are played back rather than one pre-recorded track, to be able to let the music move freely. Markov analysis can be used for generative audio. Markov analyses index how many times certain changes in music occur in a piece, and use these values to create variations on a piece. The downside to this kind of composition is that because individual samples have to be used for each note, it places too much load on the computer's memory resources. One possible solution is to use a smaller number of samples, although this would greatly decrease the sound quality.

A final method of non-linear games composition that seems to work fairly effectively is what I will refer to as 'parallel composing'. The idea behind this method is that the composer writes a track in a linear way, but at the same time writes one or two additional tracks, with the essential musical parameters like tempo and key being equal. These tracks are then played in parallel (starting at the exact same moment in-game), and can be interchanged at certain points in the tracks. Each of these tracks is composed with a different emotion in mind, much like writing music pieces one after another. The difference here is that, because composers write these at the same time, they can easily continually check if the tracks are still interchangeable. During the composition process, composers choose as many points as they feel they can afford without making the music too repetitive, at which time these tracks can be interchanged. From my experience, this comes down to approximately once every two or four bars (when using lyrical, melodic-based music), to every sixteenth note (when using highly rhythmical music, like techno). This method has some advantages: for instance, it does not overload the memory; it is not difficult to compose (since linear composition tools can be used); it offers very good adaptability, without having to use fades, transitional pieces and so on; complex elements can be played with, such as modulation, rhythmical changes, tempo changes and so on as long these happen in every parallel track; and it can be applied to most musical styles.

Of course, there are also some downsides to parallel composition. For instance, the composer still has to write a significant amount of music (at least one track for every emotion or event), meaning small-budget studios probably will not have the money to finance a good parallel composition score. It is also necessary to ensure that the song can jump at any chosen moment in the tracks to any other tracks.

In-depth adaptive music composition

Let us look in-depth at an idea for composing adaptive music using the more complex generative composition method. What we want to do is link musical elements to game-play elements, and have them be generated in real time, rather than played back like pre-recorded tracks.

First, we must pick a musical style: For this section, we will use drum'n'bass (D&B). In order to make sure that the music we are going to make is at all times within this style, we have to define the essence of the style. For this example, one of the most characteristic features of D&B is the 'Amen Break', a sample from an old James Brown record. When analysing the beat, we can derive a couple of recurring elements. If we alter any of these elements, the beat will no longer be recognizable as D&B, so we will make sure these are present at all times. The Amen Break drum pattern basically implies a 'boom-boom-tack' rhythm in the beginning, with another 'tack' on the fourth beat. The rest of the beat can be filled in semi-randomly with hi-hats, snares and bass drums. (I say semi-randomly because some logic has to be used here.) A beat with nothing but bass drum hits and the occasional snare would not be effective. It is, however, much more common for hi-hats to be played in succession. A chance value can be assigned to every sound to give the beat some balance.

Now, we have a basic computer generated D&B beat, but it is not yet interactive. We have to decide what we want to change at certain moments. A heavy bass drum and crash cymbal on top of each other, played at a high-action moment, could work very well. To make this happen, we have to have some kind of action meter in the game engine that tells the music engine when an action moment takes place, so that the music engine can trigger the 'kick and crash' cue on the beat nearest to the action moment.

At this stage, we have an interactive drum beat, but since D&B is quite an energetic style, most likely it will not be suitable for every situation in the game. Let us say there could be a calmer, exploration-orientated part of the game that the gamer can choose to enter at any time. The producer of the game requests ambient music, with a slightly dark and electronic sound to it. Because our D&B beat is generated instead of pre-recorded, we can slowly morph from it to ambient music, perhaps stripping down the beat to the bare essence (keeping only the boom-boom-tack rhythm. By slowly decreasing the tempo, switching to electronic drum sounds instead of acoustic drums and lastly filtering until the beat is silent, we can leave the D&B beat in a musically smooth way.

In the meantime, an ambient synthesizer layer could be added into our song. Let us say that we now want a synth melody to carry the gamer into a certain direction, hinting at the correct path. Again, we have to figure out what musical tools we can use to give the music a certain emotion. Varying degrees of dissonance can make us feel everything from a dreamy haze to gut-wrenching spasms of pure evil. Minor 9 chords, for instance, are usually linked to a feeling of mystique, while Major 7 chords feel light-hearted and slightly dreamy, and diminished chords often feel unsettling or strange.

Of course, such feelings can change depending on the listener's cultural or personal experiences, the instrument they are played on, the aggression with which they are played, the rhythm, the adjacent chords and so on. A Major 7 chord, for instance, can sound dreamy when played slowly note-for-note in a high register on a piano, but it can sound surreal when played aggressively on an electric guitar, followed by another Major 7 chord starting one note higher.

Since we want the melody to hint to the user to head in a certain direction, we might propose the following approach. Let us say that in a general 'in between' state in the game, where no dominant feeling is present yet, the music hangs around a C minor chord. Without other chords, this chord will generally sound fairly neutral. When followed by an A flat Major 7 chord played in somewhat the same way, the combination of these two chords brings forth a rather unsettling, unresolved feeling. However, when the C minor chord is followed by an F Major chord, the feeling is much more positive, though still unresolved. Because both of these combinations are small and unresolved, they can easily fit into our composition. Another option would be to take a fairly neutral bit of music (like the single C minor chord) and slightly shift the aggression and rhythm with which certain notes in the piece are played. For instance, a C minor chord accompanied by short, aggressive low notes and medium higher notes feels much more threatening than the same chord played with long, even notes, with the middle notes slowly swelling in volume.

By 'teaching' these aspects of music composition to a music engine, a computer can pick what to play according to certain aspects of the game status. However, it is not always so easy. Human-composed and performed music has many great subtleties that exist but are very hard to analyse, such as the concept of 'the groove'. If we let a computer play the same beat as that of a human drummer, the piece may not feel 'groovy' at all. In other words, the groove may be in the nuances in the ways in which the drummer plays. When technically analysing what the drummer does, we may learn that it is tiny timing errors and differences in how hard the drums are hit that produce most of the groove. However, a drummer does not consciously play notes late or softer or louder; a lot of that happens in the way she or he approaches what is being played. The drummer might for instance think: 'okay, I've got to play this really relaxed', then attempt to convey the relaxed feeling. It is this elusive 'feel' that puts musicians above computer-played instruments (also known as virtual instruments). Although the preference is typically for human musicians, generative music must be played by virtual instruments for obvious reasons.

Another important factor is tone or the 'sound' of a certain instrument. Synthesizers used in many 1980s songs sound different from those used in modern dance songs. By playing the exact same thing on different synthesizers, the experience can be very different for the listener, because she or he has emotional values linked to these sounds. An interactive music composer should be very aware of as many of these things as possible, in order to give the computer – and thus the game – as much freedom as possible.

The usefulness of interactive music can be seen by an examination of non-interactive music, such as in the popular computer online game *Guild Wars*. In *Guild Wars* players play with or against each other over the Internet. *Guild Wars* is a game in which the player's skills build over time, both in how well the gamer is able to control the player's character and the technical 'skill' of the player character (in strength, speed and so on). The music was composed by Jeremy Soule, a popular composer of orchestral music for games. The total music length of this game was roughly one hour. The tracks were written around locations and events in the game.

The 'Hall of Heroes' is an area in the game in which players come to team up, gear up and battle each other. The track 'The Hall of Heroes' plays in this area. The track starts with low staccato strings in pairs of two notes going higher and higher, with underlying percussion, building up in energy. Imagine *ta-tam*, *ta-tam*, *ta-tam*, *ta-tam*, getting louder and louder. A quick analysis of this part can be divided into the various musical elements and associated feelings as in Table 6.1.

Table 6.1 'Hall of Heroes' Connotations

Element	Connotations (feelings)
Aggressively played strings	*danger, anger, energy*
Heavy, low percussion	*danger, strong, big*
Short staccato note patterns	*drawing near, increasing the feeling*
Long high crescendo notes	*increasing tension*

The combination of these elements gives a better idea of what feelings the music brings forth. The combination of aggressive, low, short staccato note patterns gives the impression of something drawing near, but also of building morale (getting ready for battle), a show of power and lust for battle. The high, long notes that increase in volume give the feeling of increasing danger. Coupled with the low staccato notes, the feeling of imminent battle is increased. Later, French horns come in with a slow, swelling melody, ending in powerful notes. This first part of the track resembles the purpose of the area very well. The pattern of notes is very easy to remember, almost like a 'hook' in pop music (a hook is a short catchy musical phrase). This causes the gamer to easily identify the music with the area (because the gamer remembers the hook), but it also easily causes a feeling of 'oh-this-again', because every time they enter the Hall of Heroes, this same music plays. Many players will come to a point sooner or later when they will want to turn off the music simply because they have heard it so many times. In this case, a very fitting and beautiful piece of music quickly becomes annoying because it lacks interactivity.

If we want to get rid of this build-up of annoyance every time the same track plays, we have to understand what it is that is making it annoying. The quick-and-easy answer to this is that the human brain is extremely good at identifying the playback of the exact same thing multiple times. When we hear a piece of music for the first time, our thoughts on it are often different than when we have heard it multiple times. The impact of the piece often decreases every time we hear a piece that is still (somewhat) fresh in our memory. Tiny changes to the music can reduce this effect. The minor changes in the performance keep the music fresh to our ears. Thus, generative music can easily perform this fairly simple task of introducing minor changes to musical pieces to greatly reduce the build-up of annoyance (without even introducing interactivity).

The generative way of composing is as much an indexing of musical parameters as it is the actual writing of music. To keep some artistic control in the hands of the composer, a combination of generative music and composer-written music could be used. This can be done with the help of algorithms such as the Markov chains. As mentioned earlier, Markov analysis involves looking at how many times certain jumps in notes or rhythm (but theoretically, in any parameter) occur and improvises on them. This is kind of like the quick drum'n'bass analysis we did. A Markov-based improvisational engine would divert very little from the essential D&B pattern, and alter instead the in-between notes. In this sense, composers can choose quite precisely how much composing they want to leave to the computer, and how much they want compose. This seems like a very promising way of creating interactive music, because it does not completely break with the traditional way of composing, and gives the creator enough freedom to select the degrees of generation involved.

When comparing composer-written (and recorded) music to generative compositions, the problems are evident: In composer-generated music, the music is more creative and has a definite 'feel' or emotion, although the production for games requires lengthy time-spans and enormous budgets. On the other hand, computer-generated music can be set to follow the action or other in-game parameters very closely, and the computer can generate endless variations on a piece. However, the creativity of generative music is an area which still requires much exploration, and real-time generation of music may require more processing power than that of pre-recorded music, straining the computer's resources. There is one more disadvantage to generative music, and that is that it remains a largely unproven method. Developers of multimedia have to spend a significant amount of money on many different kinds of specialists to get a product finished. As such, they want to take as little risk as possible. Since audiences are so accustomed to the playback of pre-recorded (and nearly completely non-interactive) music that they hear in film or television, there remains a preference for this style and quality of music. Generative music is not yet at the level of pre-recorded, humanly created music.

The future

In the world of games we are at a turning point of realizing very good, truly adaptive music. Developers and game consoles are now powerful enough to open up more opportunities for composers. For instance, physical modelling synthesis can make generative music possible with a very high sound quality. Physical modelling works without samples (so there is no stress on the RAM at all) but instead 'generates' the sound of the instrument that it models, mimicking the working of that instrument (including elements like the vibration of a string, the resonance of the body of an instrument, the ways in which the instrument reacts to different articulations and strengths of playing and so on). This technology is still fairly new and processor-intensive, and requires a lot of instructions from the composer, but that will all diminish over time. Storage devices (most notably hard disks) have become fast enough to stream audio directly to the processor, bypassing the memory nearly completely (and thus allowing for many more audio tracks to be played simultaneously).

However, it is my opinion that the answers lie not so much in technological advancement but in whether or not game developers and composers realize the benefit of adaptive audio, and that organizations and institutions realize that much more education and teaching material on the subject is needed. We can wait for technology to bring us answers, but unless we start to actively work on realizing adaptive music, we will not arrive there any time soon. This means that much research is still to be done, and information sources should be centralized and accessible. Composers must learn and train themselves to compose in non-linear manners, and the technology (such as interactive non-linear software) must be developed to ease both composition and implementation stages.

I recall one remark in a forum topic at the *Game Audio Network Guild* message boards on adaptive music that went something like this: 'Adaptive music has been found to be so difficult and time-consuming to produce that spending the time and money on composition and production quality instead is largely favoured.' In other words, an entire orchestra is hired to record twenty minutes of linear music instead of the game's developers opting for a much more effective adaptive score, without a real orchestra, but offering much more music in the end. The current average music–to–game-play ratio is no less than 1 to 40. Any orchestral score is going to sound repetitive after the tenth time the player hears it, and yet the player may still have to hear it 30 more times.

Developments in new media (and especially in computer games) mean that previously difficult elements are being realized all the time. It is now a matter of realizing the value of a concept such as interactive music, and therein lies one big problem: if neither the game developer nor the composer realize how much of an improvement adaptive music is, it is not implemented. All parties involved must be convinced by the benefits of adaptive music: Then – and only then – will knowledge about and the quality of game music increase.

Chapter 7

The composition-instrument: emergence, improvisation and interaction in games and new media[1]

Norbert Herber

In the conventional practice of music, the process of composition can be understood as the conception and organization of musical ideas, whereas an instrument provides the equipment necessary to realize such a work. In contemporary interactive media such as multimedia websites, computer games and other interactive applications involving the personal computer and mobile devices, this distinction remains largely the same. The composition of the music heard in these environments consists of musical statements to be heard and instructions to be executed in the course of an interaction. Often these structures call for a great deal of random sequencing and repetition following a linear structure.[2] The instrument can be designed as a software synthesizer or as a database of recordings or samples, and is used as a sound resource to suit the demands of each piece of music within the project.[3] For example, consider the iMuse engine by LucasArts. In this system branching or layered instrumental tracks act as the compositional structure and cut-up musical phrases (samples) can be mixed with synthesized instruments to realize that structure in sound.[4] Whatever the design and compositional scheme, contemporary computer games and other interactive media limit the responsibilities of composition and instrument. Each is asked to function in its traditionally separate role and is treated as distinct within the structure underlying the media product.

1   This chapter is based on a paper originally published in the Proceedings of the Audio Mostly Conference: a Conference on Sound in Games, and in *HZ* journal #9, January 2007, http://www.fylkingen.se/hz/n9/herber.html (accessed 11 June 2007).

2   Kurt Harland, 'Composing for Interactive Music', *Gamasutra* (2000): www.gamasutra.com/features/20000217/harland_01.htm (accessed 11 June 2007) and in Alexander Brandon, 'Building an Adaptive Audio Experience', *Game Developer*, October 2002, pp. 28–33.

3   Given the enormous variety of playback engines, file formats and other technical specifications, there are too many different audio technologies to mention specific cases. See the IAsig (Interactive Audio Special Interest Group) website for a comprehensive summary of the formats and technologies in current use: http://www.iasig.org/wg/index.shtml (accessed 11 June 2007).

4   Alexander Brandon, *Audio for Games: planning, process and production* (Indianapolis, 2005), pp. 86–8.

There is need for a critique of music in contemporary interactive media. And the separation of composition and instrument, while not wholly damaging to the experience of the media, should not be immune from scrutiny. Music that operates in a binary, linear mode does little to recognize the emergence, or becoming, that one experiences in the course of an interactive exchange. A traditional, narrative compositional approach leaves no room for the potential of a becoming of music. When involved in a game, a player isn't sitting back passively absorbing events as they unfold on screen; they are engaged. A player actively negotiates environments, converses with others and strives for goals. They work to build meaning and to have an experience that is only possible in the world created by the game. Their interactions in this environment are unique, and represent a kind of becoming where myriad events collide to unfold as experience in the course of their play. This kind of experience can also be described as emergent. Scientific knowledge understands emergence as complex, ordered behaviour that is initiated under random conditions and arises from local, non-linear interactions. Emergent behaviour is generated through 'bottom-up' processes rather than by 'top-down', hierarchical control[5]. Unlike a film, where a narrative dominates the trajectory of a viewer's experience, games present a player with potentialities. Their interactions with the environment, other characters and ultimately the 'rules' of the game can lead to a wide variety of possible outcomes. The non-linear and emergent experience of interactivity is incongruous with the overly repetitive, linear music that is often heard in games and other digital media. It is time to ask: what kinds of compositional techniques can be used to create a music that recognizes the emergence and the potential of becoming found in a digitally-based interaction with games and new media?

Blurring the traditionally distinct roles of composition and instrument provides one possible answer to this question. This approach allows a piece of music to play, or undergo a performance like a traditional composition. When it plays, it enables a musical experience of sound. But it can also be played like a conventional instrument. This treatment allows the musical output of the work to be modified in the course of an interaction. Such an 'instrumentalization' transforms the work into an agent for further musical expression and exploration. Thus, a composition-instrument is a work that can play and be played simultaneously.

A composition-instrument is not a specific piece of music or interactive work in itself but a means of approaching any work where music can be created and transformed. Composition-instrument is a conceptual framework that helps facilitate the creation of musical systems for interactive media, art and game environments. This chapter will discuss the historical context of this compositional approach and show how it is beginning to emerge in the current field of interactive media. The example of an original work aspires to demonstrate how a composition-instrument approach to music exhibits a congruity with the emergent nature of the medium. And finally, discussion of a contemporary computer game project exposes the potential of this musical concept in the world of games, digital art and new media.

---

5   Steven Johnson, *Emergence: the connected lives of ants, brains, cities, and software* (New York, 2001), pp. 17–23.

History

Though the idea of a composition-instrument hybrid is situated in the praxis of computer games, new media and digital art, the historical precursors to this kind of compositional approach lie in an entirely different field and stem from three different musical traditions: experimental, improvisatory and generative. Each of these traditions has established aesthetic approaches, creative processes and musical style. A historical perspective helps to reveal how these attributes can be woven into the fabric of a compositional approach for music that operates in art and media environments with telematic and digitally-based interaction.

The roots of a composition-instrument approach can be found in experimental music. American composer Earle Brown was looking for ways to open musical form and incorporate elements of improvisation into his music during the 1950s. He found a great deal of inspiration in the mobiles of sculptor Alexander Calder. Brown described them to guitarist and author Derek Bailey as:[6]

> ... transforming works of art, I mean they have indigenous transformational factors in their construction, and this seemed to me to be just beautiful. As you walk into a museum and you look at a mobile you see a configuration that's moving very subtly. You walk in the same building the next day and it's a different configuration yet it's the same piece, the same work by Calder.

Brown's thoughts on musical structure are also noted by Michael Nyman in *Experimental Music: Cage and Beyond*[7]. Brown emphasizes that one importance of composition is to be both a means of sonic identification and a musical point-of-departure:

> There must be a fixed (even if flexible) sound-content, to establish the *character* of the work, in order to be called 'open' or 'available' *form*. We recognize people regardless of what they are doing or saying or how they are dressed if their basic *identity* has been established as a constant but flexible function of being alive.

Brown was interested in approaching music with an openness that allowed every performance to render a unique musical output that retains the essential character of the work. These compositional ideas, however, were not exclusive to Brown and his music.

Terry Riley's *In C*, composed in 1964, is a seminal work in both the experimental and minimalist music traditions, and shares in the compositional approach discussed by Brown. The piece consists of 53 melodic phrases (or patterns) and can be performed by any number of players. The piece is notated, but was conceived with an improvisatory spirit that demands careful listening by all involved in the performance. Players are asked to perform each of the 53 phrases in order, but may advance at their own pace, repeating a phrase or a resting between phrases as they see fit. Performers are asked to try to stay within two or three phrases of each other

---

6   Derek Bailey, *Improvisation: its nature and practice in music* (New York, 1992), p. 60.

7   Michael Nyman, *Experimental Music: Cage and Beyond* (Cambridge, 1999), p. 70.

and should not fall too far behind or rush ahead of the rest of the group. An eighth note pulse played on the high Cs of a piano or mallet instrument helps regulate the tempo, as it is essential to play each phrase in strict rhythm.[8]

The musical outcome of *In C* is a seething texture of melodic patterns in which phrases emerge, transform and dissolve in a continuous organic process. Though the 53 patterns are prescribed, the choices made by individual musicians will inevitably vary, leading to an inimitable version of the piece every time it is performed. Riley's composition reflects the imperative of self-identification expressed by Brown, but it also illustrates some of John Cage's thoughts on experimental music,[9] when he writes that the 'experiment' is essentially a composition where 'the outcome of which is unknown'. In performance, *In C* has indefinite outcomes and yet is always recognizable as *In C* due to the 'personality' of the composition – the patterns and performance directions that comprise the work.[10]

There are links between experimental music practice and improvisatory music. Free Improvisation is a good example of this. The genre took root in Europe in the early 1960s, with London serving as a major hub in its development.[11] This genre, in spite of labels and stereotypes, still involved elements of composition. One instance of this can be found in the coalescence of performing groups. In his essay 'Les instants composés', Dan Warburton notes that 'The majority of professional improvisers are choosy about who they play with ... and tend to restrict themselves to their own personal repertoire of techniques.'[12] In this case a kind of composition takes place through the selection of co-performers to join in an improvising ensemble.

David Borgo, in a recent publication on music improvisation and complex systems,[13] acknowledges that this characteristic in Free Improvisation praxis comprises an important aspect of the musical organization and composition in these performances. Free improvised music depends upon some amount of organization, even if it is minimal. In musical situations where there is no preparation or discussion of musical intentions, an established rapport or relationship between performers serves as a kind of composition. This provides organization through familiarity and shared sensibilities. Borgo describes an improvising ensemble as an 'open system' that emerges from bottom-up processes driven by players' relationships and interactions, their training and the performance environment or overall musical situation. Likewise, listening is always an overriding compositional factor because it regulates the dynamics of the performance. Players are constantly aware of their own contributions as well as the contributions of others, and make split-second decisions based on the overall musical output of the group.

---

8   Terry Riley, *In C* (1964): http://www.otherminds.org/SCORES/InC.pdf (accessed 11 June 2007).

9   John Cage, *Silence: lectures and writings* (Middleton, CT, 1973), pp. 13–17.

10   The score for *In C* is available in PDF format at http://www.otherminds.org/shtml/ Scores.shtml (accessed 11 June 2007).

11   Bailey, *Improvisation: its nature and practice in music*, pp. 83–142.

12   Dan Warburton, 'Les instants composés', in Brian Marley and Mark Wastell (eds), *Blocks of Consciousness and the Unbroken Continuum* (London, 2005), p. 109.

13   David Borgo, *Sync or swarm: improvising music in a complex age*, (New York, 2005), pp. 124–6.

Composition in this genre can be more formalized as well. Saxophonist Steve Lacy talks very openly about how he uses composition as a means of mobilizing a performance and creating a musically fertile situation that can nurture an improvised piece. He stated:

> I'm attracted to improvisation because of something I value. That is a freshness, a certain quality, which can only be obtained through improvisation, something you cannot possibly get from writing. It is something to do with 'edge'. Always being on the brink of the unknown and being prepared for the leap. And when you go on out there you have all your years of preparation and all your sensibilities and your prepared means but it is a leap into the unknown. If through that leap you find something then it has a value which I don't think can be found in any other way. I place a higher value on that than on what you can prepare. But I am also hooked on what you can prepare, especially in the way that it can take you to the edge. What I write is to take you to the edge safely so that you can go on out there and find this other stuff.[14]

In Lacy's view precomposed material acts as a point-of-departure or primer for the improvised piece. Improvising musicians will decide on the totality of the work, but the composition helps get them there.

A similar aesthetic is evident in John Zorn's compositional approach to his game pieces, which he considered as a latter-day version of Riley's *In C*, 'something that is fun to play, relatively easy, written on one sheet of paper. Game pieces came about through improvising with other people, seeing that things I wanted to have happen weren't happening.'[15] Zorn discusses the compositional direction he followed:

> The game pieces worked because I was collaborating with improvisers who had developed very personal languages, and I could harness those languages in ways that made the players feel they were creating and participating. In these pieces, they were not being told what to *do*. You don't tell a great improviser what to *do* – they're going to get bored right away.[16]

In an interview with Christoph Cox,[17] Zorn explains his rationale behind this position. He emphasizes how the individuality of the players he selected to perform the game pieces was an essential part of the compositional process:

> I wanted to find something to harness the personal languages that the improvisers had developed on their own, languages that were so idiosyncratic as to be almost un-notate-able (to write it down would be to ruin it). The answer for me was to deal with *form* not with *content*, with *relationships* not with *sound*.

Zorn understood the musicians in his ensemble and knew what they were and were not interested in playing. He was able to situate their personal musical vocabularies

---

14 Bailey, *Improvisation: its nature and practice in music*, pp. 57–8.

15 Anne McCutchan and C. Baker, *The Muse That Sings: Composers speak about the creative process* (Oxford, 1999), p. 164.

16 McCutchan and Baker, *The Muse That Sings: Composers speak about the creative process*, p. 164.

17 Christoph Cox and Daniel Warner, *Audio culture: readings in modern music* (New York, 2004), p. 199.

in a larger structure that allowed for freedom and individual expression while also satisfying his own musical objectives.

Experimental music composition, and techniques or processes of composition found in various forms of improvised music, are similar to the work involved in modelling an emergent, self-organizing system. Generally, all involve a bottom-up structural approach that generates emergent dynamics through a lack of centralized control. The same can be said of generative music. Musician, composer and visual artist Brian Eno has been working with a variety of generative structures throughout his career. He looks at works like *In C,* or anything where the composer makes no top-down directions, as precursors to generative music. In these works detailed directions are not provided. Instead there is 'a set of conditions by which something will come into existence'.[18]

Eno's influential Ambient recording *Music for Airports* was created using generative techniques. Rather than deal directly with notes and form, generative composers create systems with musical potential. Eno refers to this as 'making seeds rather than forests', and 'letting the forests grow themselves', drawing on useful metaphors from arboriculture. An important aspect of this approach, however, is in setting constraints so that the generative system is able to produce what its creator (and hopefully others) will find to be interesting. In a dialogue with Will Wright, the designer of *The Sims* and *SimCity*, Eno explains the reasoning behind this: 'You have to care about your inputs and your systems a lot more since you aren't designing the whole thing (you are not specifying in detail the whole thing) you're making something that by definition is going to generate itself in a different way at different times.'[19] Completed in 2006, *77 Million Paintings* by Brian Eno (Figure 7.1) is an example of the artist's generative approach in a visual medium. Working from a body of predefined images, the software will generate an enormous variety of paintings by compounding these images in novel ways. Given the amount of available material, it is very unlikely that anyone will ever see two identical images.

---

18 David Toop, *Haunted Weather: music, silence, and memory* (London, 2004), p. 184.
19 Brian Eno and Will Wright, *Playing With Time*, Long Now Foundation Seminar, audio recording (San Francisco, 26 June 2006).

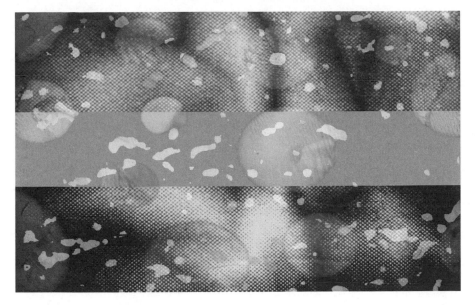

Figure 7.1   *77 Million Paintings* by Brian Eno

The steps involved in making this sort of music may at first seem vague or confusing, but in fact there is no 'secret recipe' for composing generative music. *Ovalprocess* (2000) by Markus Popp is a good illustration of this particular compositional situation and shows how a generative work can be conceived. Popp works in a very hands-on fashion; his pieces are built slowly through a laborious approach of cut-and-paste sequencing.[20] While the *Ovalprocess* CD itself was the result of his musical endeavours, it was originally distributed with a software application that simulated Popp's compositional thinking. Says Popp:

> *Ovalprocess* is a model of how I work, and is designed according to completely different ideas to making a professional audio productivity software application ... Instead, it's a very modest attempt at providing the user with one possible way to reconsider his or her expectations about working in sound or in software. In general, *Ovalprocess* is much less meant to be a statement in the software domain than it is towards being a statement in the music domain.[21]

This software enabled people to step into his mental compositional model and, using the sound material provided on the CD, create their own music.

Popp's intentions behind the *Ovalprocess* software can be found in other discussions of computers and music composition. Michael Hamman,[22] who has written

---

20 Sam Inglis, 'Markus Popp: Music as Software', *Sound on Sound*, (2002): http://www.soundonsound.com/sos/oct02/articles/oval.asp?print=yes (accessed 11 June 2007).

21 Inglis, 'Markus Popp: Music As Software'.

22 Michael Hamman, 'Structure as Performance: Cognitive Musicology and the Objectification of Procedure', in J. Tabor (ed.), *Otto Laske: Navigating New Musical Horizons*, (New York, 1999), pp. 37–52.

extensively on the subject, notes that, 'Computers become not merely tools for the making of artistic works (artefacts); they become instruments for the objectification of the very processes by which such works might be made.' The computer, as an instrument, uses software to internalize a composer's creative process and treats that process as a guide to create new musical works.[23] This scenario illustrates a sort of 'general recipe' for generative music: Take one system of musical thinking (in the specific case of *Ovalprocess*, Markus Popp's compositional method programmed as software), add a collection of sonic material to be used by this system, and listen. After it is started, and the generative music system begins to incorporate some sound material, a piece of music is revealed – of which each performance sounds potentially different than the last.

Through non-hierarchical, bottom-up compositional techniques, the sound of experimental, improvisatory and generative music exhibits emergence. In these musical works, the simple rules or relationships that form a composition act together and lead to unexpected, unpredictable or novel results. Musical gestures are not composed but take ephemeral form and emerge at the time of performance. One can also expect to encounter this quality – this becoming – in the emergence of telematic systems and in the experience of interactive games, art and media.

Contemporary related works

While a true blurring of composition and instrument has not been fully realized in contemporary practice, there are a number of works that show the potential embedded in this approach. All examples discussed here demonstrate the latent quality of 'composition-instrument' in the current art and media landscape. These works each share the characteristics asynchrony, emergence and generative-ness. Asynchrony is a key factor in the processes of interaction. An input will have an effect on the musical output of the system but it may not be immediately or fully apparent at the moment of interaction. While at first this approach may seem misleading or unresponsive, it is essential in shaping the music and the listening experience it creates. Whereas an immediate response would cause participants (more formally known as users) to focus on functionality and 'what it (the software/music) can do', a delay – however slight – helps keep them focused on listening and allows for a more gradual and introspective process of discovery. Additionally, it retains the potential for musical surprise. The listening participant can hear that the music shifts in character but is unlikely to be able to anticipate the nature of its transformation.

Change occurs by way of interaction but also through various means of generation. All of the works discussed here contain, in some way, generative processes that affect the sound as well as the visuals and overall experience of the piece. These processes occur in a variety of ways including participant, user or player interaction, random ordering and selection and computer algorithms. Depending upon the nature of the

---

23   This idea is also emphasised by Otto Laske in *Compositional Theory: an enrichment of music theory*, (1989).

work, several generative processes may be used, each in a different way, leading to a unique experience for the participant and listener.

As discussed earlier, emergence is an important quality implicit in the sound and development of experimental, improvised and generative music. It is also a fundamental aspect of contemporary digital artworks, and can arise from a variety of sources, 'ordering itself from a multiplicity of chaotic interactions'.[24] The pieces discussed here are no exception. Whether through the layering of sonic and visual patterns, navigation of a dataspace, evolutionary algorithms or telematic exchange, one cannot ignore the emergent properties that characterize these works.

Electroplankton

Electroplankton, created for the Nintendo DS game system by Toshio Iwai, was released in Japan in 2005, and later in Europe and North America in 2006. Iwai writes that the idea draws on his fascination with different objects across the course of his life – a microscope, a tape recorder, a synthesizer and the Nintendo Entertainment System (NES).[25] Some consider it a game; others a musical toy. Either way, *Electroplankton* captivates player and audience alike with its engaging use of sound and animation controlled via the touch-sensitive screen of the Nintendo DS device. Using a stylus, players are able to draw, twirl, tap and sweep an array of animated plankton characters on the screen. There are ten different plankton 'species'; each with its own sounds and sound-producing characteristics. Plankton and their behaviour are linked to a pitched sound or a short recording made by the player using the device's built-in microphone. Manipulating an individual plankton (or its environment) initiates a change in the sound(s) associated with it – a different pitch, timbre, rhythm, phrase length and so on. As multiple plankton are manipulated, a shift in the overall sonic output of the system is apparent, causing the music of *Electroplankton* to produce textural patterns and foreground/background modulations similar to those of *In C* (as described earlier).

Interactions with the plankton turn the Nintendo DS into an instrument that can be played purposely through the manipulation of the on-screen animations. Simultaneously, the software programming that links sounds to the plankton and their environment represents a musical ordering, or composition, that is implicit in *Electroplankton*. The coupling of these attributes perfectly illustrates how the combination or blurring of composition and instrument can lead to an interactive work with profound musical potential.

Additional examples

The musical qualities embedded in *Electroplankton* provide a clear – but not a sole – example of ways in which a composition-instrument approach is latent in

---

24 Roy Ascott, 'Telenoia', in Roy Ascott and Edward Shanken (eds), *Telematic Embrace: Visionary Theories of Art, Technology, and Consciousness* (Berkeley, CA 2003), p. 275.

25 Nintendo of America, *Electroplankton instruction booklet* (Redmond, WA, 2006), p. 57.

contemporary games and digital art works. Following are several short descriptions of additional projects that share a similar musical sensibility. To retain the focus of this chapter, lengthy discussions have been avoided. However, readers are encouraged to pursue further investigation into these projects beginning with the websites provided in this text.

Rez, designed by Tetsuya Mizuguchi for Sega Dreamcast and Sony PlayStation 2, is described as a musical shooter game. Players enter the cyberworld of a sleeping computer network to destroy viruses and awaken the system.[26] Each successful shot leads to the performance of sounds and musical phrases that perform/compose the soundtrack for *Rez* in real time as a direct result of the game-play. Both the visual and audio experience leads players to feel an immersive, trance-like state that makes the game incredibly captivating.[27]

Eden, by Jon McCormack, is described as an 'interactive, self-generating, artificial ecosystem'.[28] In more general terms, it is a generative installation artwork of sound, light and animation, driven by Artificial Life systems and environmental sensors.[29] *Eden* situates visitors in a room, standing outside the virtual ecosystem that is represented by a projected, cellular lattice in the room's centre. A visitor's presence in the room can impact the ecosystem favourably. Someone standing in a particular location makes the adjacent space more fertile for the creatures, or 'sonic agents', that inhabit *Eden*. The lives of these creatures involve eating, mating, fighting, moving about the environment, and central to the musical character of the piece – singing. In various ways, all of these activities lead to both the visual and aural events that comprise the work.[30] In exhibition, the *Eden* environment is projected onto two large, translucent screens arranged to form an 'X' (see Figure 7.2).[31] The audio speakers and environmental sensors required for the work are not pictured here.

---

26 Sonicteam/Sega. 'Rez Story', (2001): http://www.sonicteam.com/rez/e/story/index.html (accessed 11 June 2007).

27 More information on *Rez* can be found at http://www.sonicteam.com/rez (accessed 11 June 2007). Readers may also be interested to see other musically-focused games that require physical or 'twitch' skills such as *Amplitude*, *Band Brothers* (a.k.a. *Jam With the Band* or *Dai Gassou! Band Brothers*), *Dance Dance Revolution* (a.k.a. *Dancing Stage*), and *Guitar Hero*.

28 Jon McCormack, 'Eden: an evolutionary sonic ecosystem', (2000): http://www.csse. monash.edu.au/~jonmc/projects/eden/eden.html (accessed 11 June 2007).

29 Jon McCormack, 'Evolving for the Audience', *International Journal of Design Computing* 4 (2002).

30 More information about *Eden* and McCormack's publications can be found at http://www.csse.monash.edu.au/~jonmc/projects/eden/eden.html (accessed 11 June 2007).

31 McCormack, 'Evolving for the Audience'.

Figure 7.2   *Eden* by Jon McCormack

Intelligent Street was a telematic sound installation where users could compose their sound environment through SMS messages sent via mobile phone[32]. The piece was developed in 2003 by Henrik Lörstad, Mark d'Inverno and John Eacott, with help from the Ambigence Group. *Intelligent Street* was situated simultaneously at the University of Westminster, London and the Interactive Institute, Piteå, Sweden via live video connection. Users at either end of the connection were able to see and hear the results of their interactions. Using freely-associated, non-musical terms such as 'air' or 'mellow', participants sent an SMS message to *Intelligent Street*, and were able to hear how their contribution impacted the overall composition.[33] Simultaneously, all received messages were superimposed over the video feed to create a graphic representation of the audible sounds at any given time. *Intelligent Street* showed how music could be used to set the mood of a physical space through

32 Henrik Lörstad, Mark d'Inverno and John Eacott, 'The Intelligent Street: Responsive sound environments for social interaction', *Proceedings of the 2004 ACM SIGCHI International Conference on Advances in computer entertainment technology*, 74 (2004): 155–62.
    33 Ibid.

processes of co-operation and composition across groups of people in distributed environments.[34]

PANSE, or Public Access Network Sound Engine, is an open platform for the development of audio-visual netArt created by Palle Thayer. The project exists online as a streaming audio application, and consists of a synthesizer, two step sequencers and an effects generator.[35] PANSE creates an opportunity for artists and musicians to create interfaces that control, or animations that are controlled by, the PANSE audio stream. Information about PANSE including technical specifics for connecting to the stream and interface authoring is online at http://130.208.220.190/panse.

Composition-instrument interactions and perturbations

As a conceptual framework for music and interaction, composition-instrument cannot be understood as a series of causal, linear relationships. The framework is ultimately a system with many individual, interrelated components (see Figure 7.3). It is helpful to understand this through the lens of Humberto Maturana and Francisco Varela's 'structural coupling',[36] where ontogenetic unities are represented by the generative system and the participant engaged in the work. Rather than see the participant's interaction as a 'cause' that leads to a specific 'effect', the composition-instrument model considers each interaction as a perturbation that echoes throughout the system and affects the other components. In the composition-instrument framework there is no set beginning or definitive source of an interaction. Rather, all components – generative system, environment and participant – exist in a relationship where a perturbation from any one will affect the others and eventually be reciprocated. Any of the three components can be identified as the origination point of a perturbation and the interaction model will follow the same flow of events.

---

34 Jo-Anne Green, M. Riel and H. Thorington, 'Intelligent Street', *networked_ performance*, (2004): http://www.turbulence.org/blog/archives/000122.html. Further information about Intelligent Street is available at John Eacott's website (www.informal.org), Henrik Lörstad's website (http://www.lorstad.se/Lorstad/musik.html), and the Interactive Institute of Sweden (http://www.tii.se/sonic.backup/intelligentstreet) (accessed 11 June 2007).

35 Palle Thayer, '/PANSE', (2003): http://130.208.220.190/panse/whats.htm (accessed 11 June 2007).

36 Humberto R. Maturana and F.J. Varela, *The tree of knowledge: the biological roots of human understanding* (Boston, 1992), pp. 74–5.

COMPOSITION-INSTRUMENT INTERACTION MODEL

[based on "structural coupling" by H. Maturana and F. Varela]

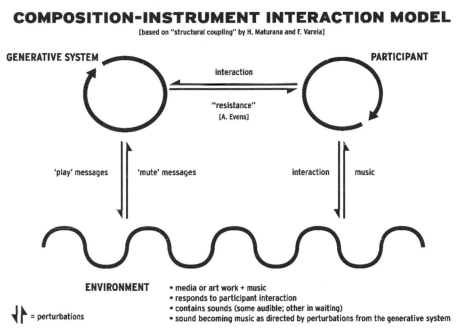

Figure 7.3   The composition-instrument framework

To make a general example, consider the case when a perturbation is first introduced by the participant. Their input will prompt a change to the internal, structural dynamics of both the generative system and the environment for interaction. A perturbation to the generative system can change the pattern determining when it decides to play a sound or sounds. A perturbation to the environment may make new sounds available and store old sounds for use a later time. These structural changes are not without consequence. Once complete they are sent back throughout the system as reciprocal perturbations. The environment sends 'mute' messages back to the generative system. Instructions from the generative system cue available sounds in the environment to become music. And most significantly, because they are listening, the music serves as a perturbation that affects the participant. What they hear in the music (their interpretation) can lead to a more complete understanding of the media environment or current in-game state. This awareness, developed in the process of interaction, constitutes a shift in the participant's internal structural dynamics, and sets the stage for further reciprocal perturbations. Maturana and Varela refer to this situation as structural coupling, where there is 'a history of recurrent interactions leading to the structural congruence between two (or more) systems'.[37] In the composition-instrument model, structural coupling is apparent in the presence of persistent perturbations. It binds the compositional order of the generative system with the sonic make-up of the environment to create an instrument that is capable of producing music in the course of participant (player) interaction.

---

37 Ibid., p. 75.

In a composition-instrument work, there is a perturbation that creates tension between the fixedness of the composition and the potential afforded by the instrument. This tension is similar to what Aden Evens refers to as the 'resistance of the instrument'.[38] It is the quality that 'pushes back' to reveal the nature, and ultimately the possibilities, of the instrument. In its resistance, the instrument is not submissive to the will of the musician. It reveals its character relative to the desire of the musician in a kind of co-operative struggle.[39] Resistance sits like a reflective pane of glass between musician and instrument; looking through it reveals that both elements merge into one. In a composition-instrument work, resistance takes the form of a generative system that is linked to participant interactions in such a way as to affect the work's musical unfolding. A perturbation will never affect a specific result, but afford a glimpse into the larger musical world implicit in both the instrument and the composition.

As a conceptual musical framework, the composition-instrument exposes its potentialities via participant interactions with a generative system. The system 'pushes back' in the form of sound and invites additional input. This exchange between participant and system ensues as a progression of interactions or reciprocal perturbations. As this exchange matures, the character of the system and the meaning it carries is revealed through sound, both in terms of what it is currently and what it could become.

The composition-instrument in contemporary projects

As stated earlier, a composition-instrument approach is latent in contemporary practice. There are many excellent projects where the seeds of this approach are visible but no single work has yet realized the full potential bound within the idea. Following is a discussion of projects that either seek – or have great potential – to embody the composition-instrument approach.

Sound Garden as a model of interaction

Sound Garden is a project developed by the author in tandem with the research that helped inform this chapter. The title alludes to the nature of interaction to be explored the work. It was created to provide an illustration of the composition-instrument idea, and to explore this model of interaction as it relates to sound, technology and location in physical and virtual space. *Sound Garden* shows how music can be composed and performed in real time via generative systems and participant interaction, as shown in Figure 7.4. At the installation site participants can make a wireless Internet connection and 'plant' or 'prune' sound files from the garden. The music of *Sound Garden* is amplified through these four speakers and can also be heard in an online web stream.

---

38 Aden Evens, 'Sound ideas: music, machines, and experience'. *Theory out of Bounds* 27 (Minnesota, 2005), pp. 160–73.

39 Ibid., p. 161.

Figure 7.4   Sound Garden: (photograph by Elizabeth Raymer)

Composition-instrument was initially defined as a work that can 'play and be played', and serves as a conceptual framework for music in interactive media and digital art. The concept seeks to find a balance; neither the ability to 'play' nor 'be played' should dominate a participant's experience. If interactions are too direct ('be played' is too apparent), the piece becomes too much like an instrument and the significance of other aspects of the artwork can be diminished. Similarly, if an unresponsive musical environment obscures interactions and 'play' dominates the experience, the work loses its novelty in being tied to the course of participant interactions. The composition-instrument approach permits equilibrium between these two and as a result, acknowledges user interactions as perturbations in the overall musical system. It does not take on the clear cause–effect nature of a musical instrument (press a key to hear a note, for example). Instead it allows interactions to manifest as sound, gradually following the course of the composition's generative system. Perturbations introduce new sounds into the composition's aural palette and can subtly reshape the musical character of the work.

Sound Garden consists of a physical installation and online interface for interaction. It is a continuous work, meaning 'performance' is not defined by any particular duration. Listeners situate themselves in the garden (either on-site or online) and remain indefinitely.

In the tradition of the physical work associated with organic gardens (planting, watering, fertilizing, weeding, pruning and so on). The online interface allows listeners to tend their sonic environment and take an active role in its composition and care. Using a web browser to make selections from a menu, participants can contribute their own digital audio files (musical material, voice and environmental recordings and so on) and become gardeners who help to form the overall sonic landscape of *Sound Garden*.

Due to the uniqueness of each sound, the 'seeds' that are planted will significantly affect the primary characteristics of the garden. A generative musical system uses Particle Swarm Optimisation[40] to grow these seeds and define the overall structure. But *Sound Garden* is also largely shaped by events that occur at the site of installation. Environmental sensors tracking ambient light levels, temperature, motion and vibration act on individual sounds that compose the garden. These sensors serve as additional layers in the musical system, and control a variety of signal processing parameters. As environmental conditions shift and change, the sensors reflect that change in the garden's constant growth and development.

In this continuous, generative work, artificial life algorithms are used to maintain performance and ensure organic development over time. This project is also an experiment in musical self-organization. Like improvising musicians, those who visit *Sound Garden* are able to make an individual contribution to the larger, group work. It could be said that this kind of freedom results in cacophony and leaves *Sound Garden* in a state of complete sonic incoherence (noise). But much in the way that improvising musicians listen to each other in the course of performance, or people contribute thoughtfully and respectfully to a community flower garden, *Sound Garden* participants generally act with sensitivity in response to the musical ecology that is created and sustained by the work.[41]

Sound Garden was created to demonstrate the musical and technical characteristics of a composition-instrument approach. The strength of the piece is in its musical expressiveness and flexibility, but it does not fully address the connection between

---

40 James Kennedy and R. Eberhart, 'Particle Swarm Optimization', *Proceedings from the IEEE International Conference on Neural Networks* 4 (1995): pp. 1942–8.

41 Photos and recordings are available at http://www.x-tet.com/soundgarden (accessed 11 June 2007).

music conceived in the composition-instrument approach and an interactive system or artwork. There are, however, other contemporary projects where the foundations of a substantial connection between music and interaction seem to be in the process of formation.

Spore – The Potential of Becoming

Spore, the current project of game designer Will Wright (*SimCity*, *The Sims*) is a project where a composition-instrument approach could be fruitfully employed. *Spore* was originally set for commercial release in the second half of 2007.[42] However, at the time this book went to press it was announced that the release date would be pushed later to early 2008 or possibly 2009,[43] which means that much of the argument offered here is speculative. Not all details concerning *Spore*'s gameplay and features have been officially confirmed. However, there have been enough published articles, screen captures, online videos and interviews with Wright to leave one with a good impression of the overall flavour of *Spore*.

In the game, players have the ability to design their own characters. These creatures can look like lizards, horses, trolls or cutesy cartoons – whatever a player decides to create. One potential difficulty with this feature then becomes animating such a creature. How can the game accurately simulate the motion of creatures that walk with tentacles or creatures that have legs like waterfowl or other exotic means of locomotion? This challenge presents one of the most promising aspects of *Spore* – the use of 'procedurally generated content'.[44] GameSpot news describes this as 'content that's created on the fly by the game in response to a few key decisions that players make, such as how they make their creatures look, walk, eat, and fight'.[45] The technology behind this aspect of *Spore* has not been revealed, but Wright describes it using an analogy: 'think of it as sharing the DNA template of a creature while the game, like a womb, builds the "phenotypes" of the animal, which represent a few megabytes of texturing, animation, etc.'[46] *Spore* also uses 'content pollination' to complete the make-up of one player's world using the assets of another player.[47] The basic sharing of resources is simple enough to grasp, but to be able to distribute

42 Andrew Park, 'Will Wright talks Spore, Leipzig, next-gen', *GameSpot* (2006): http://www.gamespot.com/news/6155498.html. 'Electronic Arts', *Next Generation-Interactive Entertainment Today* (2007): http://www.next-gen.biz/index.php?option=com_content&task=view&id=1638&Itemid=2.

43 Wikipedia contributors, 'Spore (video game)', Wikipedia, The Free Encyclopedia, http://en.wikipedia.org/wiki/Spore(video_game). See also SeekingAlpha.com, 'Electronic Arts F4Q07 (Qtr End 3/31/07) Earnings Call Transcript', 8 May 2007, http://software.seekingalpha.com/article/34946 (accessed 11 June 2007).

44 Wikipedia contributors, 'Spore (video game)', Park, 'Will Wright talks Spore, Leipzig, next-gen'.

45 Ibid.

46 Wikipedia contributors, 'Spore (video game)'.

47 Steve Boxer, 'From a germ of an idea to the Spore of a franchise', *Guardian Unlimited* (2006): http://technology.guardian.co.uk/games/story/0,,1835600,00.html (accessed 11 June 2007).

these resources realistically and allow them to engage in believable interactions with another environment must involve a complex Artificial Life (or A-Life-like) system. If the world of *Spore* is to be a fluid ecosystem as promised, there will have to be some sort of self-organizing system or generative, non-linear dynamics that underlie the entire game and allow it to unfold in a natural, organic fashion.

The generative aspects of *Spore* (whether documented in an article or speculated here) show that it has, as a central component of its functionality, the ability to *become*. Wright has commented that at one point the game was titled 'Sim Everything'.[48] Most likely this is due to the ability of the game to become any kind of world the player/designer intends. This focus on customization of experience, growth and becoming are what make *Spore* such an ideal environment for music. In addition to exploring (to name a few) the physical, dietary and architectural possibilities of culture in this game environment, it would also be interesting to explore musical possibilities. What sounds resonate with a particular species? What devices do they use to make music, and what is the sound of that music?

In a game of becoming like *Spore*, a composition-instrument approach would be very advantageous. Composition-instrument monitors interactions carefully and sees each as perturbation that will have a gradual consequence within the system where it is sensed. In the way that procedural content generation leads to a natural mode of locomotion for a creature, perturbations to the musical system lead to a natural development of sounds that define that creature and its culture. As creature and culture develop and evolve, the sounds and music that are part of their identity take on new forms and tonalities. The generative nature of *Spore* can help to sustain this development. The game maintains its own internal sense of progress and evolution as it grows new creatures and new landscapes, generates climates and pollinates one world with the contents of another. This continuous process of generation provides the exact dynamics that enable a composition-instrument piece to play autonomously, while a game player's interactions in the *Spore* world "improvise" music within this overall structure.

It was confirmed in January of 2007 that Brian Eno has been hired to compose the music for *Spore*. The only knowledge of his plans can be drawn from his demonstration of a working prototype called the 'Shuffler' at the University of Arts in Berlin.[49] Peter Chilvers, who has been working closely with Eno on the Spore project, originally designed the 'Shuffler'.[50] According to Eno, Chilvers has an early version of the 'Shuffler' on his website,[51] and was asked to develop an expanded version of this for *Spore*. Chilvers has been working with generative music since his involvement with Steve Grand's *Creatures* games.[52] In writing about his music for

---

48 Ibid.

49 Sascha Pohflepp, 'Before and After Darwin', *We Make Money Not Art* (2007): http://www.we-make-money-not-art.com/archives/009261.php (accessed 11 June, 2007).

50 Brian Eno, *E-mail interview*, 10 April 2007.

51 http://www.peterchilvers.com/generative.php (accessed 11 June, 2007).

52 Peter Chilvers, 'generativemusic.com', *Artist's web site* (2005): http://www.generativemusic.com (accessed 11 June 2007).

Creatures,[53] he discusses opting for a generative compositional approach. Each piece of music in *Creatures* is tied to a set of 'players' in a sort of virtual band. A player has its own set of instructions that will respond, for example, to the emotional state(s) of the character(s) on screen or to any threats present in a character's environment.[54] Chilvers notes that his music builds the mood and atmosphere, and that it compensates 'for the lack of information to other senses such as smell and touch. It can also impart information about thoughts and characters that is not otherwise evident.'[55]

If this same aesthetic of music and interaction carries from *Creatures* to *Spore*, and the 'Shuffler' is employed to generate music in real time drawing from the dynamics of game play, it will effectively couple procedurally generated visual content to procedurally generated sound and music. No specific comparisons can be made between the use of the 'Shuffler' system and the composition-instrument framework, but there is certainly shared currency in the use of generative systems and in their connection with the interactions and experience of a player or participant. The prospects for Spore are compelling, but how the shuffler will manifest in actual game-play will have to be seen and heard once the game is finally released. *Spore* promises to be musically sublime and is likely to represent a significant step forward in the creative potential of music for games and new media in both its commercial and artistic manifestations.

Composition-instrument as an open episteme

Interaction within the composition-instrument framework is similar to what Michael Hamman refers to as an 'open episteme'.[56] Episteme, as used in his text, refers to the process by which the description of a mechanism is revealed, and how that description forecasts an output by the mechanism. Hamman describes a 'closed episteme', one that is bound to cultural, technical or historical expectations. These leave little room for innovation because their use is assumed based on prior exposure or understanding. An 'open episteme' is one in which the frame for understanding is emergent. One's conception of its use changes relative to the particularities of an interaction with the mechanism at the time of interaction.

The open episteme offers a porous understanding, 'open to input from a particularized situation'.[57] A composition-instrument framework leads to such

---

53 This online article reads as if it were written by someone at Gameware Development. In fact, Chilvers notes that he wrote this and that it had later 'rather weirdly been shifted into third person' (Chilvers, 'generativemusic.com').

54 Gameware Development, 'The Music Behind Creatures' (2004): http://www.gamewaredevelopment.co.uk/creatures_more.php?id=459_0_6_0_M27 (accessed 11 June, 2007).

55 Ibid.

56 Michael Hamman, 'From Symbol to Semiotic: Representation, Signification, and the Composition of Music Interaction', *Journal of New Music Research* 28/2 (1999): pp. 90–104 (accessed 11 June 2007).

57 Ibid.

an understanding because the interactive systems that facilitate this approach are themselves open, and produce unique outputs relative to the myriad interactions conducted within them. This makes the frame for understanding the system emergent – its outputs will always be specific to an interaction at a certain time, in a certain place and under certain conditions. As the parameters surrounding the interaction shift, the system's output shifts. And most significantly, the person engaged in interaction experiences an emergent shift in their reception of that output and in their mental model of the system and its possibilities.

Conclusion

A composition-instrument approach embodies qualities of music formally understood as 'composed' and 'improvised'. Works that use this idea are like generative music compositions in that they have their own internal order or organization. They are also like instruments in that they can be played, or performed upon, and in the course of that performance, make an impact that modifies the character or course of the music outputted by the generative system. This 'instrumentalization' allows for perturbations in the generative system and leads to an emergent becoming of music. When coupled with an interactive game system, the composition-instrument piece becomes a soundtrack that is both responsive to the game state and autonomous in its ability to adapt and develop relative to that state. This approach to music for games, or any sort of interactive digital system, hopes to open new opportunities for music in digital art and media, and to break down the linear models that have stifled creative progress in this area.

As a conceptual framework for music in computer games, digital art and new media, the composition-instrument approach is in its infancy. It has proven to be useful in projects conducted by the author (*Sound Garden* as discussed earlier, and *Perturb*[58] completed in 2006), but has had little opportunity to stretch into other areas. *Perturb* and *Sound Garden* are both technically 'open' interactive systems such as Wikipedia or Slashdot,[59] and can be modified by anyone. 'Closed' systems, such as traditional websites, feature preset content by a single author, and are 'interactive' in that the sequence of content is chosen by a user. While it is entirely possible for the composition-instrument framework to function in a closed system, it has not yet been attempted. A game like *Super Mario Bros.* (Nintendo 1985) is technically closed but due to the richness of the world, the experience while playing can be closer to the sense one has in an open system. (Do we call it a semi-open system?) Encounters with foes, obstacles, hidden surprises and a variety of different environments lead to a kind of emergent experience through game-play. This kind of game offers the right kind of opportunities that can be exploited 'instrumentally' and used to perform the game soundtrack in real time in the course of interaction and play. Clearly these questions show the way forward for the composition-instrument framework. As research and compositional efforts progress, the idea will be the subject of much

---

58   A description, photos and sound recordings are online at http://www.x-tet.com/perturb (accessed 11 June 2007).

59   http://www.wikipedia.org and http://slashdot.org (accessed 11 June, 2007).

experimentation. With luck, it will reveal new musical potential for games, digital art, telematic systems and other emerging forms of new media.

PART 4
Techniques and technologies

Chapter 8

Dynamic range: subtlety and silence in video game sound

Rob Bridgett

With the increasing cinematization of visuals, game-play and consequently audio in recent console-based video games, several essential elements of game sound have been overlooked. Primarily, from an aesthetic standpoint, a competent use of subtlety and silence is distinctly missing from video game audio. Lack of dynamic range, over-compression of sound and music assets, not to mention narrative notions of tension and release, are among elements that video game sound can more deeply exploit in order to achieve a more cinematic feel.

This chapter will examine production practices in which sound, music and dialogue are over-compressed. It will also centre on the challenges of getting narrative tension into game-play and being able to leverage this for sound. The focus will then shift onto how these challenges can be potentially solved with the advent of software digital signal processing (DSP: effects such as reverb, compression and so on) inherent in the architecture of next generation consoles such as the PlayStation 3 and the Xbox 360. In particular, this closing section will concentrate on how real-time DSP effects and in-game mixing can be used to dynamically remove, reduce and prioritize sound in an interactive environment.

Dynamics crisis

When one examines the dynamic range of the audio output from video games, one can clearly observe that the audio assets are heavily compressed, and often overloaded. There are many reasons for this, chief among which are the demands that every sound in the game needs to be audible to the player at particular moments during game-play; dialogue, music and sound effects all compete with one another on a seemingly equal footing. This reflects a similar attitude to compression and limiting that is evident in popular music, FM radio commercials/transmissions and television commercials.[1] When one compares these heavily processed signals to waveforms from cinema soundtracks or classical music recordings, the difference in dynamic range can be easily visually recognized (compare Figures 8.1 and 8.2). By physically attending orchestral music concerts one can reveal the true extent of how much dynamic range we have lost in this age of digital reproduction.

---

1   Compression, also known as dynamic range compression or DRC, is a process whereby the dynamic range of an audio signal is reduced. Limiting is a type of compression with a higher ratio.

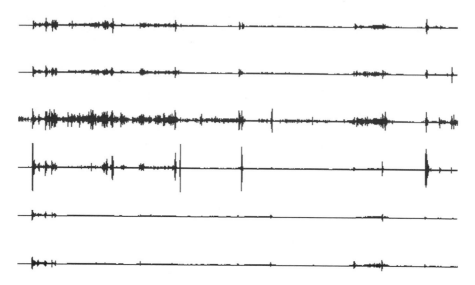

Figure 8.1   The 5.1 waveform for a recent Hollywood film (from top to bottom L, R, C, LFE, LS, RS)

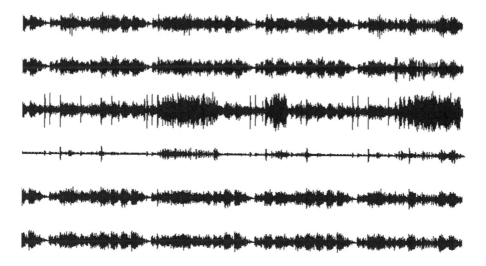

Figure 8.2   The 5.1 waveform from a recent Xbox 360 title (from top to bottom, L, R, C, LFE, LS, RS)

One possible cause for this loss of dynamic range is that the expected playback environment for popular forms of music and entertainment (the nightclub or the home) and for video games is, or was relatively similar. Video games were born in arcades where they had to compete with the sounds of other nearby games consoles for the paying public's attention. At the same time as the rise of the arcade machines, various home game systems also gained popularity. The sounds of games in the home have also had to compete with many other domestic sounds, much as the television does. However, cinematization of video games is changing this cultural positioning. Classical music and film soundtracks by comparison have a cleanly and culturally established designated attention space, what one could call a 'listening etiquette'; meaning that they are designed and expected to be listened to in isolation and given the audience's undivided attention; they are not expected to compete simultaneously with other sounds – in fact any extraneous sounds to the performance or film are considered as a woefully distracting noise and irritation, no matter how tiny. By adopting a 'film sound' or 'classical music' model to game dynamics, there of course needs to be the prerequisite that the game is to be enjoyed specifically as a 'cinematic' and wholly immersive experience without interruption.

As stated before, there are only certain kinds of games that demand this kind of immersion and attention: *God of War*, *Gears of War* and the *Silent Hill* series are good cases in point. Many games such as party games or children's games actually demand the opposite cultural environment in that they need to be heard over other sounds and potentially other participatory voices in the room, and in this case dynamic range should be treated differently. However, there is an increasing trend among console-based video games of the former category, meaning that the expectation is for these games to tell stories and to reveal narrative events to the player that rely on a filmic visual language and that immerse the player in the game world. There has of course simultaneously been a trend towards the cinematization of video game audio. Brands like THX and Dolby and their involvement in pushing game sound quality and surround technology into the 5.1 and 7.1 realms is well documented, while the use of name film composers, film actors and film sound designers all point to a similar aesthetic convergence within the worlds of games and films. However, aesthetically the convergence is still a long way from being fully realized and dynamics are a key to this.

Dynamics of narrative

The dynamics of any game-play narrative can be easily plotted on a linear graph. Each game-play element, or mission, can be plotted showing how the narrative of that mission or event will work. Simple game-play mechanics can be drawn as a simple linear curve going from easy to difficult. A similar curve can be applied to the game structure as a whole. Each of the elements of the narrative will be matched by intensity of audio and of user interaction. The audio aesthetics of these narrative dynamics can either play with the action game-play curves or play against them. They can even begin to set up expectations in the matching of audio action to game-play action, and then break those rules as the narrative progresses to provide even further excitement and immersion in game-play.

Simple ways to think about the dynamics of audio are by looking at survival horror games that have successfully taken the horror film genre's narrative dynamics and mapped game-play onto these curves. Often leading with audio, the viewer's expectations are manipulated within the horror genre. Silent or extremely quiet moments where characters (players) are listening to the world around them often precede extremely loud and violent moments in the horror film genre. This is completely by design, and survival horror games such as *Silent Hill* have taken the way that sound leads and incorporated it into a variety of game-play elements. Non-diegetic sounds are used well in this type of game-play to evoke the elements of unseen horrors within the player's imagination. Their use of visual darkness and fog effects is also exemplary within video games in allowing sound to develop an often unrevealed world outside what can be seen. Moments of silence are followed by sudden and disturbing attacks from bizarre creatures. While this genre in particular lends itself to these kinds of extreme dynamics, these are certainly ideas that can be picked up within all other game genres.

Racing games, open world games, first person shooter (FPS) games can all learn from lessons in the narrative dynamics displayed in the survival horror genre. In order to make an event seem really big, it makes sense that immediately preceding that event is a drop in action and a drop in sound levels; this will make the subsequent sonic barrage perceptually seem so much louder, even when in measured decibels it is not. One common mistake of games designers in the past has been that game-play dynamics are never really plotted out in this way until the game production has been completed. If a simple dynamics curve is applied to every game-play element, with some understanding of how to make things seem more intense by preceding them with low intensity moments, then sound, art and technology teams can use these curves in order to make critical aesthetic and technical decisions that not only match the curves and are able to deliver the intensity required when it is required, but also to play against these expectations, and magnify their effects on the player's senses.

It is this ability to draw in the audience, or player, with sound where dynamics begin to be fully realized in an artistic way. Without a suitably defined dynamic range game-play curve within which to do this, it is an uphill struggle to deliver the same high and low dynamic moments within a game as already exist in cinema or in classical music.

Games as cultural artefact

One way to help define a clearer position for the dynamic expectations of a game's audio is by thinking of the game as a cultural artefact: is it high art or is it pop art? Most games probably have elements of both, but on examination of the high-level goals of the game, examining visual style and intended audience, one can easily define the intended experience of the game relatively early in production. If a game is considered as a cultural artefact from day one of its production (which most games are, even if not consciously), then the expectations for its reception can be easily determined. The type of cultural artefact a game aspires to be ultimately tells you about the kind of environment it is expected to be played in. Is the game a pop-culture game that encourages group play and is expected to be experienced in a noisy home environment? Is the game intended to be taken more seriously? Is the player expected to immerse themselves fully in the game with as little extraneous noise and interference as possible? Once this is determined, then a reasonable and informed approach to the dynamic range of the sound can be determined.

Interactive mixing

One of the main reasons that so much sound, music and dialogue has been limited and compressed so harshly is that there has been, until recently, a complete lack of sophisticated mixing available in video games. On the older generation platforms such as the PS2 and the Xbox sound memory was limited enough to prevent hundreds of sounds from being played at the same time. In many cases, and there are numerous examples, there were still actually too many sounds playing at the same time on these consoles, resulting in an unintentional cacophony of sound. If a sound needed to cut through in this climate and always be reliably heard, that particular sound, or group of sounds, had to be limited and compressed to extremes in order to compete with other sounds and music – it can be argued that this process of limiting and compressing is simply because a sophisticated enough approach to ducking levels of other sounds did not exist. In more recent cases where simple mixing technically did exist, the ways of implementing it, via a text-script file, were prohibitive enough for it not to be artistically useful.

The shortfalls imposed by limited sound memory on older consoles were often a blessing in disguise for sound designers, even though they probably didn't think of it as such at the time. By limiting what sounds could be in memory at any one time, and limiting the number of voices available to play back these sounds, there were very strict limits placed upon the amount of sound that could physically be played back in any particular scene.

With the increased memory and available voices of next-generation consoles and more sophisticated audio compression codes, such as Microsoft's XNA and Sony's ATRAC allowing for a reasonable quality sample rate at roughly 10:1 compression, the amount of sounds that can now be played simultaneously has increased roughly tenfold. This means a heavily increased role for in-game run-time mixing in order to prevent a cacophony of sound effects from playing back during run-time. Assigning a finite amount of available voices is one particularly crude way around this, but there emerge problems of really important sounds not being played back because other important sounds are also playing. Mixing in video games, as in cinema, is concerned with sound removal and subtraction rather than pushing volumes up. In mixing, it is often very subtle fader ducking that is required to allow a more important group of sounds to be made prominent above others.

When mixing a video game, the first thing that one notices is that video games have become very loud. This is due in great part to a lack of successful calibration and reference levels available to game sound designers and mixers. Films, by contrast, have very strictly defined and calibrated output levels and much can be learned from this medium in terms of mixing and calibrating. THX Games Mode certainly helps a great deal in allowing the sound designers and mixers to know that what they are hearing is a true image. In video games it is often the case that the game being worked on is compared to another finished game, in order to gauge roughly if the volume levels are similar. More often than not, the games being compared were not mixed at reference level and were also based on other games, and there has been a tendency to make each successive game louder than the previous one, further resulting in crunching of the dynamic range. Pulling sounds back and defining maximum levels from the outset is the first step that needs to be taken for video games; once the loudest possible sound output has been defined, it is then a case of pulling everything else back from that level.

Once the maximum volume headroom is defined, it is usual to be ducking extraneous sounds as and when the relevant in-game events occur within the game-play. For example, with dialogue, rather than having to be compressed and limited so that it can be audible over gunfire in the game, and thereby making the dialogue extremely loud when there is no gunfire, it makes more sense from a dynamics point of view to duck down the gunfire slightly and perhaps any ambience or other extraneous enemy dialogue in order that the player receives the right dialogue with clarity.

One major difference with video game mixing over that of film is that it is interactive – meaning that snapshot mixers are installed at run-time to coincide with events that are occurring in the game rather than having linear mix automation. Mixer automation, in the interactive sense, is attached to the interactive events themselves, rather than curves over linear time. There are a variety of attenuations aside from volume that can be performed via interactive mixers in a next-generation console game, such parameters as high- or low-pass filters, LFE[2] levels and any kind of DSP effects. This is one of the many technical advances that have been brought about by having software DSP able to function at run-time on the next-generation consoles. In addition to this, having enough spare memory to allow for a great deal of multiple dynamic volumes to be adjusted at run-time has a profound effect on the aesthetics of game audio.

These advances give sound designers the potential to work with professional mixer personnel at the end of the project when all game design, art and the majority of game-play code has been debugged and locked down, and to concentrate on a full mix for the entire game. In this sense the dynamics of the game's audio no longer need to be considered at the level of the individual sound effect, but can in fact be defined and reconsidered at the mixing stage. The realm of a post-production audio mix can be used to strengthen and highlight an audio direction for the game, as well as making critical decisions about the aesthetic elements of the audio at this stage when all the components are together and functioning as the game has been designed to do.

---

2   LFE refers to Low Frequency Effects, or deep bass sound effects.

Interactivity: giving gamers control over dynamics

Ultimately, the playback environment in which a game is heard, no matter how it is posited as a cultural artefact, will be determined by only one person: the player. Because the amount of dynamic compression used by the game has such a profound effect on the overall sound, it is entirely possible that having an option of a software-based run-time dynamics compressor or limiter running on the audio outputs of the game (that could be turned on or off in the sound options menu by the player) would solve any issues of adapting the dynamics of a game-play environment to the way the dynamics sound in the future. This would allow the user to set the playback situation themselves, and it would also cater for an audience who do not have a calibrated 5.1 entertainment system, so they would be able to switch on the compressor and boost all the quieter moments in the game. Many of these simple user-initiated compressors already exist in digital cable television packages. At least this method allows for an adaptable approach to the dynamics of game sound by recognizing the varied playback environments available to gamers. These choices should eventually always be made by the gamers themselves, although the default setting shipped with the game can always be the one recommended by the sound designers.

Chapter 9

An introduction to granular synthesis in video games

Leonard J. Paul

This chapter is meant as an introduction to learning how granulation works, and offers some suggestions on how it might be used in games to generate and enhance engine models, dialogue, sound effects, crowds and music with a focus on their real-time use in video games. Granulation is a relatively recent method of processing sampled sound in a variety of ways. One can stretch sampled sounds in time without changing their pitch or change the pitch of a sound without changing its length and other granulation effects. Granulation of a sound can create many other unique audio transformations such as scrambling the grains to produce organic sounds similar to water or wind, as well as thinning out the number of grains until only the occasional sonic blip is heard.

Granular synthesis can be defined as using short sound events (or 'grains') in a synthesis method, such as frequency modulation (or FM), to produce a full sound texture from these grains. Grains tend to be from 1 ms to 100 ms with an envelope to reduce unwanted distortion. Granulation utilizes a sampled sound source for the grains to produce the final granulated sound. Granulation can also be performed on a real-time audio input and this is known as a granular delay-line. Figure 9.1 shows grain generation in granulation. The original waveform has a 10 ms segment taken from it which is enveloped and played as a grain. Typically there are many grains which are played each second that produce a dense sonic texture.

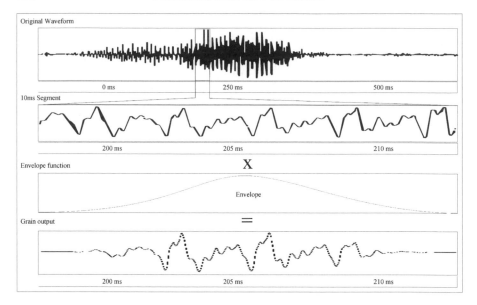

Figure 9.1   Grain generation in granulation

In its electro-acoustic music roots, granulation was often used to create long, shifting drone soundscapes by stretching a sound out many times its original length. However, this 'magnification' into the timbres present in a sound sample produces a very abstract soundscape and in games we are typically most interested in more realistic representations of sound performance. So, we concentrate on forms of granulation rather than granular synthesis, as granulation is more applicable to video game audio.

History and background

The fundamentals of granulation and granular synthesis can be seen in the work of British physicist Dennis Gabor in 1947, who outlined the notion that any sound could be created by combining very short bursts or 'grains' of sound. This theory was difficult to fully explore until computers were available, since it required a sufficient number of grains to recreate a reasonable reconstruction of a sound. Composer Curtis Roads was the first to implement non-real-time granular synthesis in 1974. The first real-time implementation of granular synthesis was by composer Barry Truax in 1986. Truax later performed real-time granulation in 1988. Since this time granulation has become more popular and more recently has been included in popular commercial audio composition software such as Propellerhead's *Reason*, *Ableton Live* and Native Instrument's *Reaktor*. The term 'microsound' has many connections to granular synthesis and is discussed at length in Curtis Roads's 2004 book *Microsound*.

Types of granulation in games[1]

Video games tend to be a representation of an alternate reality, so sounds that are based in reality, such as sampled sounds, are typically the most appropriate for games. In our effort to make things sound realistic, we might also reduce the constraint of the length of a grain to include chunks of sampled sound longer than 70 ms. One could view the granulation of longer grains more as 'units' of granulation, being a term borrowed from concatenative sound synthesis (Schwarz). Concatenative sound synthesis (CSS) is a technique related to granular synthesis that segments a source sample into units, which are analysed and matched against an existing database of unit samples from different sources. The synthesized sample is a reconstruction of the source sample from chunks of the audio database. Different methods are used to segment the units and analyse the matching of the source units to the units in the database and amount of audio processing to match source units to database units. Units can be of any length; this can be used to help preserve characteristics of the source sample and avoid modifying the sound too much through granulation. The concatenative nature of CSS means that one is typically proceeding sequentially through a sample and experiencing much less overlap than with classic granulation. So, rather than utilizing strict classic sample granulation, we can use a spectrum of techniques from granulation via grains, granulation via units and concatenate use of units to reconstruct and modify source sound. The longer the grains are, the less overlap is desired when trying to reconstruct a sound without too much colourization of the sound due to processing.[2]

A granular technique commonly used in games is to break a sound into its component parts and to use scripting or other implementation techniques to describe an algorithmic method of playback. This can be described as 'manual' granulation of a sound. One could use this method to create a jungle ambience; rather than just utilizing a sample loop that will quickly become repetitive, the sound artist might recreate the sound by breaking the ambience into its component parts and using scripting or other implementation to interactively reconstruct the ambience in real time so that it is never heard exactly the same way twice. For example, for a jungle ambience, the sound artist might create pools of short samples (or 'units') for a river, the wind, insects, birds and monkeys, then interactively play the samples back when the game is played. So, a script would be run to consecutively play river, wind and insect samples, then bird and monkey sounds would be randomly triggered by a script on a timer to play a sample every few seconds. The power of this method is that we can have it adapt interactively to game-play. So, if the player shoots their gun in the jungle, we can change the script to lower the volume of the insects, gradually fading it back in to full volume, as well as adjusting the play-back frequency of the

---

1   There are many variants to granulation whose descriptions are given an in-depth discussion in the *Microsound* and *Computer Music Tutorial* texts by Curtis Roads, who is one of the foremost pioneers of granular.

2   See Diemo Schwarz, 'Concatenative sound synthesis: The early years' *Journal of New Music Research*, 35/1 (2006): http://mediatheque.ircam.fr/articles/textes/Schwarz06b/ (accessed 10 June 2007).

birds and monkeys to be more sparse until eventually they are played as often as they used to be, once they are no longer afraid of the gun sound. This way we can create highly interactive soundscapes that react to the player's actions and make the player feel an increased sense of immersion within an interactive landscape. With programs such as Propellerhead's *Recycle*, the sound artist is able to interactively change the slicing parameters for the sample and interactively watch the points where the transient boundaries are detected.

The 'manual' method of granulation has been used in games not only to reduce the frequency of repetitive looping sounds but also to reduce the amount of memory used for ambiences and other effects. With the addition of high-quality digital signal processing in the current video game consoles, getting the layers of manual granulation to fuse together becomes much more feasible.

So, to summarize, there can be seen to be three different types of granulation which are best suited for real-time use games:

- *Granulation of sound samples via grains (short grains, automated segmentation)* Short grains, less than 100 ms, are utilized to reconstruct a sound from a source sample. Synchronous granulation can produce a result very similar to the source sample if the correct settings are found.
- *Granulation utilizing sounds via units (long grains, automated segmentation)* These units are typically segments of sound longer than 100 ms. The segmentation is done automatically and the amount of overlap of units is less than that of granulation via grains.
- *Manual granulation of sounds (long grains, manual segmentation)* Sounds are pre-split into component layers and the resulting sound is created by defining algorithms to decide how the different type of grain pools might play back. The amount of overlap of grains within pools is often quite minimal in an effort to reduce the possibility of transients causing phase cancellation and other unwanted noticeable side-effects. The advantage of this method is that the grains are chosen in a logical fashion (rather than being selected randomly) on transient boundaries, but the disadvantage is the amount of extra time it takes to construct the grain pools.

The application of granular synthesis to video games is a natural fit, as game sound artists are constantly fighting the repetitive nature of sample-based playback. In particular, the technology for handheld and mobile platforms typically lags behind that of the current generation of consoles, so the reduction of sample memory through granulation can be seen as a welcome advantage. Samples are very efficient at capturing a performance, but modifying the recording in real-time is difficult. Direct sample playback of a sound basically means that we hear an exact reproduction of the sound each time we hear a particular sample. Game platforms are able to change the playback rate (sometimes referred to as pitch) and volume of a sample on playback, but little else. Our ears are highly sensitive to repetitions in sounds and it becomes difficult for the player to hear the exact same sample played repeatedly over a several hour gaming session. Granulation has an advantage in that it is able to modify a source sample in real time, changing many elements of the sound but retaining much of the quality of the original sound. The more one uses granulation, the more one realizes that different types of segmentation algorithms work best with certain types of sample material. This is the reason that most commercial programs utilizing granulation often allow the user to choose between granulation that favours transient-based material such as drums or tone-based material such as musical pads.

Granulation in next-gen games[3]

With the inclusion of granular processing in popular software packages and the growth of the video game market, it appears to be a natural match to bring the two together to help improve the quality of game audio. Granulation has not been commonly used with games until this time due to the relatively costly computing power required and number of grain voices needed. With the seventh generation of game platforms, such as the PlayStation 3 and Xbox 360, these limitations have been relaxed, allowing for the increased possibility of real-time granulation in games.

The advantage of granulation is that it allows a high degree of control by the sound artist, who generates the initial sample but wishes to reduce the static and repetitive nature of sampled sound playback. It is also possible to input a stream of real-time audio into a granular synthesis algorithm and produce a granular delay line. With the increase of disc space and RAM, we can make the sample resolution very high in games, but without the proper tools, these samples will quickly become repetitive with repeated playback. Granulation can be a very effective process to augment the conventional sample sound pool which is played randomly in response to game events. If a sufficiently intelligent method of segmentation of grains is found, then sections of two or more similar source samples can be used to 'merge' grain playback from multiple sources. This operation is similar to the 'granular cross-fade' approach described below that allows for the merging of sampled sound sources.

In games it is much more common to wish to produce a sound similar to the original waveform rather than an entirely new sound. To do this, we choose our grains such that they step sequentially through the source sample and overlap the playback of grains in a fairly consistent manner. This is known as 'synchronous' granulation. 'Asynchronous' granulation is when the amount of overlap of grains is random and their position from the source waveform is not sequential, which produces a much more chaotic sounding result.

More modern time-stretch algorithms similar to those found at the time of writing (2007) for *Ableton Live* should be the goal of the video game audio granular synthesis toolset. The difficulty is that an effective granulation and segmentation algorithm are not trivial to produce. Granular synthesis requires the modification of many parameters and it takes focused research and experimentation to find the combination of parameters that best preserves the nature of the source sample while allowing for the modification of the sound afforded by granulation.

---

3   'Next-Gen' refers to the 'next generation' of games consoles, or Xbox 360, PlayStation 3 and Wii.

One of the key aspects to getting this granular re-synthesis to work is the transient detection algorithm. There are many methodologies and granular time-stretching algorithms that use transient detection. In the case of *FL Studio*, the user is able to select an automatic transient detection as well as rely on existing markers within the audio file to define the transient locations. Using transient detection improves the time-stretching of material with an emphasis on transients such as drum loops. Without synchronization of transients, the resulting granulation often sounds 'mushy' as the transients are largely lost.

Granular synthesis in commercial programs

Granular synthesis has become popular within modern audio software such as *Ableton Live*, Propellerhead's *Reason* and Native Instrument's *Reaktor* in varying levels of control over the granulation process. *Ableton Live* uses granular synthesis when time-warping samples in real time, but allows for little direct control over the granulation parameters. Granular effects are available through parameter controls in its Sampler plug-in to a limited degree. Propellerhead's *Reason* supports granular synthesis through its Malström synthesis component. Figure 9.2 illustrates an example of auto-segmentation by transients in *WaveLab*. By changing various parameters, the user can control how effectively the slicing is done to preserve the transients.

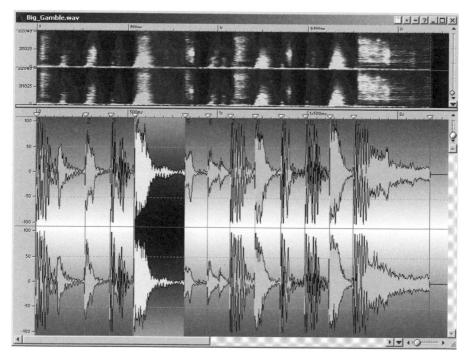

Figure 9.2   Auto-segmentation in *WaveLab*

Granulation has been commonly used to stretch out a sound to many times its original length as a 'sonic microscope' on the source sample. It has the advantage of retaining much of the harmonic content of the seed data, but is often represented as a dense sonic texture. Depending on where the grains are chosen from within the table, the size of the grains and other parameters, the resulting sound may either be similar or show little resemblance to the seed. Figure 9.3 shows the flow chart for the generation of grains in a basic granular synthesis algorithm and how the output can be distributed to a multi-channel surround sound output.

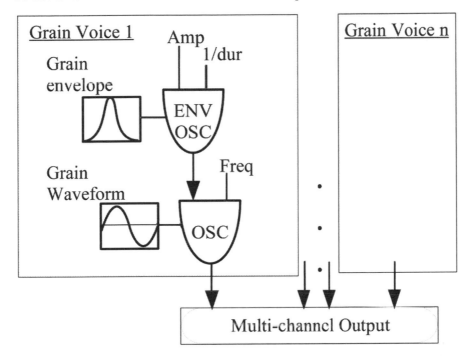

Figure 9.3   Basic granular synthesis flow chart

Granulation control parameters

Since there are often hundreds of grains of sound every second, one of the more difficult aspects of granular synthesis is how to intelligently control the grains. When granular synthesis has been used for electro-acoustic composition in the past, a common way of defining parameters, such as grain source position and grain size, was to use a range of possible values within which a value would be randomly chosen; this is also known as tendency masking. However, with games we have direct access to many real-time parameters (such as a car's RPM, velocity and more) that we can use to drive the parameters of the granulation. All we need to determine is what game events and parameters we want to use to direct the granulation and, more importantly, how these parameters are used together to guide the granulation parameters. The advantage that composers have when using the tendency mask is that they have a large amount of aesthetic control over the result. With games, the parameters from the game often do not sound very musical, so an intermediate layer must be inserted between the game and the granulation to make the granulation sound more 'intelligent'. When examining the compositional process of granular synthesis, Barry Truax noted: 'the composer functions not as an omniscient arbiter, but as the source of control messages that guide the overall process without directly determining it.'[4] This is a key concept in game audio: the sound artist may create the sound, but the sound truly comes to life when it is played in the game itself. So, the sound artist is not only responsible for creating the content or sample data but also determining the behaviour that is utilized to play the sound in the game and have it correlate to game-play. For instance, a simple example for an explosion effect might be to use number of particles to choose the number of grains and the size of the particles to control the grain size so that the granular audio density is similar to the visual density.

Typical parameters for granulation include:

- Selection order (forwards/reverse or freeze);
- Pitch shift (or playback rate);
- Amplitude range;
- Spatialization/panning (static/dynamic);
- Grain duration;
- Grain density (number of grains/second or number of grain voices);
- Envelope (ASR shape, attack/release slope or windowing function);
- DSP effect (reverb, filtering and so on.);
- Feedback amount (for granular delay lines).

The following examples of granulation in games are simply meant to be a starting point for further exploration.

Using granulation in games

Dialogue

Granulation can be used with speech to dynamically change the playback speed or pitch of the speech sample independently of another in real time. This can make the retriggering of certain speech lines ('Hey! Over here – over here!') sound a little less repetitive. The advantage (and disadvantage) of using granulation for time stretching is that it preserves transients. Transients are key in our identification of a sound. Unfortunately, when the granulation process causes transients to be retriggered when stretching a sound longer, this results in a 'stutter' sound to the transients, which is unnatural. A method of solving this difficulty is to first find the transients in

---

4   Barry Truax, 'Composing with real-time granular sound', *Perspectives of New Music* (1990): 120–34.

the granulated signal and pre-segment the sample into large grains (less than 100 ms) with a minimum amount of enveloping to preserve the transients.

The playback rate of each grain can be modified individually to change the pitch of the granulated signal. The difficulty with this method is there can be gaps between segments if the playback rate or amount of time stretching is too high, which requires repeating a previous grain, or lowering the playback rate.

If we perform a windowed Short Time Fourier Transform (STFT) on the incoming signal at regular intervals, looking for changes in phase values in the frequency domain, and then convert back to the time domain while overlapping the output (commonly 75 per cent), we basically arrive at a phase vocoder. The phase vocoder can sometimes preserve the quality of the source sample better than granulation, but can smear the transients as it is unable to detect rapid phase changes.

Sound effects

Granulation is a good choice for special effects, notably science fiction effects. Using an analogue synthesizer sound as a source for rich harmonics, we can granulate the sound to create clouds of sounds with very specific envelopes. The possibilities for granulation of regular sounds such as footsteps allow for variation, yet preserve the character of the original recording. One interesting effect is to step through the source sample in reverse, but have the granulation play the grains normally. To find interesting timbres, move slowly through the source sample and widen the playback range to modulate the sound. Working with granulation is an interesting way to really magnify a sound and listen to the inner details and timbres present in a waveform.

Ambiences

I have already discussed the example of the jungle ambience being reconstructed via granulation, but there are many other granular effects possible to enhance ambiences in games. Although digitized samples are great at capturing human performance, they are not as good at being manipulated in real time and avoiding becoming repetitive upon repeated plays. Granular synthesis allows independent change of pitch and tempo which allows for a myriad of possible real-time effects.

Car engines

Car engines are a common area in games in which the sound often becomes repetitive. With the current generation platforms it is very difficult to make good engine loops with the limited memory and number of voices available. We can segment the signal into variable natural-length grains which can be seen as a 'syllable-like' segmentation. The engine sound is segmented and organized into large grains which naturally lead one into the next. The appropriate grains are played back to suit the respective RPM and a certain amount of 'jitter' applied to reduce the amount of repeated grains.

Crowd sounds

Granulation can be effectively used to generate the background din of a large crowd. The difficulty of repeated noticeable sounds in conventional crowd loops can be largely eliminated as the sound does not repeatedly play the same way through the sample table. Phasing issues can occur, but larger seeds, transient detection, pre-segmentation and more grains are techniques that can be used to reduce this difficulty. One of the advantages of granulation is that the different crowd intensities can utilize a granular cross-fade rather than an amplitude cross-fade, which can increase the realism of the crowd. Basically, experimentation is key to finding the proper balance between number of voices and noticeable cross-fades. Large-grain granulation can be used to reduce the repetition of crowd loop ambience by choosing large grains and effectively chaining randomly through the sample data. Figure 9.4 shows a crowd engine for a roller coaster ride from the Canadian company Audiokinetic's *Wwise* program. Rather than just using static loops, granulation could be used to increase the variation of the sample data and perform granular cross-fading to blend between loops more naturally. A second layer of more identifiable samples could be layered on top of the granulation layer to increase the level of realism.

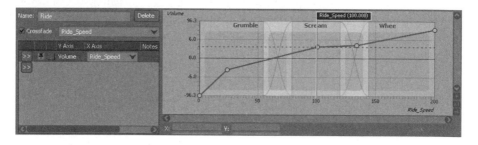

Figure 9.4   Example of a crowd engine for a roller coaster ride from *Wwise* blend groups

Granular delay-line

Rather than just using a static sample waveform as the input data for granulation, it is also possible to granulate a real-time audio input. This is known as a granular delay-line and can be explored in the software program *AudioMulch*. Try using the 'DLGranulator' object in *AudioMulch* and experimenting with various inputs. One of the additional parameters for delay-line granulation is the possibility of feedback of the output back into the delay-line. Riding the feedback level at the edge of over-saturation can produce some very unique audio effects, especially when combined with pitch transposition of the grains. In contrast to fixed waveform granulation, real-time granulation can cause inconsistencies when the grain source read pointer attempts to read ahead of the start of the buffer or past the end of the delay-line buffer when the granulation tempo is set too fast or too slow respectively. In games, one could use delay-line granulation as an additional layer to car or crowd engines to add some sonic grit to the loop playback.

Granular cross-fading/morphing

Granular 'morphing' is done by playing grains from two (or more) source samples simultaneously and adjusting the amount of grains chosen from each source dynamically. To control the level of the cross-fade or morph, the density of one set is raised and the others lowered while attempting to maintain an even output signal level. With a granular cross-fade, the spectral elements of the crowd can be mixed together slowly, which makes the transition between crowd samples more natural and smoother. To reduce the possibility of an overly noticeable shift in timbre when cross-fading, a spectral analysis could be done to select similar grains from the destination sample as compared to the source sample. This spectral analysis process is very similar to techniques used in some forms of concatenative sound synthesis.

Surround sound

Granulation can be a great way to diffuse a sound into a surround field. This technique has been used in the past in electro-acoustics with live performance of material through multi-speaker diffusion systems. Granulation into surround simply distributes the grains with their own individual surround panning. This process works best with ambiences such as water and wind that have few identifiable elements in the source sample. The panning of the grains can be dynamically modified and Doppler shift can be applied to give a strong feeling of a moving sound field, such as insects.

Granular synthesis in music

The first use of granular synthesis was in the area of electro-acoustic music production, so there is an extensive history to draw upon when using granular synthesis for music. Granulation is good at producing long, pad-like, shifting sonic textures that imply both motion on the micro layer and stasis on the macro layer simultaneously. I typically use granular synthesis on source sounds which have a strong formant and resonant signature to them, such as sung phrases and stringed instruments.

Granular musical textures can be very rich in timbre, occupying a large spectral bandwidth due to the upper harmonics generated by the steepness of the grain. One effective way to break up the 'wall' of granular synthesis is to quantize the grains to a specified BPM. One can also equalize the grains so that only certain frequencies are present. This produces a slightly different result than filtering the entire granulated signal, as much of the timbre is produced by the enveloping of the grains.

With the next-generation platforms, we have the possibility of using a software synthesizer (soft-synth) composition program similar to *Ableton Live* to render the score in real time and have it react to game events. This idea is not new, but the power offered by soft-synths, sample processing and real-time effects allow for much more flexibility than previous adaptive methods utilizing MIDI and sampled instruments. The 'ultimate' goal would be to move the composer's composition environment entirely onto the game platform and avoid having to pre-render the entire score to static wave files in order not to overload the CPU of the game platform. However, when looking historically, game systems, by their nature of being affordable and special-purpose computing systems, will always lag behind the capabilities of the cutting-edge desktop computers utilized by composers. The step from current-generation composition tools to next-gen tools will likely take several years.

Conclusions and resources[5]

Granulation is a powerful new tool in the hands of an experienced game sound designer. As granulation techniques make their way into sound drivers for games, the techniques covered in this chapter will become as commonplace as granulation in current audio software applications. For further investigation into the use of granular synthesis in music, see Curtis Roads's *Microsound*, and the writings of Barry Truax provide deep explorations into granular synthesis composition techniques and aesthetics.[6]

For those of you who wish to try your hand at coding your own granulation algorithm, there are several good locations from which to begin your efforts. Starting points for implementing granulation include Ross Bencina's 'Granular Synthesis Toolkit' (RB-GST), the Granulate class from the Synthesis Toolkit (STK) and the source for the syncgrain~ PD object. Implementing granular synthesis isn't a difficult process, but care should be taken to optimize the efficiency of the grain algorithm as well as spending time tuning the resulting granular texture from the system. A great explanation of the implementation of a granulation algorithm is Ross Bencina's paper 'Implementing Real-Time Granular Synthesis', available on his website.

Each granulation algorithm has its own distinctive characteristic sound. This is largely due to the fact that the overall sound is highly coloured by the nature of the grain processing itself, which is repeated each time a single grain is played. Very similar to chaos theory, small changes in a granulation algorithm can cause large changes in the resultant granulated sound. It takes continued research and refinement to arrive at a granulation algorithm that sounds good with both the sample data and

---

5   For copies of software, see *Ableton Live* (http://www.ableton.com), *Crusher-X* (http://www.crusher-x.de), *Csound* (http://csound.sourceforge.net), Cycling '74 *Max/MSP* (http://www.cycling74.com), Image Line *FL Studio* (http://www.fruityloops.com), KTGranulator (VST Plug-in, at http://www.koen.smartelectronix.com/KTGranulator), Miller Puckette's *Pure Data* (http://www-crca.ucsd.edu/~msp/software.html), PD port of Nobuyasu Sakonda's Max/MSP Granulation Patch (http://www.videogameaudio.com), *Supercollider* (http://supercollider.sourceforge.net), *Synthesis Toolkit* (STK http://ccrma.stanford.edu/software/stk/), Audiomulch (http://www.audiomulch.com/~rossb) (accessed 10 June 2007).

6   For further reading, see Ross Bencina, 'Implementing Real-Time Granular Synthesis' in K. Greenbaum and R. Barzel (eds), *Audio Anecdotes II: Tools, tips, and techniques for digital audio* (Natick, MA, 2004); Simon Price 'Granular synthesis: How it works and ways to use it', *Sound on Sound* (December 2005); Curtis Roads, *The Computer Music Tutorial* (Cambridge, MA, 1996) and *Microsound* (Cambridge, MA, 2004); Barry Truax, 'Composing with real-time granular sound'; 'Time-shifting of sampled sounds with a real-time granulation technique', *1990 ICMC Proceedings* (San Francisco, Computer Music Association, 1990), pp. 104–107.

the type of processing that one wishes to perform on it. Finding an algorithm that works well with many types of input data takes time not only tuning the granulation algorithm itself, but also the data that is used to control the grains over time. Don't be too discouraged if your initial efforts are unsuccessful.

The tutorials here are meant as a starting place for your own experiments with granulation methods. Have fun experimenting with various types of granulation as it holds great potential for the modification of and exploration into the inner details of sounds.

Audiomulch granular tutorials

To begin the tutorial, you will need to obtain a copy of *Audiomulch* online.[7] *Audiomulch* is available for the PC and runs well on Intel Macintosh machines running the Windows OS. The software comes with a generous trial period which should be sufficient for beginning to experiment using its granulation functions. The author used *Audiomulch* extensively for granular compositions for the Canadian documentary *The Corporation*. It has a wide range of audio processing features besides granulation not commonly found in other audio software applications.

This first tutorial in the *Audiomulch* manual is meant to get you up and running with *Audiomulch*. After getting comfortable with *Audiomulch*, you can work through the following tutorial to get started making some granular sounds. This tutorial covers how to perform granulation in *Audiomulch* and how to change the synthesis parameters and how this changes the resulting sound. For this example patch and more, see the author's website.[8]
1. Install *Audiomulch*.
2. Get audio working (see *Audiomulch* 'A Beginners Tutorial' tutorial in the Manual).
3. Add the 'Bubbleblower' object
4. Set the parameters to the following values:
    a) Amplitude = 0.18;
    b) Pan = Full (one slider at top and bottom of range);
    c) Inskip = 0 (minimum), 1900 (maximum);
    d) Trans = 0 and 0 (no transposition);
    e) Density = 2000 (maximum);
    f) Quant = 0 (no quantization of grains);
    g) GrainDur = 5 ms (minimum).
5. Experiment with some example parameters, and build some presets.
6. Experiment with placing some of the presets on the Metasurface.
7. Explore the sonic possibilities of granulation interactively with the Metasurface.

---

7   http://www.audiomulch.com (accessed 10 June 2007).
8   See http://www.videogameaudio.com (accessed 10 June 2007).

Pure data tutorial

The granulation patch in Pure Data runs on the Windows extended version of Pure Data 0.37 and above. The PD community is a strong one, but similar to many open source projects, it is difficult to guess where the best place to find the extended version of PD that will support the project will be at the time this book is being read in the future. The author has included a version of PD that will run the granular PD patch on his website.

This patch implements synchronous granular synthesis, which is good for more transparent sound manipulation. It is based on the Max/MSP patch by Nobuyasu Sakonda and the PD port by Bill Orcutt. It uses eight grains in total and is able to produce very smooth-sounding transformations given that it is only using eight voices. As it does not perform any sort of transient detection, it tends to work better with samples that have fewer transients. For samples with more transient information in them, the result tends to sound 'phasey' or 'washed out' as the grains are overlapping each other and causing various cancellations to the transients in the signal.

The patch gives you control over position and pitch independently, surround panning location, playback rate (pitch), grain size and window type for the grains. The control mode choices allow you to have the patch control the playback position automatically (being the default in 'choice 1') or to manually define the playback position ('choice 2'). When in automatic mode, the grain position sliders define the size of the range that the patch uses while moving through the entire sample. In manual mode, the sliders determine the absolute source sample position range that the grains are chosen from. If you set the speed to negative, then the playback position runs in reverse while the grains are playing the sample information forwards.

The two blue grid objects are great ways to play around with the parameters of this patch. When scrubbing the position and pitch grid, you can hear how easily granulation is able to change the quality of the voice that is used as the demonstration sample. The surround panning allows the creation of a strobe-effect behind the pointer as new grains catch up to the current pan position. It shows how easily granular synthesis can spread a sound into a surround image.

The different window types show how the smoother the slope of a window is, the less 'crackle' in the upper harmonics are added to the granulation. The options are for a triangle, cosine, rectangular and trapezoidal envelope from left to right. The only real noticeable change occurs with the rectangular envelope, which causes clicks at the grain boundaries as the audio is being cut in and out, as this is equivalent to no enveloping of the source segments at all.

This patch loads up with a repeating speech phrase. Experiment with this patch by utilizing the blue grid that controls the pitch and position (or tempo) of the granulation independently. Try loading in different samples that you might use in a game, such as explosions, screams and engine loops.

When first opened, the patch defaults to automatically updating the playback position ('choice 1'), so the grid gives control over pitch and tempo of the grain selection position. Try experimenting a bit with how the quality of the voice changes when the parameters are changed interactively. When small modifications are done, you can make the voice sound like it is someone else speaking or even rushing their speech. These slight modifications in a game could allow a game character's speech to react in real time to game-play, such as slowing down their speech when an awesome or horrific event is witnessed.

When you switch to manual position updating ('choice 2'), you are able to scrub backwards and forwards through the sound file. This is less applicable to games, but recognizable gestures can be made when modifying the grain source position. You can also adjust the 'Grain Position' sliders and widen the window that the grains are chosen from. If you set them to extremes, then you hear grains being randomly played from any position in the source sample.

PART 5
Audio and audience

Chapter 10

Chip music: low-tech data music sharing

Anders Carlsson[1]

Ever since I was very young, I have been using Commodore computers to make music. As a teenager I fiercely defended low-tech computing in the face of more user-friendly systems. This purism was put to the test as I started collaborating with people from different backgrounds: when the Spanish designer duo Entter produced my first video clip, they showed an IBM PC instead of what should have been the Commodore 64. This was hard for me to accept, since the old computers were the basis of my music and had important symbolic value to me as an alternative to contemporary technology. Today I am not such a purist, but to me the question remains: how important is it to use 'authentic' technology when making music?

Nowadays, it is common to see influences from old video games within popular culture. In media publications this re-use is often explained by the fact that during the past 25 years, children in the Western world have grown up with rapidly evolving video games. Consequently, these games play important roles in their childhood memories. But there is another reason for the recent nostalgia: the growth of file sharing. Digital subcultures have been spreading free software on an international level since there were home computers with modems in the mid 1980s. This spreading started out with the distribution of home-made applications as well as commercial software and evolved into the spreading of audio-visual presentations, and more recently stand-alone music. This musical style has become known as 'chip music', music composed by using, emulating or sampling old digital sound chips. At present there are thousands of chip music songs available on the Internet for free. In many cases this music is presented in an open-source format, including the source of the music, which can be changed or adapted by the user. This practice of open sharing distinguishes parts of the chip music scene from most other music genres and scenes.[2]

To the uninitiated, chip music is often perceived as homogenized, mostly due to its distinctive sound, and therefore is often categorized as one specific musical genre. The artistic freedom, based on the technological constraints of old chips, has, however, produced 'bleepy' music that sounds very different from the songs of the 1980s' video games, as today's composers are influenced by more contemporary

---

1   I would like to thank Rosa Menkman for assistance, and also 4-mat, Autoboy, Aleksi Eeben, Linus Walleij, Johan Kotlinski, Rambones and Julian Van Aalderen.

2   Here I define 'scene' as an 'active creation of infrastructure to support ... bands and other forms of creative activity'. Alan O'Connor, 'Local Scenes and Dangerous Crossroads: Punk and theories of Cultural Hybridity' *Popular Music* 21/2 (2002), p. 226.

musical genres and are not obliged to make the songs fit into a game. In this sense, it could be argued that the technological minimalism of chip music is the most significant defining element of the music: no matter what is done with a sound chip in terms of harmony, structure or rhythm, it is still chip music. There is, however, a difference between regarding chip music as medium and chip music as form. I will discuss this difference below.

The purpose of this chapter is to discuss chip music with a historical perspective based on the 'demoscene', a subculture of creative computer users submitting their work to competitions with audio-visual productions programmed to be generated in real time for the viewer. Since today's chip music scene is essentially non-commercial, the commercial industry of video games is out of the scope of this text.[3] There is not much literature on either the demoscene or chip music, and so much of this text is based on my own experiences from the northern European music and demoscenes of the Commodore 64 and Amiga.

The demoscene

The demoscene grew out of the movement of removing copy protection from games, commonly known as 'cracking'. This view of making software freely available for the public has roots in both hacker ethics and free software movements. Parts of the cracker community have ideals similar to those of hackers and phreakers[4], but it seems likely that a lot of early crackers were kids cracking games for fun, for intellectual challenge and for 'street credibility'.[5] The European cracking scene (from out of which the demoscene formed) stems from the 1979 American Apple II and the Atari 800 cracker scene, which was linked to Europe through modems and the BBS (Bulletin Board Service) culture.[6] Hackers and phreakers were, however, generally more 'underground' than the game-crackers, in the sense that the nicknames of crackers would appear on hundreds of thousands of screens while kids were loading the cracked games. Although most people did not know or care who 'Mr.Z' or 'Dynamic Duo' were, these names would, for some, represent mysterious heroes who provided them with countless hours of free entertainment. For the crackers (usually boys in their early teens), this was an exciting way of obtaining notoriety. Crackers would compete to make the best cracks and to be first to have a game released on an American BBS for international use. This activity required both programming skills and the ability to make free international calls.

The cracking scene has been compared to graffiti culture mainly because the two both involve illegally invading corporate and public space in a search for identity or

---

3   Chip music has been used in more commercial purposes such as with Malcolm McLaren's launch of chip music as the new 8–bit punk, and will be discussed more later on in the chapter.

4   Linus Walleij, 'Copyright Finns Inte' (1998). Online English Version, Chapter 5 http://home.c2i.net/nirgendwo/cdne/mainindex.htm (accessed 12 February 2007).

5   Lassi Tasajärvi, *Demoscene: The Art of Real-Time* (Finland, 2004), p. 12.

6   Walleij, 'Copyright Finns Inte', Chapter 5.

fame.[7] Initially the crackers' name tags (nicknames) started as basic text messages but gradually included more complex programming and graphics, and became known simply as 'crack-intros' or 'intros'. Around 1985, crack-intros were released separately from the games and were made famous within the scene by groups such as 1001 Crew and The Judges, both from the Netherlands.[8] By this time, the demoscene was starting to form in Western Europe, although it was connected to the one in Australia, and to lesser extent those in North America and Eastern European countries.[9] The key demoscene computers were those of Commodore, Atari and Sinclair – very similar to those now part of the chip music scene, although today the USA and Japan have a lot more prominence, and Nintendo products have become popular.

A 'demo' (abbreviated from 'demonstration') demonstrated what a user could do with a specific technology. Everything seen and heard would be generated by the computer in real time and running at full frame rate. Demos can be understood in opposition to animation that consists of a big file of pre-generated data that is exactly the same every time you play it. Originally, animations were not used in demos because they used too much memory. Later on in the demoscene, as programmers had memory to spare for animations, real-time generated audio and visuals were still used and it became an important convention in the demoscene.

Tasajärvi uses a metaphor to explain how a theatre director instructs the actor who then performs the script live, as opposed to a film that has a final fixed product.[10] A demo, a theatre play and a pure chip music song are normally generated as the listener is experiencing it, rather than being pre-recorded. Just as a theatre director can play with the rules of what theatre is supposed to be, the demosceners and chip music composers found ways to work beyond technological boundaries thought to be unbreakable. Demosceners would, for example, launch new graphic modes to expand resolutions and colours, work around bugs in the sound chips, experiment with samples and expand the computers' possibilities in general. These tricks were not rational mathematical programming, but rather trial and error based on in-depth knowledge of the computers used. Demosceners managed to accomplish things not intended by the designers of the computers.

During the 1980s the programming was more important than the graphics and music in demos, but by the 1990s so-called 'design demos' started appearing, a term which implies how much the programming dominated the previous demos. These more recent demos were based on graphical and musical concepts, rather than maximizing the hardware through programming. The Danish/French group Melon Dezign has been credited with starting this movement in the Amiga demoscene in the early 1990s. As for the music, there would be a growing gap between bleepy chip

---

7 Tasajärvi, *Demoscene: The Art of Real-Time*, p. 31. Sky Frostenson, 'Bombing the System', Winter ACE Seminar: Virtual Identities (2004). Walleij, 'Copyright Finns Inte', Chapter 5.

8 Támás Polgár, *Freax: The Brief History of the Computer Demoscene* (Winnenden, Germany, 2006), p. 57.

9 Polgár, *Freax: The Brief History of the Computer Demoscene*, pp. 58–68.

10 Tasajärvi, *Demoscene: The Art of Real-Time*, p. 17.

music and songs that sounded more like studio music. The studio-oriented music would typically sound like jazz funk or techno, a unique style of the demoscene that became known as 'doskpop'. Swedish artist Lizardking was the father of doskpop, which can be described as soft digital disco music, somewhere in between 1980s electronic disco music such as Laserdance and Vangelis.[11]

In the 1980s most home computer set-ups were identical, but in the 1990s the market for hardware expansion grew bigger. This meant that one Amiga set-up could be so different from another set-up that you could not run the same demos; a problem most notable in the IBM PC demoscene. This meant that demos had to be more system-friendly to work on different set-ups of CPUs, memory and graphic and sound cards. Traditional demoscene norms of making the computer do 'impossible' things would weaken on the PC as possibilities expanded. Some demo groups would start using Windows' 3D software or MP3 files in their demos, stepping away from the older norms of the demoscene towards music videos. However, certain people would stick with tradition to only use default hardware and programming everything themselves – which became known as 'dogma-demos'.[12] With demos increasingly taking the form of music videos, the gap between the demoscene and the major music industry decreased. Demoscene composers began to appear on large record labels, such as Brothom States on Warp and Bogdan Raczynski on the Rephlex label.

The many improvements in technology were one of the reasons some demoscene artists returned to the older machines, like the Commodore 64 and ZX Spectrum. In addition, the Nintendo Entertainment System (NES), Super Nintendo (SNES) and Game Boy also gained popularity as new developments in hardware and software for hobbyists appeared. Although the ever-present demoscenes of the 8-bit machines remain underground today, the PC demoscene has gained popular recognition, as has chip music in general.

A brief history of chip music

Computer-based music took its first steps in the 1950s, although analogue electronic music already had a 50 year head start.[13] In 1951 the Australian mathematician Geoff Hill was the first to generate music in real time.[14] In 1957 Max Mathews began programming music software for the IBM 704 in the USA. During the next decades digital music was experimented with by pioneering multimedia artists, *musique concrète* composers and scientists, and began to appear in video games such as Atari's *Pong* (1972).[15] By 1975 a computer was playing 'Daisy Bell', realized by having an Altair 8800 manipulating a nearby AM radio, which was made by the

---

11 Polgár, *Freax: The Brief History of the Computer Demoscene*, p. 134.

12 Tasajärvi, *Demoscene: The Art of Real-Time*, p. 68.

13 See Peter Manning, *Electronic and Computer Music* (Oxford, 2004), pp. 19–100.

14 Paul Doornbusch, *The Music of CSIRAC: Australia's First Computer Music (Altona, Australia, 2005), Online version* http://www.csse.unimelb.edu.au/dept/about/csirac/music/introduction.html (accessed 19 December 2006).

15 Karen Collins, 'From Bits to Hits: Video Games Music Changes its Tune', *Film International* 13 (2004), pp. 4–19.

hobbyists in the Homebrew Computer Club[16] and has been described as the world's first demo.[17] Although the generated sounds were not digital and it is therefore problematic to describe the song as a demo, this example is of interest here since it is an early example of hobby users playing music with a computer.

In the 1970s video games and arcade games music was not a primary concern for manufacturers. During the 1980s, however, this sentiment changed, making sounds and music more important for interactive game-play.[18] During the 1980s all of the music in video games, computer games and arcade games used basic sounding chips, meaning all computer music was 'chip music'.[19] From quite early on there was music software available on home PCs, such as *Commodore Music Maker* (1982) for the Commodore 64, using traditional notation techniques. However, these programs were not efficient enough to be used for games and demos, and composers basically had to be programmers as well because of the need to use assembler or even machine code (basically only a list of numbers) to make instruments and sequence notes.[20] The first popular music program for games and demo music on the Commodore 64 was *Soundmonitor*, made by Chris Hülsbeck in 1986. Instead of using a programming language to make music, it became possible to use this interface to make music. Although some artists still preferred the low-level composing techniques which offered more flexibility and efficiency, such as the game composer Rob Hubbard and the demoscener Laxity, *Soundmonitor* proved to be an important step towards the most popular tool for making chip music: the tracker format.

In *Soundmonitor*, a composer did not have an overview of a song, since she or he had to switch between the song arrangement screen and the pattern editor where the notes were sequenced. The composer would write small sequences of notes with his or her instruments of choice, and could add portamento, arpeggio or transpositions. This note and effect data was written straight into a specific place in the memory. For example, the computer could store a 32-byte sequence (including more than just note data) between B200 and B21F in the memory, and then point to it in the song arrangement screen with B200. All of the numbers in *Soundmonitor* were written in hexadecimal form, which remains common among trackers even today.

In 1987 Karsten Obarski released *Soundtracker* which turned the Commodore Amiga into a very price-worthy tool for composers, using 8-bit samples up to 29 kHz. It was disassembled and improved upon to be re-released by numerous programmers in the demoscene, the most popular releases being *Noisetracker* (1989) and *Protracker* (1990). With these releases, it was possible to use 32 samples and sequence them in a more user-friendly tracker style, adding effects in an effect

---

16 Sheet Music/BASIC listing of 'Fool on the Hill' played on the Altair 8800 computer, Digibarn Computer Museum, http://www.digibarn.com/collections/weirdstuff/altair–sheetmusic/index.html (accessed 19 December 2006).

17 Polgár, *Freax: The Brief History of the Computer Demoscene*, p. 41.

18 Collins 'From Bits to Hits: Video Games Music Changes its Tune' p. 6.

19 'Chiptune', *VORC Internet Chiptune Encyclopedia*, http://www.vorc.org/en/info=Chiptune (accessed 15 May 2007).

20 Thomas Egeskov Petersen, 'Music Recollection', *Music Recollection Issue 2*, http://www.atlantis-prophecy.org/recollection/?load=online&issue=1&sub=article&id=11 (accessed 15 May 2007).

column right next to the notes. The songs created with these trackers were called 'modules' or 'mod-files' for short. These trackers were the most popular form for composition in the demoscene, and were also used in the game industry to create music for games. Two disks of sampled sounds were provided with *Soundtracker* – known as ST-01 and ST-02 – and were used so frequently that they created a distinct aesthetic in the sound of Amiga.

In 1989 the British composer 4-mat, along with contemporaries such as Turtle and Duz, started using sample-based trackers to make chip music. Previously, the bleepy chip music style had been made with waveforms straight off the sound chip (as with C64 or Spectrum), or with software synthesized waveforms (as with *Future Composer* on the Amiga), but the new technique meant taking samples and cutting them up into tiny segments of 200 bytes or less, and then looping them. This would generate a tone, which would sound different depending on the waveform of the sample, but basically sounding like different kinds of completely static 'bleeps'. On computers such as the Commodore 64, however, the tone was generated in real time by the chip itself, and the sounds could be modulated to sound different every time they were played. In an Amiga *Protracker* chip song, these dynamics would instead be programmed by having several similar bleep sounds that the composer would rapidly switch between, or would add effects to in the patterns. Effects such as pitchbend, portamento, arpeggio, vibrato and volume envelopes were entered straight into the pattern data, which made it easier than the effect handling on the Commodore 64 trackers. The sample-based chip music, then, offered a different way of creating sounds for chip music.

When releasing songs in games or demos with the tracker format, it was possible to look into the memory to see how the song worked in terms of the routine that defines how to access the sound chip, and the key was to tweak the chip to its fullest. It was therefore useful to look into the code to see how artists would produce sounds. One programmer known as 'Predator', for instance, made a tracker based on the code of games composer Rob Hubbard. When releasing a song, it was possible for users to access the player routines, along with instruments, note data, effects and samples. Even though these elements could be hidden with various techniques, there would usually be a way to hack into the code, which is why it is possible to find most Commodore 64 games songs released online today (for instance, in the High Voltage SID Collection). As long as a user has the tracker that was used for making the song, it is possible to load the song into an editor and gain total control of the song. This practice has been more heavily used on the Amiga since the mod format was more standardized, and it was possible to access the actual sample data. Today, however, chip music is not often released in its original format, but rather as an inadaptable MP3.

In the 1990s the most popular trackers in the demoscene were *Fasttracker* on the PC and *Protracker* on the Amiga, although *Little Sound DJ* (*LSDJ*) is probably the tracker that has gained most attention outside of the demoscene. *LSDJ* is a music program for the Game Boy in which patterns are individual for each track, much like *Soundmonitor*, but which has a new way of creating chains of patterns that could be then arranged in a song view. This is why the creator Johan Kotlinski 'doesn't really see it as a tracker'.[21] *Little Sound DJ* brought trackers into the mainstream and the Game Boy came to be a popular symbol for the art of chip music composing and performance. *LSDJ* offered more possibilities than any tracker before, both in arranging the song and in editing notes, effects and instruments in real time.

Although composing with old sound chips is usually accomplished with trackers today, there are other options. In addition to traditional notation software, there are alternatives for trackers in text-based format like *Prophet64* (C64), *Nanoloop* (Game Boy) and *Midines* (NES). *MCK* is one program to make NES music, and is arguably the most popular text-based composing tool today, especially in Japan. Today, non-purist chip music is often made with modern software like *Cubase* and *Reason* with VST instruments emulating the old sound chips. There are also modern trackers like *Renoise* that combine the *Soundtracker* tradition with more modern approaches such as MIDI and VST. Some chip music purists, preferring trackers running on the original hardware, condemn this practice and prefer not to label these compositions chip music, leading to a difficulty in defining the genre.

Defining chip music

Although I have chosen to use the term 'chip music' throughout this text, alternatives to this term exist, such as 'chiptune' and '8-bit' with several lesser-known subgenres such as 'bitcore' and 'chiphop'. 'Chiptune' was probably first used in the Amiga demoscene in the early 1990s, and is used today as widely as 'chip music'. 8-bit is more specific to music being made with 8-bit technology, which I will discuss further below. Sometimes this music is referred to as 'micromusic' and 'bitpop'. The term 'micromusic' stems from the community micromusic.net and usually refers to music made with home computers or video game consoles that is more or less inspired by 'old school' computer sounds. Bitpop is similar, but includes the use of analogue synthesizers, and is even more oriented towards poppy dance music than other styles. Chip music, on the other hand, is a broader term which can refer both to music made with old sound chips and bleepy sounding music made with other hardware.

Chip music is often defined by technology, which is to say that chip music is often defined as all music made with old sound chips. The problem with this distinction is that, generally speaking, it can be hard to tell the difference between simple waveforms being played by a 1980s sound chip or a modern synthesizer or emulator. A strict technological definition also brings the problem of defining which sound chips are acceptable to the community. There are, for instance, sound chips in toys, alarm clocks, mobile phones, doorbells and Game Boy Advance, and then there is also General MIDI and FM synthesis. Which of these would be included in a technological definition of chip music? One option would be to only accept sound chips up to those of the 16-bit era, but most sound chips are not easily defined as 4-, 8- or 16-bit, since different parts of the chip works with different resolutions. For

---

21 Tasajärvi, *Demoscene: The Art of Real-Time*, p. 43.

example, the Commodore 64's SID chip has 16-bit envelope control and 16-bit pitch register, although the chip is typically referred to as 8-bit.

As chip music has gained popularity, it has influenced and been influenced by other kinds of music, making it hard to maintain a purist technological definition. Even as the term was popularized on the Amiga, it referred to sample-based music, as mentioned above: It was not about the medium, but rather the form the composition took. However, *Protracker* on the Amiga was also used to make music very far from bleepy C64 nostalgia. In the Dutch gabber scene there were, for example, *Protracker EP* (1993) and *The Three Amiga's EP* (1993) by Neophyte. In Australia, Nasenbluten and Xylocaine released hardcore *Protracker* songs on records, and Digital Hardcore Recordings in Germany had artists such as Patric Catani (under various pseudonyms), eq8or and Christoph de Babalon who used similar trackers. Although these artists used the tracker format, their music is not generally considered chip music. It is chip music as a medium, but not chip music as form. In the 1990s sample-based chip music became more a conscious choice of style rather than a direct consequence of the hardware and software used to create it. Although chip music songs were originally used in the demoscene due to their small file sizes, there would soon grow a small scene of dedicated chip music creators and listeners.

Some composers have more recently turned away from the technologically imposed sounds to impress the listener. In the C64 demoscene programmers and composers would evolve the sounds with new tricks in order to beat the competition, and on the Amiga the capability of sampling led to some music resembling studio recorded music with, for example, the works of Audiomonster or Moby. However, the chip music composers on the Amiga were often embracing the (arguably) simplistic sounds of the C64 and its games, giving it a value and aesthetic in and of itself. For the most part, more recent chip songs have been short and happy-sounding loops in 4/4, often flirting with C64 music from the 1980s,[22] but composers have used chip sounds to make songs sounding like jazz, noise, death metal or even hip-hop.

Chip music after 2000

Chip music today has grown in popularity and in style. One important part of the evolution of chip music has been the website micromusic.net, formed in 1999 and still very much alive. It offers a selection of user-uploaded songs merging old and new computer sounds, usually dance-oriented, but also some quite experimental songs. The website has become an important name in the blossoming media coverage of 'chipoid' music, but with founders from the subversive Internet art scene, it has effectively stayed clear of labels and generalizations. Through the website, chip music has started appearing on stages mainly around Europe. Some of the artists that would make pure chip music popular outside of the demoscene in Europe are Rolemodel, Gwem, Lo-Bat, Firestarter, Teamtendo, Bodenständig 2000, Puss (the latter being nominated for a Swedish Grammy in 2003) and Goto80. In North America, artists such as 8-bit Construction Set, Bitshifter and Nullsleep, along with the 8bitpeoples

---

22 Personal e-mail correspondence with 4-mat, December 2006.

label have become important figures. Japan's chip music scene has also gained notoriety, with artists such as Cow'P and Hex125.[23] Despite the popularity, chip music also remains tied to its origins, with some cracked software for PC having spread composers like Maktone once again into the homes of computer users.

Fuelled by a growing popularity of 1980s culture, chip music has enjoyed success far beyond video games and demos. In 2003 punk pioneer Malcolm McLaren wrote an article in *Wired* magazine that would bring chip music even more into the media spotlight. After having worked with fashion and music projects like the Sex Pistols, he then launched a view of chip music as the new 8-bit punk. Chip music was described as a subversive and cheap way of making Game Boy music for vinyl releases, deliberately staying underground.[24] His statements upset a lot of chip music people, who feared he would commercialize the music, as described by micromusic. net.[25] Although McLaren's hype of chip music led to positive attention for a lot of artists, his outsider perspective also cultivated some unfortunate misunderstandings, such as the claim that subversive chip music composers hacked into video games to make music.[26] This is a rare part of the chip music scene, as most chip music composers simply copy a program that someone else has made and use it to make music. Chip music composers can, however, be called subversive in the sense that they do perhaps 'abuse' corporate technology by not using it for its intended purpose. The software is usually developed by hobbyists in the demoscene with the intent of maximizing and reaching beyond the hardware's limits, and then disseminating it free of charge. Some of the machines used by chip music artists were not even meant to be musical devices. Although some chip music artists do have ideological or artistic motives, these are not usually outwardly expressed in the music. One of the problems for McLaren would have been to generalize chip music. Judging from media coverage and online chip music archives, the dance and pop approaches are in the majority, but especially after 2000, chip music has been merged with a lot of genres and instruments. Some of the more prominent approaches of adding traditional instruments and vocals to chip music come from David Sugar, Mark DeNardo, Bodenständig 2000, Bud Melvin, Anamanaguchi, Gwem and Superdöner. The noisier chip music, often released on low bit-rate Internet labels such as North American Hardcore or 20kbps Rec, has some common ground with the *Protracker* hardcore music in the 1990s. Some artists are either by choice or 'accident' not really a part of the traditional chip music forums, as for example Patric Catani or the frequently touring DJ Scotch Egg.

There are also major commercial artists incorporating the sounds of chip music into their songs, such as Beck's 'Hell Yes' (2005) and also Nelly Furtado's song 'Do

---

23 'VGM or Chiptune of the Year 2002', *VORC*, http://www.vorc.org/en/columns/hally/2002best10e.html (accessed 5 June 2007).

24 '8-Bit Punk', *Wired Magazine* 11/11 (November 2003), http://www.wired.com/wired/archive/11.11/mclaren.html (accessed 15 May 2007).

25 'Open Letter to Malcolm McLaren', *Micromusic* (2004), http://micromusic.net/public_letter_gwEm.html (accessed 15 May 2007).

26 Peter Culshaw, 'So I pitched my Oscar Wilde film to Spielberg', *Guardian Unlimited*, 21 March 2004, http://arts.guardian.co.uk/features/story/0,11710,1175408,00.html (cited 15 May 2007).

It' (2006), produced by Timbaland, which ran into trouble after it sampled a song by the Scandinavian demosceners GRG and Tempest without credit. It has also been my experience that various TV channels and radio channels have used my own music without credit. The question I asked myself after these incidents was: is it more wrong when a big business company does it? To me this is an interesting conflict with chip music. These examples and other uses of chip music without credit to the original authors have raised discussions about how chip music composers could protect their work from illegal use. The question of free distribution is undoubtedly something to keep in mind when speaking about the future distribution of chip music. Chip music has its roots in the demoscene where music was traditionally shared in open-source formats and extracted in parts, but as the music is now available for any Internet user, the question is how to handle 'unlawful' use of chip music especially by mainstream artists and companies. In the discussions on the forums at micromusic.net, it seems that most people defend the traditional copyright laws and not the demoscene style of sharing: especially not when there is money involved. Although chip music artists do not necessarily want to make more money from their work, with the growing possibility of more commercial activities, there might arise a conflict between the ideologically driven file-sharers and culture-jammers on the one side, and more traditional record-releasing artists on the other. Compromises have been reached, such as with the American label 8bitpeoples, which sells music but also offers it free for download.

Another interesting thought is what will happen to chip music when kids are no longer raised with bleepy video games. It leads to the question of whether the digitally primitive interfaces and sounds have something unique to offer, or if it is just a nostalgic fad. This brings me back to my initial question of how much importance one should put on using 'authentic' hardware when making music and what consequences it has on the creative processes. To me, starting as a purist chip music composer, I have gradually learned to appreciate chip music as something other than a result of the medium. Ultimately the music is more interesting than the technology, and there have been very exciting recent developments in chip music. However, I also strongly believe that composing on old computers and consoles gets the composer closer to the machine, which has an effect on the music. There is something beautiful about learning how to use the so-called constraints of old technology to expand creativity. It would therefore be interesting to see some more research on how chip music tools are used and how the use of these tools affects the realization of musical ideas.

Chapter 11

Left in the dark: playing computer games with the sound turned off

Kristine Jørgensen

In audio-visual contexts we often get the impression that the use of audio is merely ornamental and present only for the purpose of supporting a specific atmosphere. Although this is an important and interesting feature of audio in such contexts, it is only one of several roles that audio may have. Audio may also work to provide specific information about a setting and situation, and may have direct influence on actions and events in the environment. In the context of computer games, audio has clear usability functions in addition to supporting a specific mood and the sense of presence in the game environment. This chapter will take the role of game audio into account by demonstrating how playing without any sound affects the game experience, both on the level of the game environment and on the level of the game system.

Recently, game audio has become a hot commodity in the game industry. This is demonstrated by an increased awareness during the last couple of years of the need to implement audio in games in innovative ways. One example is the *Grand Theft Auto 3* games in which the player may change in-game radio stations when driving around in the city, and another is how the Xbox 360 game console allows the player to add music from his or her computer hard drive into the game she/he is currently playing. This may be seen as a symptom of the golden rule in game audio design, which is to never let the player become annoyed or bored by the repetitiveness of the sound. By allowing the player to be in charge of the music, the developer may avoid players turning off the music intended for the game. In the context of this chapter, however, the question is whether (and if so, how) removing the implemented game audio influences the game experience. I will argue that taking away the sound has consequences for the player's orientation and awareness in the game world. In addition, certain kinds of information are harder to grasp when sound is removed. The argument is based on qualitative studies of empirical game players' understanding of game audio in context, and how they experience the game without any sound present. Since theories specifically aimed towards game audio at the time of writing are scarce, the empirical data will be further supported by auditory display studies and film theory. Auditory display studies will emphasize game audio as a usability feature, while film theory underlines game audio as a support for the game environment.

In audio-visual contexts it is often believed that sound and image work as two complementary information systems that compete in the meaning making process.

Michel Chion describes the relationship between sound and image in films as an audio-visual contract in which sound always will transform the meaning of the image to a certain extent.[1] However, the informative value that sound brings to the image tends to give the impression of stemming from the image itself. Because of its added value, sound is often given a lesser role in films than it deserves. Such a problematic relationship does not exist in games, however. Since the temporal relationship between sound and image is dynamic in games, and not fixed as in films,[2] talking about the relationship between sound and image as the central one for understanding what is going on in computer games is not the right focus. In computer games it is important to examine how sound and image affect the game experience and the game as activity. In most computer systems the visual and the auditory channels are the only ways in which the system can communicate with the user. This means that both should be utilized in order to provide all necessary system information to the user. In games both sound and graphics therefore have the function of providing usability information and supporting the sense of presence in the game environment. When sound is removed from this context, one of the two only channels for communication on the part of the system is lost, and the user runs the risk of losing important information. Even though this information is often provided by visual output, the user may not be able to pick it up if the visual system has a lot of other information to keep track of,[3] a point which will be demonstrated below.

Although research into game audio is young at the time of writing, scholars have tried to identify the role of sound in gaming contexts. Stockburger outlines a range of sound objects in order to demonstrate the important informative role game audio has in orienting the player and providing a sense of spatiality in the game environment.[4] Stockburger's sound objects are sounds connected to objects and events in the game environment, and should be seen as discrete elements that provide information about a specific object, event or location. His overview is useful for identifying sounds and their relationship to the game environment, but it does not go into detail of how sound is relevant for how the player experiences the game system and the game dynamics. Collins moves further in this direction and describes game audio as dynamic in the

---

1   Michel Chion, *Audio-Vision. Sound on Screen* (New York, 1994), p. 9.

2   Axel Stockburger, 'The Game Environment from an Auditory Perspective', in Marinka Copier and Joost Raessens (eds), *Proceedings: Level Up: Digital Games Research Conference* (Utrecht, 2003), http://www.audiogames.net/pics/upload/gameenvironment.htm (accessed 28 April 2007).

3   Carrie Heeter and Pericles Gomes, 'It's Time for Hypermedia to Move to Talking Pictures', *Journal of Educational Multimedia and Hypermedia*, Winter 1992, http://commtechlab.msu.edu/publications/files/talking.html (accessed 31 January 2007). G.B. Kramer, T. Bonebright, P. Cook, J. Flowers, N. Miner, J. Neuhoff, R. Bargar, S. Barrass, J. Berger, G. Evreinov, W. Fitch, M. Gröhn, S. Handel, H. Kaper, H. Levkowitz, S. Lodha, B. Shinn-Cunningham, M. Simoni and S. Tipei, *The Sonification Report: Status of the Field and Research Agenda* (Santa Fe, 1999). http://icad.org/websiteV2.0/References/nsf.html (accessed 31 January 2007).

4   Stockburger, 'The Game Environment from an Auditory Perspective'.

sense that it may either respond to game events or player actions.[5] She also points out that this goes both for game sounds with a perceived source existing within the game universe (diegetic sounds), and game sounds with no realistic in-game source (extra-diegetic sounds). This puts emphasis on game audio as different from other kinds of audio in the sense that it is always closely related to player actions and in-game events, and needs to be understood from that perspective. Whalen goes further in how he understands game audio by claiming that game music may either expand the concept of the game world, or draw the player forward through sequential game-play.[6] This means that game music works to support the sense of space and presence in the game environment, or that it helps the player to progress through the game. This view is not very far from the view I will pursue in this chapter, since my claim is that game audio works as support for the game world and the usability of the game system.[7]

Empirical background

As mentioned above, this chapter is based on findings from qualitative studies of empirical players. In connection with my PhD research, thirteen studies were carried out in which players were observed while playing either the real-time strategy game *Warcraft III* (Blizzard 2002) or the stealth game *Hitman Contracts* (Io Interactive 2004). The participants were experienced computer game players who played the game in question under normal conditions for about 15–20 minutes before the sound was turned off. Then they played for additional 10–15 minutes with no sound. The playing was recorded by video capture software, which allowed us to have a conversation based on the actual playing immediately after the playing session. This conversation focused on the players' description of what they were doing in the game with special attention paid to how sound related to their choice of actions.

It should be kept in mind that game audio plays different roles from game to game and from genre to genre. The two games in question were chosen because they are representatives of genres that present very different challenges to the player. In addition, the two games place the player in very different positions, which has important consequences for the use of sound. Categorized as a stealth game, *Hitman Contracts* demands the player be discreet, stealth-like and tactically focused. Cast in the role of a professional assassin, the player must take violent action to take out his targets, but the player gains bonuses for executing the missions without being exposed

---

5 Karen Collins, 'An Introduction to the Participatory and Non-Linear Aspects of Video Game Audio', in Stan Hawkins and John Richardson (eds), *Essays on Sound and Vision* (Helsinki, 2007).

6 Zach Whalen, 'Play Along: An Approach to Video Game Music', in *Game Studies. The International Journal of Computer Game Research* 4/1 (2004): http://www.gamestudies. org/0401/whalen (accessed 28 April 2007).

7 See also Kristine Jørgensen, 'On the Functional Aspects of Computer Game Audio', in *Proceedings of the Audio Mostly Conference 2006* (Piteå, Sweden, 2006); Kristine Jørgensen, *'What are those Grunts and Growls Over There?' Computer Game Audio and Player Action*, Ph.D. dissertation. (Copenhagen, 2007).

by guards or civilians. The game is played through an avatar, which is the player's personification in the game, positioned as an actual character within the game world. *Warcraft III*, on the other hand, is a real-time strategy game in which the player plays against human or computer opponents. The game is real time, which means that each participant develops and manages his/her military base and his army simultaneously and with no interruptions in order to beat his/her competitors. The player does not have an avatar in this game, but controls a number of semi-autonomous units. These are given specific orders such as build, patrol or attack, which then are carried out until the unit dies or is given a new order by the player.

In *Hitman Contracts* sound is important as a system that informs the player about his/her own status in relation to the game environment. Guards will shout at the avatar if he/she acts suspiciously, and the background music will change according to whether the situation is calm or critical. This makes sound an important feature that works to inform the player about how characters in the environment will react to his/her presence, at the same time as it works to create mood. Also, the sombre music often tends to blend with the environmental ambient background sounds, creating a mood that suggests a continuous danger state, while also discretely reflecting the life of a professional assassin as one coloured by moral dilemmas. In *Warcraft III* the sound is important for different reasons. The high pace of the game, and the focus on controlling several processes at the same time, makes it necessary to keep the player updated at all times on events taking place both on- and off-screen. The game is set in a medieval fantasy world, and each unit has verbal responses that reflect their place in a feudal society and underline the units as caricatures. This creates a light-hearted and humorous mood on the audio side. It is also important to point out that the player's representation in the two games has consequences for the realization of audio. In *Hitman Contracts* the game system may communicate to the player through the avatar, by making all sounds address the avatar instead of the player. In *Warcraft III*, on the other hand, there is no avatar, and instead the game system communicates directly with the player situated outside of the game world. This means that communication stays within the boundaries of the diegetic game world in *Hitman Contracts*, while in *Warcraft III* units that are represented as characters within the virtual world communicate with a space located outside the diegetic world of the game.

Consequences for the game as virtual world and as usability system

The participants in the study did not know beforehand that the sound would be removed from the game half way through the session, and their immediate reaction towards this sudden modification was that they thought playing without sound would be problematic. They felt that they lost control, and described this feeling in terms of other perceptions. One of the participants felt that he was being left completely in the dark (Petter, answer 31), while another compared it to losing a leg (Nils, answer 46). It was also underlined by a few that the game felt less engaging without any sound (Geir, answer 25; Stian, answer 34). One participant admitted that he never thought that sound would affect a game like *Warcraft III* very much, but that this view had changed during the course of the research session:

> I knew I thought it's duller to play without sound. But I didn't know I would think it affected the game so much. But it's like, I have seen people play Counter-Strike without sound and that doesn't work [laughter]. (Nils, answer 38).

In specific genres such as first-person shooters like *Counter-Strike*, where two teams play each other in a hostage scenario, this participant believed sound was an important feature, but he did not think that the same applied for a strategy game before participating in the research. Nevertheless, after playing with a certain focus on the auditory part of the game, he realized that sound also plays an important role in this genre in relation to how successfully he could play the game. Below we will see how the absence of sound decreases the sense of control in the game, and how the sense of presence and a lifelike universe is affected. We will also see that although the absence of sound changes the attentive focus of the player, it does not lead to a decrease in attention. In addition, it will be demonstrated that in certain situations, removing the sound also contributes to removing certain distractions from the game experience.

Information and orientation

One of the reasons why the players experienced a loss of control and a sense of helplessness when the sound was removed was that one of the two access points between the game and the player had disappeared. This has specific consequences for the players' ability to orient themselves in the game environment. Compared to visual perception, auditory perception has the fortunate advantage that it does not require a listener to be oriented in a specific direction. This means that sound is useful in situations where the visual system is not available, for instance to provide information about events located out of line of sight, or when the visual system is busy with other tasks.[8] Removing sound from a computer game will therefore decrease the player's ability to locate enemies and receive information about specific events. This is also demonstrated by Stockburger, who points out that sound objects connected to specific visual objects or events have the ability to situate objects in the game environment.[9]

In *Hitman Contracts* the avatar positions the player as a character existing within the game world, and the game environment therefore reacts to the player's presence. This means that everything that goes on in the surroundings may affect the player's character directly, and the sound of a door opening behind the avatar may therefore contain crucial information about the situation. One of the participants believed that removing the sound in this game severely constrains the player's understanding of what goes on in the game:

---

8   G.B. Kramer et al., *The Sonification Report: Status of the Field and Research Agenda*.

9   Stockburger, 'The Game Environment from an Auditory Perspective'.

> You don't get any feedback from the surroundings ... [The sound] contributes to placing you in ... when you hear a door open up behind you, or hear a door opening and there're no doors before you, you think it's behind you. But it's like ... you don't want to end up in that situation (Geir, answer 25).

The playing situation becomes a very different one without sound, since there is no possibility that the players can orient themselves in relation to events outside range of sight. The result is that the sense of spatiality disappears, and consequently the players have no way of understanding the specific situation. According to Stockburger, providing information about what is going on in other locations is one of the most critical roles of game audio, and he calls it the acousmatic function with reference to Pierre Schaeffer and Michel Chion's use of the term.[10] The acousmatic function refers to the situation where one can hear a sound but cannot see the source. In games, acousmatic sounds are important since they provide information to the player in situations where the visuals have no power to do so. In *Warcraft III*, for instance, the player monitors a range of processes and events simultaneously, and in this respect acousmatic sound is a vital orienting system. When the player visually attends to one part of the game, there may still be processes going on offscreen in different parts of the game. For instance, when the player is moving his army in the direction of the enemy base, there will still be processes going on in his own base. In order to keep track of what is going on back home, the sound works as an important system of information:

> If you're working on one part [of the map], doing many things and then you get 'summoning complete' or 'building complete', then perhaps you start thinking, what was that I was building which should've been finished [by now] (Anders, answer 16).

Here the player is allowed to concentrate on different tasks when a process has been started, since acousmatic sound will provide information about changes in status. Without these sounds the player must double-check visually on all processes, thereby having less control over all situations. Worse, the player would run the risk of forgetting processes he/she had already started:

> If I'm out with a couple of men and my hero's hunting xp [experience points] for the next level, and I don't hear anything from the town, I would've ignored the town. Would have had like, three thousand gold and three thousand trees and only five buildings (Lars, answer 18).

In this sense sound also becomes a reminder that helps the player keep track of processes. These examples demonstrate Stockburger's emphasis on the importance of acousmatic sounds, and supports the view of auditory display and sonification theories that sound is a tool that is beneficial in monitoring and alarm situations.[11]

Sound may also be used as an informative system that enables listeners to pick up a higher amount of data compared to the visual system, and sound is therefore

---

10 Stockburger, 'The Game Environment from an Auditory Perspective', p. 10.

11 G.B. Kramer et al., *The Sonification Report: Status of the Field and Research Agenda*.

suitable when providing a lot of simultaneous information to a listener.[12] In computer games this means that the player will receive less detailed information about events and processes in the absence of sound. One of the *Warcraft III* participants explains that in chaotic situations, it is not easy to see what is going on. This is especially evident in battle situations. The player cannot see how much health enemy units have left, but sound indicates when units die, what kinds of units are involved and how large the armies are:

> I recognise the attack sounds and death screams of some of the units. So I notice – if I hear a lot of bows, sounds from archers attacking, then I know they're attacking, so if I suddenly hear the death scream of one of the heroes I think, ha ha. There! My archers got him (Richard, answer 27).

The participant here knows from experience that his army has archers, while the enemy does not. Thus, hearing a lot of bow strings compared to the sound of enemy units is a good thing. When he also hears screams from an enemy hero, the participant knows that his army has been able to take out one of the most central enemy units. Although it is possible to see a difference between the units, it is hard to register exactly which units die and which stand without a high level of visual attention due to the large number of units in play. Using sound instead, the game frees the visual system from unnecessary tasks, at the same time as auditory information provides more detailed information than the visual system could do alone. We see a similar example in *Hitman Contracts*, where the participant was able to identify whether he hit or missed the enemy with a piercing weapon based on the sound:

> [The sound of] the knife and the meat hook. They are ok, since then you know you've done something. Also because … yes, there it was again. The sound when I fail to hit something, too (Anders, answer 10).

In this game the player has no visual meter that monitors enemy health. Instead he/she must evaluate the situation based on the sound, which has a different characteristic related to whether the player hits or misses. In this sense, sound contributes to an identification of the situation and supports the process of playing the game.[13] The usability role of sound as a response system that provides immediate feedback to player actions becomes very evident in this situation.[14] When sounds like these are absent, the player has a less detailed information system telling him/her how he/she is doing in specific situations. Although lack of sound in these contexts does not make the game unplayable, it makes the player's status in relation to the opponent uncertain.

These examples also demonstrate how the absence of sound isolates the player from certain information, and that usability messages become harder to apprehend.

---

12 Scaletti and Craig cited in G.B. Kramer et al., *The Sonification Report: Status of the Field and Research Agenda*.

13 Collins, 'An Introduction to the Participatory and Non-Linear Aspects of Video Games Audio'.

14 Stockburger, 'The Game Environment from an Auditory Perspective', pp. 6, 9. See also Jørgensen, 'On the Functional Aspects of Computer Game Audio', p. 49.

Without sound, the visual system alone must interpret and notice events and information that normally would not require much attention.[15] In this situation the eye perceives more slowly because it has too many tasks to which it must attend.[16] One of the participants described how he repeatedly clicked a unit because the game did not provide any response to the fact that an object had been selected:

> Sometimes I sit like, I often hear 'click', then you hear 'not enough gold', and perhaps I click once or twice more. But now it was 'click-click-click-click-click-click'. Oh shit. [laughter] Nothing came up. So it took me a little longer to notice things (Richard, answer 34).

When the sound was removed, the participant experienced clicking several times before realizing that the order had already been carried out. Thus, the player's ability to know whether an order has been received or not decreases when the auditory system is removed. The participant also noticed an increased reaction time, since he was dependent on actually seeing what was going on before knowing for certain that the system had accepted his order. This also supports the idea that channel redundancy, that is, presenting the same information on several channels, increases the likelihood that the information will be received.[17]

When reaction time increases, the player's overall performance also decreases. This can be traced back to the acousmatic function of sound discussed above.[18] One of the participants explained that the reason for the decrease in performance was that he did not receive information about events that happened off-screen, that still had equal relevance to what was within range of sight in the game world:

> The first thing I notice is that my time of reaction has increased by ten. For example, in the beginning I sent a farmer through the woods at midnight … And I noticed at once when he was attacked because of the sound. But now … My whole base was attacked three centimetres below [the edge of] the screen, and I didn't notice anything. And it changes things very drastically, you're not able to move things where you want them, and you're not able to build defences as fast as you would've wanted to (Lars, answer 33).

The participant reported that his playing generally became less successful, since the environment failed to inform him what was going on in the surroundings. In addition to being connected to the fact that certain pieces of information cannot be attended to or are harder to grasp, performance also decreases because the player needs to refocus his/her attention on the visual channel. This sudden change is unfamiliar, and contributes to making the whole game seem different from ordinary playing circumstances. All in all, the sense of lack of control is connected to the fact that the player cognitively must adjust him/herself to new mental models since new ways of relating to limited game output must be learned.

---

15 Heeter and Gomes, 'It's Time for Hypermedia to Move to Talking Pictures'.
16 Chion, *Audio-Vision. Sound on Screen*, p. 11.
17 Heeter and Gomes, 'It's Time for Hypermedia to Move to Talking Pictures'.
18 Stockburger, 'The Game Environment from an Auditory Perspective', p. 10.

Emotional connections to the game world

Another issue that felt very pressing for all participants was that the sense of presence in the game world disappeared together with the sound. Presence is an important concept in the study of virtual environments, and refers to 'the successful feeling of "being there" in a synthetic environment'.[19] The sense of presence demands that we direct our perceptions to a different reality than that of which we are currently part. This means that feeling present in a game is feeling that you are part of the environment in question, and that you understand the world presented as a three-dimensional reality that can be interacted with in a similar way to our own world. According to Alison McMahan, an increase in the sense of presence can result from a range of different factors. Most important for this chapter, one of these factors is the graphical and auditory realism of the environment,[20] or how well the environment sounds and looks like the real world. The degree of immersiveness generated by the interface is a second important contributor to the sense of presence.[21] The sense of presence is enhanced by how the users perceive the space, in terms of how well they can orient themselves in space.[22] Stockburger also points out that specific sound objects have the power to aurally define and identify specific areas in the game environment.[23] He states that music is often connected to specific locations in a similar manner. Since music generally has a huge emotional impact on listeners, it also works to enhance the player's engagement in the game world.[24] The thoughts of both McMahan and Stockburger support Whalen's idea that game audio may expand the game world by creating an awareness of the game space and providing characteristic auditory features of it.[25] The importance of sound in creating a sense of presence, and a feeling that one is in the environment in computer games, suggests that the absence of sound would affect the feeling of the game world to a great degree. One of the participants believed that *Hitman Contracts* did not feel right when played without sound:

> It's like [gun scenes] don't work right, because it's like you're reminded that this actually is a computer game. So when there's no sound, it's just like two animated figures standing there, shooting at each other (Rasmus, answer 13).

The sound normally provides the environment with a sense of life, and when the sound was removed, the participant was reminded that what he saw were just computer

---

19 Marie-Laure Ryan, *Narrative as Virtual Reality: Immersion and Interactivity in Literature and Electronic Media* (Baltimore, 2001), pp. 67–8.

20 Alison McMahan, 'Immersion, Engagement, and Presence. A Method for Analyzing 3-D Video Games', in Mark J.P. Wolf, and Bernard Perron (eds), *The Video Game Theory Reader* (New York, 2003), p. 72.

21 McMahan, 'Immersion, Engagement, and Presence. A Method for Analyzing 3-D Video Games', p. 73.

22 McMahan, 'Immersion, Engagement, and Presence. A Method for Analyzing 3-D Video Games', p. 75.

23 Stockburger, 'The Game Environment from an Auditory Perspective', p. 8.

24 Stockburger, 'The Game Environment from an Auditory Perspective', p. 9.

25 Whalen, 'Play Along: An Approach to Video Game Music'.

graphics, and that the figures shooting at each other were animated features. In this sense, the illusion of an actual world disappears and the artificiality of the virtual surroundings becomes clearer. The sense of presence disappears in this situation because the game world does not seem consistent anymore[26]. In the natural world objects produce sound when manipulated, and when they do not do that in the game world, the environment loses part of its similarity to the real world environment. One of the participants playing *Warcraft III* had a similar experience to that above. He described how the military units felt more artificial with no sounds present,[27] and described them as nothing but 'numbers':

> It becomes like, you become more systematic, they become almost like numbers. Like, that unit fell, that unit fell, and now I lost one and stuff. There's almost no emotion behind the fact that they're falling (Stian, answer 36).

From providing an impression of being living human beings, the units are now reduced to nothing but a large number of entities. This observation is supported by Stockburger, who points out that sound effects objects create a cognitive link between a visual object and a sound, and enables the orientation of objects in space.[28] In this sense, removing sound is also removing a sense of physicality from game objects and units.[29] The lack of lifelikeness without sound makes the player become less emotionally engaged, since the virtual world seems to have fallen apart. Consequently, the player becomes more distanced from the game world, or feels even alienated, as the participant above described.

A last interesting effect related to the sense of presence is that in the case of *Hitman Contracts*, one of the participants reported becoming more scared and even a little paranoid when the sound was removed. Since he could not receive any auditory information about what was happening out of the line of sight, he felt that dangers may be hiding in the shadows everywhere around him:

> Yes, first you get like plugs in your ears, and it was just a lack of hearing. But after a while, then ... I get much more paranoid. I become actually a little scared when there's no sound, because you need to hear if things are around you, as it were. Where things are (Jonas, answer 26).

The player's sense of helplessness when playing without sound affected his sense of being within the game world. The participant became especially aware of the informative and orienting roles of sound when not being able to use audio for getting a sense of what was going on around him in the game environment. The sense of distance to objects and events disappeared, leading to a situation that was even more frightening than hearing enemies around. This reaction strongly supports Stockburger's emphasis on the acousmatic role of game audio,[30] and shows that

---

26 McMahan, 'Immersion, Engagement, and Presence. A Method for Analyzing 3-D Video Games', p. 69.

27 Chion, *Audio-Vision. Sound on Screen,* p. 14–15.

28 Stockburger, 'The Game Environment from an Auditory Perspective', p. 6.

29 Whalen, 'Play Along: An Approach to Video Game Music'.

30 Stockburger, 'The Game Environment from an Auditory Perspective', p. 10.

game audio that refers to off-screen events may be even more important than audio connected to onscreen events.

Although a lot of information disappears in the absence of game audio, there are also many distractions which disappear with the sound. In the quote above, Stian described how he played in a more systematic way when he became emotionally detached from the game world as a result of the lack of sound. It was easier to concentrate on the tasks in the game without sound, without getting distracted by the mood following the auditory atmosphere of the game. This became very evident for one of the participants, who played *Hitman Contracts* in an aggressive manner that made non-playing characters run around in fear of the uncontrolled gunman:

> It's a very chaotic situation, and when the sound was on, I played in a chaotic way. But now when the sound's turned off and I became more systematic, it was partly because the immersion in that chaos was equal to zero. It's almost the same as in role playing games. If you don't immerse yourself into the character, you can per definition play more effectively. But it becomes much worse role playing (Lars, answer 27).

When playing in an aggressive manner, the participant found that the situation became very chaotic. Guards and civilians were running around shouting and screaming, accompanied by up-beat and fast-paced music. In this situation, the sound became yet another feature of distraction. With the sound turned off, the distractions decreased and the participant found it easier to concentrate on the objectives of the game. He compared it to pen and paper role playing games, where being 'in character', or playing the role of a specific personality, may exclude some behaviours and strategies. In a similar manner, sound affects the player's experience of the game emotionally, with the consequence that the player plays the game in a more or less calculated manner. This example demonstrates that too much sound may lead to an overload of information, and that in such cases, it may ease performance and concentration to remove some of the sources of information, in this case audio.[31] Another participant also explained how his concentration in *Warcraft III* was taken away from what was important because of information overload:

> Well, sometimes the sound can take away some of your concentration. You're working on something and then you hear that a building you've been waiting for is finished, then you want to jump right to it although perhaps you should've done other things. So it may … be a little too much sometimes (Anders, answer 39).

The participant knew that sound was important for performance in this game, and that it provided usability information about processes and events. When he heard sounds that signalled a change in status, such as a finished process, he wanted to check on it immediately, even when he was busy with other tasks that might be more pressing. In this situation the absence of sound appeared for the participant as a sudden opportunity to concentrate on what was important, instead of trying to attend to all sounds at once. In this sense, overload of sound decreases the player's ability to distinguish between more and less important pieces of information.

---

31 Heeter and Gomes, 'It's Time for Hypermedia to Move to Talking Pictures'.

Although Collins argues that sound can serve to focus our attention,[32] it also seems that the player's attention changes when the sound is removed. Without sound, the player must utilize visual perception of data that earlier would be provided through auditory information. In this sense, the player must change his/her attentive focus from relying on both auditory and visual perception to visual perception only. This sudden new focus is unfamiliar, and the participants were discontent in having to read certain messages instead of listening to them, since they often failed to notice them in the absence of sound:

> I noticed that I had to start looking much more at the messages displayed down here, and that was annoying sometimes, and I didn't always notice things happening (Richard, answer 26).

Since the utilization of sound frees the visual system from attending to a lot of data, such as written messages rolling over the screen, it becomes easier to process a lot of simultaneous information. This is also supported by the fact that presenting the same information over different perceptual channels increases the likelihood that a message will be understood.[33]

Since sound has the property to enhance a visual or haptic display by providing a second channel of information,[34] we may easily believe that the ability to attend to and comprehend what is going on in the game world decreases in the absence of sound. Nevertheless, even though attention and apprehension do change when the game is modified in this manner, the level of attention apparently remains the same. One of the participants believed that what changed was the balance between auditory and visual perception:

> Well, the level of attention remains the same. Although I actually think it increases when I play with no sound, because it's like you're deaf or something (Rasmus, answer 12).

The participant claimed that he had the same high level of attention as before, but now the auditory part disappeared and what remained was the visual attention. The visual attention became sharpened since it remained the only perceptual threshold between him and the game.

It is also important to note that even though the game experience changes, and the system becomes less responsive, the most experienced players already have a very close relationship to the game as system, and know that the system responds even when they do not receive the information aurally. One of the participants was convinced that unfamiliarity was the reason why difficulties in playing occurred immediately after the sound was turned off:

> Yes, in fact, the first seconds ... I became a little, like, woah – what's happening now. But I soon got used to it. My reaction became much slower, I'm certain about that. But I don't

---

32 Collins, 'An Introduction to the Participatory and Non-Linear Aspects of Video Games Audio'.

33 Heeter and Gomes, 'It's Time for Hypermedia to Move to Talking Pictures'.

34 G.B. Kramer et al., *The Sonification Report: Status of the Field and Research Agenda*.

know ... The difference isn't really that great, I'm so familiar with what's happening, I'm so used to attacking in a specific manner if a spot turns up, then I have to do this and that (Stian, answer 33).

The participant had a certain routine when it came to playing the game, and he always reacted in the same manner. His style of playing also utilized the visual markers such as text and spots on the mini-map, which meant that he still received the information although the sound was gone. The participant did, however, believe that his reaction time increased, which underlines that redundancy increases the performance of the players.[35]

Conclusion

All in all we see that the games were affected on two levels when the sound was removed. On the one hand, the usability of the system decreased, since the players did not receive any responses from the system regarding their own actions and commands. Likewise, the players received no warnings or alerts from the system about abnormalities. Although both responses and alerts often can be detected visually as movements, text or as highlighted interface elements, these may be difficult to grasp when the eyes are busy with other tasks. On the other hand, the mood, sense of presence and the feeling of a lifelike world disappeared, and the games revealed themselves as nothing but animated graphics on a screen. In this sense, the games suffered both as user-oriented game systems and as virtual worlds when sound was not present, which means that both the progression through the game and the sense of presence in the game environment were affected.[36]

However, we see that these consequences have different relevance in different games. The strategy game *Warcraft III* was most severely affected on the level of the usability of the system, while the stealth game *Hitman Contracts* was most clearly affected on the level of presence in the game world. In *Warcraft III* the players experienced problems receiving important information. Alerts about enemy attacks were harder to grasp, and the system became less responsive. Status notifications about off-screen processes were also lost without sound. The reason for this is first and foremost because of the player's positioning in the game. As an external force situated outside the game world, the player's role is to command units and manage situations from an indirect point of view. This means that the player has no control over every single action that the units take, and must often leave them alone while attending to other tasks. In such situations audio becomes a necessary acousmatic information tool. In *Hitman Contracts*, on the other hand, the sense of presence was affected to a greater degree when sound was removed. This became especially evident when participants reported that distractions became fewer when the sound was removed. *Hitman Contracts* has a gloomy soundtrack supposed to reflect the not-so-glorious life of a professional assassin, and the audio team behind the game underlined a desire to put the players in an unpleasant mood when playing the game.

---

35 Heeter and Gomes, 'It's Time for Hypermedia to Move to Talking Pictures'.
36 Whalen, 'Play Along: An Approach to Video Game Music'.

When this was removed from the game, the player was freed from a specific bias, which indirectly may have caused them to act more carefully in the game.

It should be kept in mind that removing sound may have additional effects in other genres. For instance, in a dancing game like *Dance Dance Revolution* it is likely that the players would be physically constrained since there would be no rhythm that they could follow. From an overarching perspective, the dual role of game audio to serve as a central usability feature while also adding to the sense or presence of a lifelike universe is connected to a specific ideal in software design, that the computer system appears invisible or transparent. Sound is a major contributor in that respect, since it may remove parts of the visual interface while maintaining or even increasing the usability of the system. This means that sound helps change the player's attention from the visual interface to other, more pressing tasks.[37] However, when audio partly takes over for the visual interface, it merges with the depicted virtual world. In doing this, audio may support the usability of the system in different ways. Sounds that seem to be motivated by a sense of realism in the game world are given usability functions. This was the case with guards shouting in *Hitman Contracts* – in this sense, diegetic characters produce the sound, but from the point of view of the game rules, the sound works as a warning signal. Alternatively, auditory system messages with a clear usability role are implemented into the game world as diegetic sounds. We find this in *Warcraft III* when units produce utterances as 'what do you need' in response to manipulation. Extra-diegetic game music may also appear as joint mood providers and usability features when a change in melody signals an event in the game environment. When merges like these happen, it may feel intuitive to claim that the usability sounds become 'unheard'.[38] Usability oriented signalling sounds are normally meant to be heard and reacted to consciously, but when they merge with the virtual environment, they become seamlessly part of the game environment. In this sense, their communicative role may become more transparent, but it is important to see that transparent and 'unheard' are not equals. Although masked as mood-enhancing features, the sounds are still important usability signals and it is crucial that the player apprehends them. This means that they are still heard and reacted to consciously, which is emphasized by the fact that players' performance is indeed affected when the sound is removed from the game.

---

37 Heeter and Gomes, 'It's Time for Hypermedia to Move to Talking Pictures'.

38 See Claudia Gorbman, *Unheard Melodies? Narrative Film Music* (Bloomington, IN, 1987).

Chapter 12

Music theory in music games

Peter Shultz

What do expert *Dance Dance Revolution* players have that beginners don't? Everyone who has played that game, or any other music-based video game, has experienced the fumbling first attempt, the physical awkwardness of learning a new visual interface and a new set of gestures. Those who have persevered know the gradual transformation of an overwhelming flood of arrows (or discs or lines) into a transparent representation of physical gesture. Music games, such as the *Dance Dance Revolution* series (hereinafter *DDR*), *Guitar Hero*, *Karaoke Revolution* and so on, require players to relearn habits of movement and thought, and the pay-offs are amazing: what was difficult becomes effortless, and what was impossible becomes simple. In this chapter I would like to investigate what sorts of concepts and skills these music games entail.

Of course, every game teaches skills and concepts of one sort or another. James Paul Gee observes that since video games are judged in part by their length and difficulty, the only way they can hope to win an audience is by building in mechanisms to encourage 'good learning'. He proceeds to examine several games in different genres and derives 36 'learning principles', including these:

- Achievement Principle: For learners of all levels of skill there are intrinsic rewards from the beginning, customized to each learner's skill, effort, and growing mastery and signalling the learner's ongoing achievements.
- Practice Principle: Learners get lots and lots of practice in a context where the practice is not boring (i.e., in a virtual world that is compelling to learners on their own terms and where the learners experience ongoing success). They spend lots of time on task.
- Ongoing Learning Principle: The distinction between learner and master is vague, since learners, thanks to the operation of the 'regime of competence' principle listed next, must, at higher and higher levels, undo their routinized mastery to adapt to new or changed conditions. There are cycles of new learning, automatization, undoing automatization, and new reorganized automatization.
- 'Regime of Competence' Principle: The learner gets ample opportunity to operate within, but at the outer edge of, his or her resources, so that at those points things are felt as challenging but not 'undoable'.[1]

---

1 James Paul Gee, *What Video Games Have to Teach Us About Learning and Literacy* (New York, 2003), pp. 208–209. In Gee's list these are rules 11 through 14.

These four principles strongly recall Mihaly Csikszentmihalyi's characterization of 'optimal experience' as a continuous 'flow' of ever-increasing challenge, accompanied by constantly increasing ability. The concept of flow is shown most simply by a graph as in Figure 12.1, in which flow results from a balance between challenge and ability. If the challenge level of a task exceeds the learner's ability, she experiences anxiety, and if the task is too easy, she experiences boredom.[2]

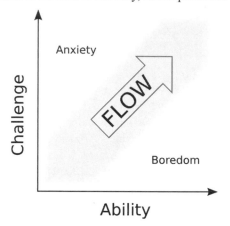

Figure 12.1   The flow region (adapted from Csikszentmihalyi)

Although Csikszentmihalyi formulated his theory mostly from interviews with artists and athletes, its applications to education and game design are immediately apparent. In a discussion of flow in video game design, Jenova Chen points out that different players have different expectations of what constitutes a fair level of challenge: 'hardcore' players expect steep challenges at all times, whereas other players may prefer to learn more gradually, as shown in Figure 12.2.[3] Games that wish to appeal to a wide audience must give the players sufficient options for difficulty at any moment, so players can choose appropriate levels of challenge at each moment in order to keep the game within their 'flow' regions.

---

2   Mihaly Csikszentmihalyi, *Beyond Boredom and Anxiety* (San Francisco, 1977), p. 49.

3   Jenova Chen, 'Flow in Games (and Everything Else)', *Communications of the ACM* 50/4 (April 2007): 31–4.

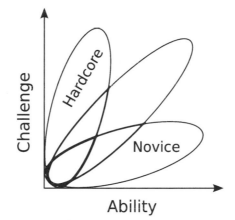

Figure 12.2   Different players have different flow regions (adapted from Chen)

But what is the player learning in a music game? Certainly there is some truth to the popular characterization of video games as tests of speedy reflexes; many games reward fast reaction times and the ability to process new information quickly. Equally important, however, is the player's development of a conceptual framework that allows them to deal efficiently with new information. Gee's principles of learning focus on semiotic structures, with three major dimensions comprising the core of a game's 'content'. Players simultaneously:

- learn to interpret the game's signs and appreciate the relationships between them;
- achieve fluency in its 'semiotic domains' and gain the ability to participate in their affinity groups; and
- learn to think critically (on the 'metalevel', in Gee's terminology) about the relationships these have with other semiotic domains.[4]

In a game like *SimCity*, for example, players explore the relationships between taxation, commerce, natural disasters and so forth. As they master this conceptual vocabulary, they also develop beliefs and theories about these relationships, which they can discuss with other players. And all the while they probe the game's simulation based on their beliefs about 'real-life cities' and evaluate the game's responses against these beliefs. They are certainly doing many other things as well, but these examples will serve to illustrate Gee's point.

---

4   Gee, *What Video Games Have to Teach Us About Learning and Literacy*, pp. 13–50. Gee explains the term 'semiotic domain' on page 18: 'By a semiotic domain I mean any set of practices that recruits one or more modalities (e.g., oral or written language, images, equations, symbols, sounds, gestures, graphs, artefacts, etc.) to communicate distinctive types of meanings. Here are some examples of semiotic domains: cellular biology, post-modern literary criticism, first-person-shooter video games, high-fashion advertisements, Roman Catholic theology, modernist painting, midwifery, rap music, wine connoisseurship – through a nearly endless, motley, and ever-changing list.'

Although music games do not usually teach musical skills and concepts directly, nor do they generally employ traditional Western instruments or notation (more on this later), they nonetheless prompt players to master semiotic domains related to traditional musical pursuits, and to examine those relationships critically. Thus even when players do not learn musical concepts or performance skills per se, the skills and concepts they develop translate easily to those domains. Brent Auerbach has used a game in the *DDR* series to teach rhythmic dictation, and he reports that 'Because it is so well-designed to model musical performance, undergraduates take to it quite naturally and quickly sense its relevance to their applied music studies.'[5]

Having distinguished properly musical activities from their simplified in-game models, I would now like to undo this distinction and examine music games as a species of pedagogical treatise that reflects interesting concepts of musical space and parses complex musical phenomena into groups of simpler structures, much like traditional analytical reductions. Of course these concepts are not 'music theory' in the academic sense of published analyses and systems, but rather in the more inclusive sense articulated by Lawrence Zbikowski, who sees music theory as 'a response to a problem. The problem is that of musical understanding: how it is that we can make sense of sequences of non-linguistic patterned sound, that we can do so with amazing rapidity, and that (often as not) we can return to these or similar sound sequences and find continued reward.'[6]

Zbikowski's formulation seems particularly apt here, since the music in these games is itself explicitly framed as a problem that demands a response. As with most games, quick reflexes alone do not guarantee success: a player's physical response must be driven by a sufficiently robust conceptual response, a theory about the game's musical system. As I mentioned earlier, video games rarely, if ever, use traditional Western music notation. The games that come closest, Nintendo's *Mario Paint* (1992) and *Animal Crossing* (2001), are not usually considered music games at all. They provide staves on which players can place note-heads to compose simple tunes, but only as diversions within larger game worlds. This is not altogether surprising, since most music games demand little nuance in pitch, certainly not enough to justify the full apparatus of tonal notation. But even rhythm-based games tend to use customized, idiosyncratic systems to indicate duration, rather than Western note shapes.

Flow theory suggests a simple explanation for game developers' rejection of Western rhythmic notation: its complexities, in particular the menagerie of note shapes used to indicate duration, could frustrate a novice player. By devising more intuitive systems of visual representation, game designers can offer players a wider range of challenge levels, which broadens their games' appeal.

But what makes these systems intuitive? They vary from game to game, but they almost all have one feature in common: they map musical time directly to physical

---

5   Brent Auerbach, 'Pedagogical Applications of the Video Game *Dance Dance Revolution* to the Undergraduate Aural Skills Classroom' (paper presented at the annual meeting for the Society for Music Theory, Los Angeles, California, 3 November 2006).

6   Lawrence Zbikowski, *Conceptualizing Music: Cognitive Structures, Theory, and Analysis* (New York, 2002), p. x.

space. Longer notes appear longer on the screen, exactly in proportion to their duration; if one note looks twice as long as another, it is to be played twice as long. Thus musical time appears in these games as a *res extensa* that can be understood and manipulated as a physical object.[7] By contrast, Western notation maps time to space only in the loose sense that time always proceeds rightward: the width of a printed measure implies nothing about its duration, as it is the shapes of the notes and rests (and expressive markings such as fermatas or ritardandi) that show the relative durations of musical events, not their placement on the page.

This analogy between musical time and physical space is not unique to video games but appears throughout music software of all types: waveform editors, MIDI sequencers, drum machines and module trackers all represent duration spatially. Even in printed notation some precedent exists in the twentieth-century use of graphic scores for electro-acoustic and experimental music, and in the use of 'time unit box system' (TUBS) notation for ethno-musicological transcription. Brent Auerbach has also compared *DDR*'s notation to the pedagogical 'proto-notation' developed by Gary Karpinski.[8]

Although most music games have a 'time axis', it appears in different orientations in different games, as shown in Figure 12.3. The arrangement shown in 12.3 is the most similar to Western notation, with time progressing left to right and pitch arranged vertically. I have labelled it the 'reading mode', as its layout resembles that of a musical score: the game's camera pans over the score from left to right (that is, in the direction of the diagram's time arrow), and the note events approach from the right. The *Karaoke Revolution* series uses this mode with rising and falling lines to show pitch contour, and the resemblance to a musical score is unmistakable. The drumming game series *Donkey Konga* and *Taiko Drum Master* use a modified version of reading mode: since there is no need to indicate pitch, they arrange the notes into a single horizontal line and use shape and colour to indicate 'quality' (left/right/both drums, clap or rim shot).

---

7 This claim does not quite hold for games such as *Elite Beat Agents*, *Mad Maestro* and *Samba de Amigo* that give action cues from several different directions, or in several different arrangements. These games cannot be said to have a single 'time axis', but they still map musical time to physical space in that the player can interpret distance and speed in the game's display to judge the amount of time remaining until an action is required.

8 Brent Auerbach, (unpublished).

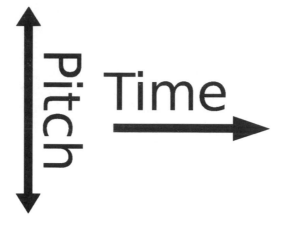

Figure 12.3   Reading mode

Another common arrangement is the 'driving mode', shown in Figure 12.4. Here the player moves 'into the screen' as the music progresses (again following the time arrow), so that the note events seem to approach from the front. This presents the song as a space through which the player drives.

Figure 12.4   Driving mode

We should note that these two spatial arrangements also have a history in video game genres: games in reading mode can be considered a species of side-scroller (a term that usually denotes platform games like *Super Mario Bros.* and shooters like *Gradius*), while games in driving mode recall 3D flying and (unsurprisingly) driving games. Thus the designers of rhythm games did not invent these patterns of spatial organization specifically for music, but more likely borrowed them from other genres in which they had worked.

By contrast, the 'falling mode' shown in Figure 12.5 seems to be almost unique to the *Dance Dance Revolution* series and its imitators, with little precedent in other genres.[9] Here the notes rise up from the bottom of the screen as if the player is falling past them.

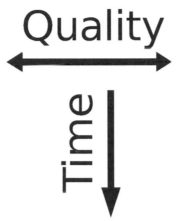

Figure 12.5   Falling mode (*Dance Dance Revolution* style)

The orientation of the notation forces the player to think about motion in unfamiliar ways and, in conjunction with the difficulty of coping with unexpected steps, threatens constantly to throw her off balance. The French writer Roger Caillois recognized the pleasure of this kind of disruption in his four-part taxonomy of games: competition (*agon*), chance (*alea*), mimicry and vertigo (*ilinx*, after the Greek word for 'waterfall').[10] Disorientation and vertigo are part of the challenge of *DDR*, so it is not surprising that its on-screen spatial orientation would suggest an unstable, unfamiliar bodily motion.

Each of these modes of orientation proposes a different mode of bodily engagement with the musical and gestural spaces the game projects, but they all rely on a common foundation: the identification of musical time with physical space. These games, along with the examples of music software and graphic notation mentioned above, illustrate more or less literally a pair of conceptual metaphors involving time: TIME IS A LANDSCAPE WE MOVE THROUGH and TIME IS SOMETHING MOVING TOWARD YOU.[11] George Lakoff, who introduced the term 'conceptual metaphor', sees them as deeply ingrained patterns of cross-domain understanding that surface in many types of human activity, most obviously in figures of speech like 'The new

---

9   Puzzle games like *Tetris* and shooters like *Galaga* often have vertically-orientated playing fields, but whereas *DDR*'s note arrows move upwards on the screen, *Tetris* blocks and *Galaga* enemies move down. The only other instances of falling mode that I am aware of are the puzzle game *Tetris Attack* (which gives much more of a sense that the blocks are rising than that the player is falling) and short sections of platform games such as *Battletoads*.

10   Roger Caillois, *Man, Play, and Games*, trans. Meyer Barash (Chicago, 2001).

11   George Lakoff, 'Metaphors with Target Domain: Time', University of California, Berkeley. http://cogsci.berkeley.edu/lakoff/targets/Time.html (accessed 11 June, 2007).

year is looming on the horizon' and 'The deadline for this project is approaching faster than any of us would like to admit.'[12]

Earlier I suggested that game designers invent these idiosyncratic systems of notation because they are particularly intuitive with respect to rhythm. Now we see that they are intuitive precisely because they draw on this common understanding of time. But only part of the challenge of music games derives from their rhythmic notation. Sometimes the physical gestures are just difficult to perform accurately and require more practice, and sometimes complicated sequences of gestures are hard to grasp. While the former problem is probably best resolved by lots of practice (see Gee's rule #12), players can achieve a holistic, synoptic understanding of elaborate gestures by learning to understand them in terms of simpler units. This learning strategy is most vividly illustrated by games that offer multiple difficulty settings for each song, so that the player experiences several gestural perspectives on the same recorded piece of music. As we will see, different games suggest markedly distinct models of musical complexity.

So far in this discussion we have ignored the element of scorekeeping. For this purpose, music games tend to prioritize quantifiable elements such as rhythm and pitch over more expressive aspects of performance such as excitement or charisma, although many games keep track of something along those lines (such as 'musical tension' in *Mad Maestro* or 'star power' in *Guitar Hero*), based on the player's cumulative accuracy in pitch and rhythm, and represented by the level of enthusiasm of an on-screen crowd. This apparently myopic musical view makes sense from the perspective of flow theory, as it allows the game to give clear feedback based on well-defined criteria of success. One has only to imagine how frustrating a game would be that graded players on 'excitement', with no further explanation, to see why these games depend so much on mechanical accuracy.

This derivation of expressive parameters directly from mechanical ones becomes a problem only when it drives the game to a flagrantly misconceived evaluation of the aesthetic value of a performance. Players who have mastered a song in *Guitar Hero*, for example (and who may be edging down into the 'boredom' area of Csikszentmihalyi's flow graph), can whip the virtual crowd into a frenzy with the whammy bar even while playing every note a semitone flat, and since *Karaoke Revolution* grades only on pitch accuracy, players are awarded the same score even if they invent their own words to the song or play it on a kazoo. These subversive strategies reflect what Gee calls 'metalevel thinking' about the semiotic domain of musical performance: by playing 'against the grain', players demonstrate not only fluency with the game's musical systems, but also a recognition of their differences from full-fledged musical performance.

Just as *Guitar Hero*'s scoring system favours some musical elements as more important than others, the structure of difficulty levels marks some musical events as more important than others. Every song offers four difficulty levels (Easy, Medium, Hard and Expert), and a perfect playthrough, in which every note of the song is triggered, will sound the same on every level. The differences lie in how many

---

12 Lawrence Zbikowski discusses conceptual metaphors for pitch in his book *Conceptualizing Music: Cognitive Structures, Theory, and Analysis*, p. 65–8.

triggering events are required, and how many frets may be employed. In Expert mode players generally trigger each musical note individually, using all five fret buttons on the controller. In Easy mode, a single stroke on the controller may trigger a short sequence of notes in the soundtrack, sometimes four or more in a very fast song, and the player uses only the lowest three frets. Therefore, a player who practises a song on progressively higher difficulty levels will learn a few 'key notes' on Easy mode, then gradually flesh out the details between them as they move up the ladder toward Expert. By the time they reach Expert level, their gestures rhythmically match the soundtrack, and they are using all five fret buttons to play more complex melodic contours. The idea of this arrangement is that novice players can approximate the gestures of familiar songs by playing a basic framework without being overwhelmed with musical detail. Then, as their skills develop, they gradually add more and more detail until they arrive at the finished product.

In effect, the developers employ a kind of reductive analysis to select certain notes as more important than others, allowing these important notes to percolate down into the easier difficulty levels, so that only the most structurally important notes make it down into Easy mode. This process should sound familiar to music theorists, who are accustomed to analysing music, particularly tonal music of the last four centuries, as simple structures decorated by progressive elaboration. This sort of reduction has a long, and as yet largely unexamined, history in music pedagogy, where students learn strategies for simplifying difficult passages, then gradually build them back up to their full complexity as they practise them. This is precisely what happens when a *Guitar Hero* player learns a song on Easy mode, then gradually moves up to Expert.

Academic music theorists try whenever possible to formalize these strategies for reduction, stating clearly the criteria on which they are based. Undoubtedly the most influential formalized reductive methodology is the late theory of Heinrich Schenker, who claimed that the entire universe of tonal music derives from the recursive elaboration of a few generic background structures.[13] Since Schenker presents his theory in generative terms, we should hesitate to call it a 'reductive' theory. Nevertheless, the practice of Schenkerian analysis is at least partly reductive, beginning with a finished piece of music and undoing these elaborations to expose a clear path to the background structure.[14]

There are other models of musical reduction as well. More recently, Fred Lerdahl and Ray Jackendoff have reinterpreted Schenker's ideas of progressive elaboration through a Chomskyian structural-linguistic model of hierarchy. Their theory, as outlined in *A Generative Theory of Tonal Music* and Lerdahl's *Tonal Pitch Space*, provides a set of explicit 'preference rules', algorithms to determine hierarchical

---

13 Heinrich Schenker, *Free Composition*, trans. Ernst Oster (New York, 1979).

14 A more nuanced view is that the analyst keeps the possible background structures in mind during the analysis, and so considers each interpretation from both the reductive and generative direction. This has been compared to Friedrich Schleiermacher's 'hermeneutic circle', a method of text interpretation that shuttles constantly between the detail and the whole.

relationships based on relationships of pitch and rhythm.[15] On a more abstract level, Robert Morris developed a system for representing melodic contour that permits systematic reduction by preserving the local extrema (highest and lowest points) of a line while smoothing out the passages in between.[16] These are just a few influential models from current music-theoretic practice; the history of music theory provides many more of greater and lesser degrees of formality.

The reductions in *Guitar Hero* are less formally consistent than those mentioned above, but they often reveal interesting and important musical structures that are not apparent from an examination of the musical surface alone. As an example, let us examine the riff from the chorus of 'Less Talk More Rokk', performed by the band Freezepop and used in *Guitar Hero II*. Figure 12.6 shows a sketch of the beginning as it appears in the game on Expert level, and Figure 12.7 shows transcriptions of the note events that represent it at every difficulty level, with each staff line corresponding to a fret button (three frets on Easy level, four on Medium and five on Hard and Expert. On the bottom staff is a transcription of the version heard on the game's soundtrack. The slurs on the Expert staff show opportunities for hammer-ons and pull-offs; only the first note in a slur group needs to be strummed, although every note must be fingered:

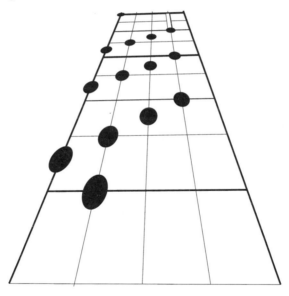

Figure 12.6   'Less Talk More Rokk' in *Guitar Hero* notation

---

15 Fred Lerdahl and Ray Jackendoff, *A Generative Theory of Tonal Music* (Cambridge, MA, 1983). Fred Lerdahl, *Tonal Pitch Space* (New York, 2001).

16 Robert Morris, 'New Directions in the Theory and Analysis of Musical Contour', *Music Theory Spectrum* 15 (1993), pp. 205–28.

Figure 12.7   'Less Talk More Rokk' in transcription

The rhythm on the Expert level is identical to that of the soundtrack version; every note counts as a musical event and must be fingered at the right time. In order to fit nine pitches onto five fret buttons, the developers have reduced the riff's contour, sacrificing the overall rising line of each measure in order to preserve the relationship between each pair of consecutive notes. Looking up at the Medium difficulty (skipping over Hard for now), we see just the opposite situation: the riff appears as a rising line, with none of the oscillations that were so prominent in Expert mode. By comparing the contours of Medium and Expert modes, we can see that Hard mode provides a transition between the two: it marries the rising line of Medium with the oscillations of Expert.

The procedure for rhythmic reduction is clear enough in this example: keep notes that fall on strong beats. Going from Expert to Hard level, this means preserving notes on quaver beats, and the transition from Medium to Easy simply repeats this process to retain notes that fall on crotchet beats. However, there is an exception both times: the last beat of the second bar retains more rhythmic detail than the rest of the riff. I read this as a pedagogical aid to the player: by introducing faster notes in small numbers and in a consistent location, the game eases the transition between difficulty levels. As we saw above, the contour in Hard mode can be read in a similar way, as a transitional guide to help the player progress from Medium to Expert mode.

This points to an interesting feature of the game's analytical system: it makes connections between the musical reductions used at different difficulty levels, encouraging the player to hear and think about each level in terms of the ones they have already played. To the extent that this happens (and I believe it usually does), the game becomes an advocate for a hierarchical order of musical awareness: players conceive of difficult patterns as elaborated versions of simpler ones, in a manner analogous to Schenkerian and other reductive or generative theories of music.

Notice that in this excerpt the rhythmic relations across difficulty levels are strictly inclusive; in other words, every time-point that carries an Easy note also carries a Medium note and so on, always adding notes without removing or shifting any as the difficulty increases. This is almost a universal feature of *Guitar Hero* difficulty levels.[17] This consistency of approach encourages a metrically hierarchical hearing of rhythm. With contour, however, there is no simple hierarchy of reductions. The Medium and Expert levels emphasize complementary aspects of the riff's contour; one could not be derived from the other. While the Expert riff is the most rhythmically faithful to the soundtrack, it is not simply the most accurate representation of the contour: each reduction here is like a shadow cast from a different direction, capturing different features of the whole. The experience of practising the riff from Easy mode up through Expert is thus like taking a walk around it in order to 'see' it from different angles.

This is perhaps even more the case in *DDR*, where the dance steps bear no predetermined relationship to the melody, and exhibit greater variation between difficulty levels. Brent Auerbach distinguishes between 'beat-based' and 'rhythm-based' songs: the former feature steps that align with the metric hierarchy, while the latter mirror some element of the musical texture (very often the vocal melody), with syncopations and other irregularities intact. The game interface projects the distinction between strong and weak beats by using differently coloured arrows. In order to succeed at the game and interpret these cues correctly, *DDR* players need to understand the relationship between rhythm and metre, and must be able to feel (literally) syncopations as displacements from strong to weak beats.

Some readers may object that these interpretations give players too much credit as intellectual music theorists, since these games ultimately require them merely to press the right buttons at the right times. However, those simple physical actions need support from a rich conceptual structure. Even if most players do not consciously consider all of these relationships, I would argue that they work behind the scenes to inform and structure musical learning. As players learn to interpret the games' notational systems, they also learn to process larger and more complicated musical units at a time and to examine the relationship between performance in the game and in conventional musical circles.

---

17   The few exceptions are riffs in Easy mode where a syncopated note might be shifted to the nearest downbeat rather than eliminated altogether. Generally, however, the game prefers to leave the syncopations in place, even if it means dropping out notes that would fall on the notated downbeat in order to preserve the contour.

Selected Annotated Bibliography[1]

Erica Kudisch

Some Notable Video Game Books in which Audio is Included

David Freeman, *Creating Emotion in Games: The Craft and Art of Emotioneering* (Berkeley, CA: New Riders, 2004). While this text deals more with the narrative aspect of game aesthetics, it does touch on music. Freeman notably compares the role of video game music to film music, and dwells on music's role in cutscenes as opposed to non-linearity. His analysis is not theoretical and does not use musical terminology, but the work as a whole is an entertaining and colloquial read and provides insight, geared at those in literary positions within a game design framework, so that they may elucidate their narrative intentions to the composers and other technical design staff.

Steven L. Kent, *The Ultimate History of Video Games* (Roseville, CA: Prima Publishing, 2001). Of all of the histories of video games available, this is perhaps the only one to mention music and sound technology as a component of the developing hardware and software. Displaying a marked bias towards popular games as opposed to unsung innovators, and encompassing a rather broad definition of 'video game'(including pinball machines, for instance), it offers perhaps the most comprehensive and well-conveyed history of the technical and commercial aspects of the medium.

Chris Kohler, *POWER-UP: How Japanese Video Games Gave the World an Extra Life* (Indianapolis: Pearson Education/BRADYGames, 2005). Chapter five, 'Game Music, Music Games', provides an invaluable English abstract of *Sou da, Game Music wo kikou!* (*All right, let's hear that Game Music!*: Micro Magazine, Tokyo, 2002), in addition to an example discography and two composer/designer interviews. Kohler conducts no theoretical analysis but a lot of qualitative analysis, and his profile of the gaming industry's role in the proliferation of its music is insightful.

Katie Salen and Eric Zimmerman, *The Video Game Design Reader: A Rules of Play Anthology* (Cambridge, MA: The MIT Press, 2006). Articles range from technical guidelines to comparative aesthetic studies. There is no theoretical analysis of game music, but various contributors discuss music's artistic role within the game's construction.

---

1   The works listed here are all in the English language and do not include technical manuals.

A Few Notable Video Game Audio Books

Alexander Brandon, *Audio for Games: Planning, Process, and Production* (Berkeley, CA: New Riders Games, 2004). As the title suggests, this book deals primarily with the planning and production workflows of game audio implementation. Recommended to anyone interested in the production process of game audio, and to those who wish to learn the basics of audio implementation.

Paul Hoffert, *Music for New Media: Composing for Video Games, Websites, Presentations, and Other Interactive Media* (Boston: Berklee Publishing, 2007). The book is divided into several sections. The first arc deals with hardware and software constraints, the second with composing for the disparate mixed media, with chapters seven and eight devoted entirely to game music; the third arc hones in on bureaucracy, including issues of collaboration with development teams. The layout incorporates a valuable lexicon and prose analysis of the different subsets of game music. Hoffert's goal is to educate the coming generation of game composers on the relevant statutes of the past and establish a canon, and his textbook accomplishes this with clear language, an expert layout and well-designed assignments.

Aaron Marks, *The Complete Guide to Game Audio* (Lawrence, KS: CMP Books, 2001). An industrial exposé masquerading as a how-to guide, Marks's book is the first of its kind. Though it lacks a theoretical bent, and though its CD components and directories are now somewhat dated, together with the book these serve as a historical insight into and documentation of the prior state of the industry.

George Sanger, *The Fat Man on Game Audio: Tasty Morsels of Sonic Goodness*, (Berkeley, CA: New Riders Games, 2003). An easy-to-read overview of game audio from one of the industry's most famous composers. It is written somewhat anecdotally, but includes a significant amount of advice and history for composers.

Articles in Scholarly Journals and Books

David Bessell, 'What's That Funny Noise? An Examination of the Role of Music in *Cool Boarders 2, Alien Trilogy* and *Medievil 2*', in Geoff King and Tanya Krzywinska (eds), *ScreenPlay: Cinema/Videogames/Interfaces* (London: Wallflower, 2002). A theoretical examination of video game music, Bessell's study is considered one of the pivotal papers in the field. As one of the earlier print sources on game audio, it lays some ground for future video game music scholarship.

Karen Collins, 'Flat Twos and the Musical Aesthetic of the Atari VCS', *Popular Musicology Online* (Issue 1, 2006). Collins describes her inspiration for this paper as wondering precisely why there had been so many flat twos (minor seconds) in the music of the Atari VCS; upon discovering that the supposed aesthetic trend was actually perpetuated by a hardware constraint, she set out to isolate the exact capabilities of the system. Her analysis is hardware-heavy and includes charts of an Atari VCS tuning system. The article is particularly useful for anyone who desires to commit to a similar deconstructive study.

Karen Collins, 'From Bits to Hits: Video Game Music Changes its Tune', *Film International* 13 (2004): pp. 4–19. In this history of game audio, Collins fills in most of the gaps in music left by non-specific video game histories.

Karen Collins, 'Loops and Bloops: Music of the Commodore 64 Games', *Soundscapes: Journal on Media Culture* 8 (2005). With this specific analysis of the role of the C64 chip in determining the sound output of its respective gaming consoles, Collins maps out what a hardware-to-composition analysis could look like; a discussion of the system's innate capabilities, followed by transcribed musical examples and elucidation of the technological constraints.

Karen Collins, 'An Introduction to the Participatory and Non-Linear Aspects of Video Games Audio' in Stan Hawkins and John Richardson (eds), *Essays on Sound and Vision* (Helsinki: Helsinki University Press, 2007). A theoretical paper dealing with the functions of games audio, as well as the various levels of diegesis within a game, focusing on distinguishing games audio from that of film.

Stephen Deutsch, 'Music for Interactive Moving Pictures', in Diane Freeman, Jerry Snider and Larry Snider (eds), *Soundscape* (London, 2003). *Soundscape* is a compilation of conference reports and lectures given on film and media music at the annual School of Sound conference in London. Deutsch staunchly correlates music for games with music for film, as the title asserts; his lecture and the rest of those in the compendium elucidate the views shared by the film music and game music communities.

Anahid Kassabian, 'The Sound of a New Film Form', in Ian Inglis (ed.), *Popular Music and Film* (London: Wallflower, 2003): 91–101. In this article Kassabian suggests that elements of game audio (such as the massive sound chaos presented by the lack of real-time mixing in games) have been incorporated into recent film sound design.

Axel Stockburger, 'The Game Environment from an Auditive Perspective' (2003). Conference paper presented at: DIGRA Level Up Conference (University of Utrecht, 2003): http://www.audiogames.net/pics/upload/gameenvironment.htm (accessed 10 March 2007). Stockburger's examination of the role of sound in the game experience is a model paper of its kind. He scrutinizes the various implications of recorded sound and its homogeneity, and postulates that the choice of sound and sound origin in video games can serve as a vehicle for the designer's intent. While the article is less about music and more about the technical aspects of design, Stockburger nonetheless lays firm groundwork for future study.

Zach Whalen, 'Play Along: An Approach to Video Game Music', *Game Studies* 4/1 (November 2004). Whalen's goal is analysis of the music as text from the outset. In addition to his supposition of illustrative cues in animation as the forerunners to video game audio functions, he provides transcriptions, sound clips and score excerpts from *Super Mario Bros.* alongside Berlioz's *Symphonie Fantastique*.

Internet Resources:

Chudah's Corner http://www.chudahs-corner.com. One of the most comprehensive resources for lyrics, liner notes, interviews and translations.

OverClockedRemix http://www.ocremix.org. OCRemix, spearheaded by programmer David Lloyd (DJPretzel), is a peer-reviewed and heavily moderated site boasting thousands of enthusiasts' reinterpretations and analyses from hundreds of games in all genres.

Video Game Music Archive http://vgmusic.com. Committed to the preservation of all video game music, David Lawrence's project collates the tens of thousands of files in question by console (or PC system) in MIDI format. The site is historically motivated and emphasizes the archiving of early game music.

The Video Game Music Preservation Foundation http://www.thealmightyguru.com/vgmpf. The VGMPF aims for the dissemination of game audio rips. It accepts submissions from all interested parties and the tracks are readily available, but the service exists only for games that have no published recordings, and the aims of the Foundation are historical.

Zophar's Domain http://www.zophar.net/music.html. Unlike the abundant MP3- and MIDI-centric repositories, Zophar's Domain gathers direct rips from the games as opposed to their adjunct CD soundtracks, providing the hardware equivalent of manuscript versus published score. These rips require special emulator software to play.

Relevant Academic and Industry Organizations:

Academic Gamers http://www.gameology.org. A public forum and article series by several individuals; the bulk of the site content is calls for papers and hard ludological analysis. There is a small musical community among the moderators and members, and these conduct unpublished discourse.

DiGRA http://www.digra.org. The Digital Games Research Association is a non-profit, international forum for game studies, and offers its members the means to publish and disseminate their findings. In addition to its interactive online community, DiGRA holds conferences and supports other colloquiums and research.

G.A.N.G http://www.audiogang.org. Game Audio Network Guild is an organization geared at developers, composers and academics, with a clear mission: to educate the world by bettering the resources available for its proponent members. Once one has established some clout, the G.A.N.G. can be the extra push necessary to seal that conference deal or publish that paper.

Interactive Audio Special Interest Group http://www.iasig.org/about.shtml. The IAsig works on developing tools and technologies for interactive audio development, as well as sharing information and opinions about game audio. The organization hosts Working Groups dedicated to a particular task, such as proliferating game audio education, developing a particular kind of software or reporting on a particular means of design.

Further Resources (by Tim Van Geelen)

There was a speech by Michael Kelly and Jason Page of Sony Computer Entertainment Europe, at the Game Developers Conference of 2007, about how MIDI could very well return as a standard for producing real-time in-game music. With the power of current-generation consoles like the Playstation 3, Xbox 360 and Wii, playback of (many) multiple streams of audio in perfect synchronization has become possible, and the biggest problems of MIDI seem to have been overcome. The General MIDI music of yesterday has a very distinct artificial sound to it, which has pushed composers towards using live instruments and high quality sample libraries to record tracks in CD, or near CD quality. This artificiality was largely due to the fact that samples had to be very, very small, due to memory constraints. Often, a recording of one or two notes was used to produce all of the notes of an instrument. The pitch shifting involved made these instruments sound more or less (often more) unreal. Current generation systems, however, have enough memory to be able to load in many more samples per instrument, making MIDI sounds much more realistic.

Now that we know that adaptive music is possible, let us look a bit more at how to compose it, and what tools we can use. The very near future brings us some very interesting tools, including iXMF, *WWise*, Sequitur and the IAsig WIKI. iXMF is a new file format for which the specifications are currently being designed by the Interactive Audio Special Interest Group (the IAsig). Its predecessor, XMF, is a file format that bundles musical data (which notes are played, by which instruments, how loud and so on.) and audio files (the actual sounds being played) in one file. This allows the composer more control. However, it is not used much today, and not many programs can create XMF files. iXMF will also allow for these elements, with the addition that it includes rules for interactive music ('play this part only when player has reached this point, mute this when health is below 50, play part A louder when part B is also playing X' and so on). Because these controls are in the hands of the composer, interactive music made for and with iXMF is much more likely to succeed than other formats, because there is no need for any programmer to do extensive, often advanced coding. This is also very important because unlike a composer, the programmer does not need to have any kind of musical knowledge.

After the specification document has been published, sequencer developers must implement the protocol into their software, in order for the format to actually be used. This is perhaps the biggest threat to any new file format, and it is therefore essential that software developers understand the need for and benefit of implementing the format.[2]

Wwise is a new game audio middleware engine created by Montreal company Audiokinetic. A game audio engine is a software package that runs in a computer game and handles all of the audio tasks. Some audio engines, including *Wwise*, also provide a way of easily integrating sounds and music into the game. The new *Wwise* 2007.1 version promises some exciting interactive music features, bringing the power to the composers and sound designers, without the need for programmers to code audio.[3]

Sequitur is a freeware sequencer that is being developed by a small group of people. At present it features no more than basic MIDI functionality and some minor algorithmic features, but the aim is to create a sequencer that allows easy interactive composition.[4]

---

2   See the IAsig WIKI homepage, http://www.iasig.org/wg/ixwg/index.shtml (accessed 7 June 2007).

3   See Audiokinetic's homepage, http://www.audiokinetic.com (accessed 5 May 2007).

4   See http://www.angryredplanet.com. See also Scott Patterson, 'Interactive Music Sequencer Design', *Gamasutra*, 2001 http://www.gamasutra.com/resource_guide/20010515/patterson_01.htm (accessed 15 May 2007).

Bibliography

(Note: all websites up to date as of 6 June 2007.)

Ahlroth, Jussi, 'Stadin kundi Ville Valo palasi kotiin', *Helsingin Sanomat* (29 December 2005): C1.

Alkio, Jyrki, 'Valtion riskirahaa ilmakitarapeliin', *Helsingin Sanomat* (7 February 2007): B5.

Altman, Rick, 'Silence of the Silents', *Musical Quarterly* 80:4 (1997): 648–718.

Altman, Rick, *Silent Film Sound* (New York: Columbia University Press, 2007).

Ascott, Roy, 'Telenoia', in Edward A. Shanken (ed.), *Telematic Embrace: Visionary Theories of Art, Technology, and Consciousness* (Berkeley: University of California Press, 2003).

Auerbach, Brent, 'Pedagogical Applications of the Video Game *Dance Dance Revolution* to the Undergraduate Aural Skills Classroom' (paper presented at the annual meeting for the Society for Music Theory, Los Angeles, California, 3 November 2006).

Bailey, Derek, *Improvisation: its nature and practice in music* (New York: Da Capo, 1992).

Banjeree, Scott, 'The Labels Have Seen EA Games Break New Bands: The Last Word: A Q&A with Steve Schnur', *Billboard*, (15 May 2004): 86.

Banks, Jack, 'Video in the Machine: The Incorporation of Music Video into the Recording Industry', *Popular Music* 16/30 (1997): 293–309.

Barron, Lee, '"Music Inspired By...": The Curious Case of the Missing Soundtrack', in Ian Inglis (ed.), *Popular Music and Film* (London: Wallflower, 2003): 148–61.

Bates, Bob, *Games Design*, Second Edition (Boston: Course Technology, 2004).

Bell, Catherine, 'Electronic Arts boss just wants our music for free', *Music Week* (15 November 2003): 16.

Bencina, Ross, 'Implementing Real-Time Granular Synthesis', in K. Greenbaum and R. Barzel (eds), *Audio Anecdotes II: Tools, tips, and techniques for digital audio.* (Natick, MA: A.K. Peters, 2004).

Berschewsky, Tapio, 'Ken on heistä kaikkein kauhein', *MikroBitti* (January 2006): 58–61.

Bessell, David, 'What's that funny noise?', in Geoff King and Tanya Krzywinska (eds), *Screenplay: Cinema/Videogames/Interfaces* (London: Wallflower Press, 2002).

Bisgaard, Lars, 'Musikalsk hermeneutik på hierarkisk grundlag – bidrag til en musikalsk Fænomenologi', in *Dansk Årbog for musikforskning* nr. 16 (Copenhagen: Danish Musicological Society, 1985).

Borgo, David, *Sync or Swarm: improvising music in a complex age* (New York: Continuum, 2005).

Boxer, S., 'From a germ of an idea to the Spore of a franchise', *Guardian Unlimited* (2006): http://technology.guardian.co.uk/games/story/0,,1835600,00.html.

Boztas, Senay, 'Computer games the new MTV for bands', *The Sunday Herald* (21 November 2004): 8.

Brandon, Alexander, 'Building an Adaptive Audio Experience', *Game Developer* (October 2002): 28–33.

Brandon, Alexander, *Audio for Games: planning, process and production* (Indianapolis: New Riders, 2005).

Brown, Mark, 'Depeche Mode try a new style: en dough cheeky-a-vunch', *The Guardian* (4 March 2006): 13.

Burnett, Robert, *The Global Jukebox: The International Music Industry* (London: Routledge, 1996).

Burnett, Robert and Patrick Wikström, 'Music Production in Times of Monopoly: The Example of Sweden', *Popular Music and Society* 29:5 (2006): 575–82.

Cage, John, *Silence: lectures and writings* (Middleton, CT: Wesleyan University Press, 1973).

Caillois, Roger, *Man, Play, and Games*, trans. Meyer Barash (Chicago: University of Illinois Press, 2001).

Chen, Jenova, 'Flow in Games (and Everything Else)', *Communications of the ACM* 50/4 (April 2007).

Chion, Michel, *Audio-Vision. Sound on Screen* (New York: Columbia University Press, 1994).

Christensen, Jørgen Riber, 'Multimedier og det postmoderne', in Jens F. Jensen (ed.), *Internet, World Wide Web, Netværks-kommunikation* (Ålborg: Ålborg Universitetsforlag 1999).

Collins, Karen, 'From Bits to Hits: Video Games Music Changes its Tune', *Film International* 13 (2004): 4–19.

Collins, Karen, 'An introduction to the Participatory and Non-Linear Aspects of Video Game Audio', in Stan Hawkins and John Richardson (eds), *Essays on Sound and Vision* (Helsinki : Helsinki University Press, 2007).

Collins, Karen, 'Grand Theft Audio? Popular Music and Intellectual Property in Video Games', *Music, Sound and Moving Image* 1:1 (Spring 2008).

Consalvo, Mia, 'Console Video Games and Global Corporations: Creating a hybrid culture', *New Media & Society* 8:1 (2006): 117–37.

Cook, Nicholas, *Analysing Musical Multimedia* (Oxford: Oxford University Press, 1998).

Cox, Christoph and Daniel Warner, *Audio culture: readings in modern music* (New York: Continuum, 2004).

Csikszentmihalyi, Mihaly, *Beyond Boredom and Anxiety* (San Francisco: Jossey-Bass Publishers, 1977).

Culshaw, Peter, 'So I pitched my Oscar Wilde film to Spielberg', *Guardian Unlimited* (21 March 2004): http://arts.guardian.co.uk/features/story/0,11710,1175408,00.html.

Deltour, Romain, and Cécile Roisin, 'The LimSee3 Multimedia Authoring Model', DocEng 2006, ACM Symposium on Document Engineering, 10–13 October 2006 (Amsterdam, 2006): 173–5.

Donaton, Scott, *Madison and Vine: Why the Entertainment and Advertising Industries Must Converge to Survive* (Blacklick, OH: The McGraw-Hill Companies, 2004).

Doornbusch, Paul, *The Music of CSIRAC: Australia's First Computer Music. (Altona, Australia:* Common Ground, 2005).

Dyndahl, Petter, 'Hypertekst og musikalsk spatio-temporalitet', in Sissel Furuseth (ed.), *Kunstens rytmer i tid og rom* (Trondheim: Tapir Akademisk Forlag, 2005).

Evens, Aden, 'Sound Ideas: music, machines, and experience', *Theory out of Bounds* 27 (Minneapolis: University of Minnesota Press, 2005).

Farrell, Nick, 'Ballmer blames pirates for poor Vista sales', *The Inquirer* (19 February 2007): http://www.theinquirer.net/default.aspx?article=37721.

Faye, Jan, 'Den gådefulde tid', in David Farverholdt (ed.), *Hvad er tid?* (Copenhagen: Gyldendal, 1999).

Fitzgerald, Kate, 'By the demo: music for the ages', *Advertising Age* 74/30 (2003): 3–4.

Fluck, Zsuzsanna and Anthony W. Lynch, 'Why Do Firms Merge and Then Divest? A Theory of Financial Synergy', *The Journal of Business* 72/3 (1999): 319–46.

Fox, Mark, 'E-commerce Business Models for the Music Industry', *Popular Music and Society* 27/2 (2004): 201–20.

Frith, Simon, *Performing Rites: On the Value of Popular Music* (Oxford: Oxford University Press, 1996).

Frost, Laurence, 'Video games drive music sales' *USA Today* (26 January 2006), http://www.usatoday.com/tech/gaming/2006-01-26-music-stars_x.htm.

Frostenson, Sky, *Bombing the System*, Winter Arts Computation Engineering Seminar: Virtual Identities (Irvine, CA, 2004).

Gee, James Paul, *What Video Games Have to Teach Us About Learning and Literacy* (New York: Palgrave Macmillan, 2003).

Gorbman, Claudia, *Unheard Melodies? Narrative Film Music* (Bloomington: Indiana University Press, 1987).

Gorbman, Claudia, 'Aesthetics and Rhetoric', *American Music* 22:1 (2004): 14–26.

Green, Jo-Anne, M. Riel, and H. Thorington, 'Intelligent Street', *networked_performance*, http://www.turbulence.org/blog/archives/2004_08.html.

Hakulinen, Silja, 'Salakavalat listaykköset', *Skenet.fi* (2005): http://www.skenet.fi/index.html?menuid=364&aid=995.

Hamman, Michael, 'From Symbol to Semiotic: Representation, Signification, and the Composition of Music Interaction', *Journal of New Music Research* 28/2 (1999): 90–104.

Hamman, Michael, 'Structure as Performance: Cognitive Musicology and the Objectification of Procedure', in J. Tabor (ed.), *Otto Laske: Navigating New Musical Horizons* (New York: Greenwood Press, 1999).

Harland, Kurt, 'Composing for Interactive Music', *Gamasutra* (2000) http://www.gamasutra.com/features/20000217/harland_01.htm.

Hawkins, Trip, 'Making Mobile Phones the Ultimate Game Platform', Games Developers Conference presentation (San Francisco, 2007).

Hayden Porter, 'Sonaptic discusses JSR-234 3D Audio', http://sonify.org/tutorials/interviews/jsr234.

Heeter, Carrie and Pericles Gomes, 'It's Time for Hypermedia to Move to Talking Pictures', *Journal of Educational Multimedia and Hypermedia* (Winter 1992): http://commtechlab.msu.edu/publications/files/talking.html.

Hesmondhalgh, David, *The Cultural Industries* (London: Sage, 2002).

High, Kamau, 'In search of all the young men with big bulging wallets', *Financial Times* (24 May 2005): 14.

High, Kamau, 'Industries in tune too woo young fans', *Financial Times* (6 September 2005): 14.

Honing, Henkjan, 'Issues in the Representation of Time and Structure in Music', *Contemporary Music Review* 9 (London: Routledge, 1993).

Hull, Geoffrey P., *The Recording Industry* (Boston: Allyn and Bacon, 1998).

Hunter, William, 'The Dot Eaters Videogame History' (2000), http://www.emuunlim. com/doteaters/play3sta1.htm.

Inglis, S. 'Markus Popp: Music as Software', *Sound on Sound* (2002): http://www. soundonsound.com/sos/oct02/articles/oval.asp?print=yes.

Jensen, Jens F, 'Multimedier, Hypermedier, Interaktive Medier', in Jens F. Jensen (ed.), *Multimedier, Hypermedier, Interaktive Medier* (Ålborg: Ålborg Universitetsforlag, 1998).

Johnson, Steven, *Emergence: the connected lives of ants, brains, cities, and software* (New York: Scribner, 2001).

Jones, Steve, 'Music and the Internet', *Popular Music* 19/2 (2000): 217–30.

Jørgensen, Kristine, *What are those Grunts and Growls Over There? Computer Game Audio and Player Action*. PhD dissertation. Department of Media, Cognition and Communication, (Copenhagen: Copenhagen University, 2007).

Jørgensen, Kristine, 'On the Functional Aspects of Computer Game Audio', in *Proceedings of the Audio Mostly Conference 2006* (Piteå, Sweden, 11–12 October 2006): http://wood.tii.se/sonic/images/stories/amc06/amc_proceedings_low.pdf.

Kassabian, Anahid, 'The Sound of a New Film Form', in Ian Inglis (ed.), *Popular Music and Film* (London: Wallflower, 2003): 91–101.

Kennedy, James and R. Eberhart, 'Particle Swarm Optimization', *Proceedings from the IEEE International Conference on Neural Networks* 4 (1995):.1942–8.

King, Geoff and Tanya Krzywinska (eds), *ScreenPlay: Cinema/Videogames/ Interfaces* (London: Wallflower, 2002).

Klepek, Patrick, 'Frag to the music: Record labels, games publishers see licensed music as booming biz', *Computer Gaming World* 250 (April 2005): 32–33.

Kline, Stephen, Nick Dyer-Witheford and Greig de Peuter, *Digital Games: The Interaction of Technology, Culture, and Marketing* (Montreal: McGill-Queen's University Press, 2003).

Koistinen, Olavi, 'Suomalainen pelitalo saa Vistasta nostetta', *Helsingin Sanomat* (3 February 2007): B5.

Kramer, Jonathan D., *The Time of Music* (New York: Shirmer Books, 1988).

Kramer, G., B. Walker, T. Bonebright, P. Cook, J. Flowers, N. Miner, J. Neuhoff. R. Bargar, S. Barrass, J. Berger, G. Evreinov, W. Fitch, M. Gröhn, S. Handel, H. Kaper, H. Levkowitz, S. Lodha, B. Shinn-Cunningham, M. Simoni and S. Tipei, *The Sonification Report: Status of the Field and Research Agenda*. Report prepared for the National Science Foundation by members of the International

Community for Auditory Display. (Santa Fe, NM: ICAD 1999): http://icad.org/websiteV2.0/References/nsf.html.

Lakoff, George, 'Metaphors with Target Domain: Time'. Berkeley, CA: University of California: http://cogsci.berkeley.edu/lakoff/targets/Time.html.

Laske, Otto, *Compositional Theory: An Enrichment of Music Theory*. Interface, 18/1 2 (1989): 45–59.

Lerdahl, Fred, *Tonal Pitch Space* (New York: Oxford University Press, 2001).

Lerdahl, Fred and Ray Jackendoff, *A Generative Theory of Tonal Music* (Cambridge, MA: MIT Press, 1983).

Lörstad, Henrik, Mark d'Inverno and John Eacott, 'The Intelligent Street: Responsive sound environments for social interaction', *Proceedings of the 2004 ACM SIGCHI International Conference on Advances in computer entertainment technology* 74 (2004): 155–62.

Lübcke, Poul, *Tidsbegrebet* (Copenhagen: Gads forlag, 1981).

Luukka, Teemu, 'Työryhmä esittää kulttuuriviennille kymmeniä miljoonia lisää tukea', *Helsingin Sanomat* (2 March 2007): C1.

Mander, Johathan, 'Poets of the Fall: Oopperaakin on laulettu', *Plaza – Kaista*, (15 February 2005): http://plaza.fi/kaista/musiikki/haastattelut/poets-of-the-fall-oopperaakin-on-laulettu.

Manning, Peter, *Electronic and Computer Music* (Oxford: Oxford University Press, 2004).

Marks, Lawrence E., *Unity of the Senses* (New York: Academic Press, 1978).

Marshall, Sandra K. and Annabel J. Cohen, 'Effects of musical soundtracks on attitudes toward animated geometric figures', *Music Perception* 6/1 (Berkley, CA: University of California Press, 1988).

Maslow, Abraham H. and John J. Honigmann, 'Synergy: Some Notes of Ruth Benedict', *American Anthropologist*, New Series, 72:2 (1970): 320–33.

Maturana, Humberto R. and F.J. Varela, *The Tree of Knowledge: the biological roots of human understanding* (Boston: Shambala, 1992), pp. 74 5.

McCormack, Jon, 'Eden: an evolutionary sonic ecosystem' (2000): http://www.csse.monash.edu.au/~jonmc/projects/eden/eden.html.

McCormack, Jon, 'Evolving for the Audience', *International Journal of Design Computing* 4 (Special Issue On Designing Virtual Worlds), Sydney (2002).

McCutchan, Ann, *The Muse That Sings: Composers speak about the creative process* (New York: Oxford University Press, 1999).

McMahan, Alison, 'Immersion, Engagement, and Presence. A Method for Analyzing 3-D Video Games', in Mark J.P. Wolf, and Bernard Perron (eds), *The Video Game Theory Reader* (New York: Routledge, 2003).

Miles, Stuart and Adam Sherwin, 'Sir Cliff is displaced by a halo', *The Times* (27 November 2004): Home News 45.

Moore, Catherine, 'A Picture is Worth 1000 CDs: Can the Music Industry Survive as a Stand-Alone Business?', *American Music* 22:1 (2004): 176–86.

Morris, Robert, 'New Directions in the Theory and Analysis of Musical Contour', *Music Theory Spectrum* 15 (1993): 205–28.

Muikku, Jari, *Musiikkia kaikkiruokaisille: suomalaisen populaarimusiikin äänitetuotanto 1945–1990* (Helsinki: Gaudeamus, 2001).

Murray, Simone, 'Brand loyalties: rethinking content within global corporate media', *Media, Culture & Society*, 27/3 (2005): 415–35.

Nyman, Michael, *Experimental Music: Cage and beyond* (Cambridge: Cambridge University Press, 1999).

O'Connor, Alan, 'Local Scenes and Dangerous Crossroads: Punk and theories of Cultural Hybridity', *Popular Music* 21/2 (2002).

Öhman, Tiia, 'Poets of the Fall – fanit odottelevat Uudessa-Seelannissa', *Tuhma* 2 (2005): 36–7.

Øhrstrøm, Peter, *Tidens gang i tidens løb* (Århus: Steno Museets venner, 1995).

Paoletta, Michael, 'EA Scores One for New Music With "Madden', *Billboard* (13 August 2005): 10.

Park, A., 'Will Wright talks Spore, Leipzig, next-gen', *GameSpot* : http://www.gamespot.com/news/6155498.html.

Patterson, Scott, 'Interactive Music Sequencer Design', *Gamasutra* (2001): http://www.gamasutra.com/resource_guide/20010515/patterson_01.htm.

Petersen, Thomas Egeskov, 'Music Recollection', *Music Recollection Issue 2*: http://www.atlantis-prophecy.org/recollection/?load=online&issue=1&sub=article&id=11.

Pihkala, Kari and Tappio Lokki, 'Extending SMIL with 3D Audio', In the Proceedings of the 2003 International Conference on Auditory Display. (Boston: 6–9 July 2003): 95–8.

Pimentel, Sergio, '7 Deadly Sins of Music Licensing', *Game Developers' Conference 2007* (San Francisco: 5–9 March 2007).

Pohflepp, S. 'Before and After Darwin', *We Make Money Not Art*: http://www.we-make-money-not-art.com/archives/009261.php.

Polgár, Támás, *Freax: The Brief History of the Computer Demoscene* (Winnenden, Germany: CSW Verlag, 2006).

Price, Simon, 'Granular synthesis: How it works and ways to use it', *Sound on Sound* (December 2005): http://www.soundonsound.com/sos/dec05/articles/granularworkshop.htm?print=yes.

Roads, Curtis, *The Computer Music Tutorial* (Cambridge, MA: MIT Press, 1996).

Roads, Curtis, *Microsound* (Cambridge, MA: MIT Press, 2004).

Rona, Jeff, *The Reel World: Scoring for pictures* (San Francisco: Miller Freeman Books, 2000).

Rosmarin, Rachel, 'Why Gears Of War Costs $60', *Forbes.com* (12 December 2006): http:// www.forbes.com/technology/2006/12/19/ps3-xbox360-costs-tech-cx_rr_game06_1219expensivegames.html.

Ryan, Marie-Laure, *Narrative as Virtual Reality. Immersion and Interactivity in Literature and Electronic Media* (Baltimore: Johns Hopkins University Press, 2001).

Sabaneev, Leonid, *Music for the films* (London: Pitman and Sons, 1935).

Sadoff, Ronald H., 'The role of the music editor and the "temp track" as blueprint for the score, source music, and scource music of films', *Popular Music* 25/2 (2006): 165–83.

Schenker, Heinrich, *Free Composition*, trans. Ernst Oster (New York: Longman, 1979).

Schnur, Steve, 'Video games and music have a strong relationship', *Music Week* (1 November 2003): 16.

Schnur, Steve, 'Electronic Arts is happy to pay for its music', *Music Week* (6 December 2003): 15.

Schnur, Steve, 'Playing for Keeps: Videogames Have Changed The Way We Hear Music' *Billboard* (6 November 2004): 10.

Schwarz, Diemo, 'Concatenative sound synthesis: The early years', *Journal of New Music Research* 35/1 (2006): http://mediatheque.ircam.fr/articles/textes/Schwarz06b/

SeekingAlpha.com. 'Electronic Arts F4Q07 (Qtr End 3/31/07) Earnings Call Transcript', [Online, 8 May, 2007] Available at: http://software.seekingalpha.com/article/34946.

Selfon, Scott, 'DirectMusic Concepts', in Todd M. Fay (ed.), *DirectX 9 Audio Exposed: Interactive audio development* (Texas: Wordware Publishing, 2004).

Smith, Jacob, 'I Can See Tomorrow In Your Dance: A Study of *Dance Dance Revolution* and Music Video Games', *Journal of Popular Music Studies* 16:1 (2004): 58–84.

Smith, Jeff, *The Sounds of Commerce. Marketing Popular Film Music* (New York: Columbia University Press, 1998).

Stanley, T.L., 'Music world hits new high note', *Advertising Age* 75/21 (2004): 4.

Stockburger, Axel, 'The Game Environment from an Auditory Perspective', in Marinka Copier and Joost Raessens (eds), *Proceedings: Level Up: Digital Games Research Conference.* (Utrecht University 2003): http://www.audiogames.net/pics/upload/gameenvironment.htm.

Tasajärvi, Lassi, *Demoscene: The Art of Real-Time* (Finland: Even Lake Studios, 2004).

Tolonen, Jussi, 'Pelimaailman pelimannit', *Nyt* 44 (2006): 45.

Toop, David, *Haunted Weather: music, silence, and memory* (London: Serpent's Tail, 2004).

Träskbäck, Jocka, 'Poets of the Fall', *Stara.fi* (2005): http://www.stara.fi/?p=165.

Truax, Barry. 'Composing with Real-Time Granular Sound', *Perspectives of New Music* 28/2 (1990): 120–34.

Truax, Barry. 'Time-shifting of sampled sounds with a real-time granulation technique', *1990 ICMC Proceedings* (San Francisco: Computer Music Association 1990): 104–107.

Valentino, Nicky, 'Lara Croft Tomb Raider: Legend Review', *GameZone Xbox* (2006): http://xbox.gamezone.com/gzreviews/r26199.htm.

Varinini, Giancarlo, 'The soundtrack for EA Sports' latest basketball game is the first video game soundtrack to go platinum' (2003): http://videogames.yahoo.com/newsarticle?eid=360530&page=0.

Walker, Rob, '50 Cent Is Calling: Rap's biggest star is now appearing on cell phones near you', *Slate* (24 June 2003): http://www.slate.com/id/2084756.

Wall, Tim, *Studying Popular Music Culture* (London: Arnold, 2003).

Walleij, Linus, 'Copyright Finns Inte' (1998): Online English Version, Chapter 5 http://home.c2i.net/nirgendwo/cdne/mainindex.htm.

Warburton, Dan, 'Les instants composés', in Brian Marley and Mark Wastell (eds), *Blocks of Consciousness and the Unbroken Continuum* (London: Sound 323, 2005).

Weidenbaum, Marc, 'Musique for Shuffling': http://www.disquiet.com/kirschner. html.

Weiss, Aaron, 'From Bits to Hits', *NetWorker* (March 2004): 19–24.

Whalen, Zach, 'Play Along: An Approach to Video Game Music', *Game Studies. The International Journal of Computer Game Research* 4/1 (2004): http://www. gamestudies.org/0401/whalen.

Zbikowski, Lawrence, *Conceptualizing Music: Cognitive Structures, Theory, and Analysis* (New York: Oxford University Press, 2002).

Zhang, Hao, 'US Evidence on Bank Takeover Motives: A Note', *Journal of Business Finance & Accounting* 25/7&8 (1998): 1025–32.

Index